Agrarian Reform and Peasant Organization on the Ecuadorian Coast

by

M. R. REDCLIFT

UNIVERSITY OF LONDON
Published for the
Institute of Latin American Studies
THE ATHLONE PRESS
1978

Published by
THE ATHLONE PRESS
UNIVERSITY OF LONDON
at 4 *Gower Street, London* WC1
Distributed by Tiptree Book Services Ltd
Tiptree, Essex

U.S.A. and Canada
Humanities Press Inc
New Jersey

© *University of London* 1978

British Library Cataloguing in Publication Data
Redclift, M. R.
  Agrarian reform and peasant organization on the
  Ecuadorian Coast. – (University of London.
  Institute of Latin American Studies. Monographs; 8)
  1. Ecuador – Rural conditions
  I. Title II. Series
  301.35′2′098663   HN313.5

ISBN 0 485 17708 0

ISSN 0076 0846

Printed in Great Britain by
WESTERN PRINTING SERVICES LIMITED
BRISTOL

To my Parents

ACKNOWLEDGEMENTS

I am grateful to the Institute of Latin American Studies and Wye College, University of London, for the support given to the research on which this book is based. In addition a number of people in Ecuador helped me with the field research. Foremost among them were the staff of 'CESA-Litoral' in Guayaquil, under Ramón Espinel. The work also benefited from long conversations and interviews with peasant leaders and *campesinos* throughout the Guayas Basin, whom I met in 1975 while undertaking research in the area.

I also owe a considerable debt to colleagues in Britain. Among those who undertook to read and comment on a draft of the whole work were: Raymond and Rosemary Bromley, William Bell, Bryan Roberts, Cristóbal Kay, David Rock and David Corkill. I am particularly grateful to them. Professor John Lynch made a number of useful comments on an earlier draft and provided editorial guidance and encouragement. Valuable criticism of sections of the manuscript, and conference papers based on the research, was made by David Lehmann, Terry Byres, John MacDonald, Jean Carrière and David Goodman. None of the above is responsible, of course, for the opinions expressed in the final version. Sue Briant and Sheila Kingsnorth typed several manuscript drafts with quiet efficiency and patience. Finally, I am especially indebted to my wife, Nanneke, for her comments and advice throughout the writing of the book.

Michael Redclift

CONTENTS

MAP

GLOSSARY OF TERMS

aparcero (aparcería) sharecropper/sharecropping
arrendatario cash tenant
asentamientos former estates now run as 'cooperatives' under Chilean agrarian reform
campesino (loosely) peasant
ciudad agraria 'agro-town' as employed by SIPPTAL
colonato system of 'unfree' labour employed on *haciendas*
comerciantes market dealers, middlemen
concertaje the forced conscription of the Indian population
criollo 'white', i.e. Spanish
cuadra unit of land equal to 1·56 hectares
Decreto 1001 decree making it illegal to employ rice tenants (December 1970)
desmonte (desmontero) the preparation of land for rice cultivation which tenants were named after in rice zone
dirigentes leaders of the peasants' movement
empresa agrícola (literally) agricultural enterprise, term used for former rice estates favoured under the agrarian reform
encomienda system under which the *Conquistadores* could draw on Indian labour during the Colonial period
eventuales casual labourers
explotación land-holding worked as one unit
finquero tenant usually growing cocoa on Ecuadorian Coast
fomentador Coastal money-lender
huasipungo (huasipungero) plot of land allocated by highland landlord to labourer (cf. *colonato*) in Ecuador (*arrimado* in southern Ecuador)
jornalero wage labourer in agriculture
Junta Administrativa the committee of members that manages a rice cooperative
latifundia large extensively-worked estates
lote comunal plot of land that is both communally owned and communally worked on a rice cooperative
mayordomo 'overseer' of rural labour force on an estate
minifundia smallholdings worked by *campesino* families

mita   Indian labour force recruited by Spanish from villages during the Colonial period

montoneras   largely peasant militias from the Coast which supported Alfaro during the 'Liberal Revolution' of 1896. Later (in the 1920s) they were directed at landlords on the Coast

montuvio   Coastal peasant

piladora   rice mill where by-products are also extracted as well as the grain

precarismo   'precarious' tenure: used of many types of non-cash tenant (including *huasipungeros*). In the context of the rice zone it refers to a particular type of leasehold tenant-in-kind (*precarista*)

redención   system of tenancy for crops of longer growing cycle (such as bananas, cocoa and coffee) under which landlord repossessed the crop cultivated by a tenant immediately before the harvest

rentier   an absentee landlord or one who takes little part in entrepreneurial decision making on his estate

rice zone   the provinces of Guayas and Los Rios on the Euadorian Coast

serrano   person from the Ecuadorian *sierra*

suburbio   urban 'squatter' settlement in Guayaquil

técnico   professional or technician

Velasquismo   refers to Velasco Ibarra, five times president of Ecuador

ACAE   *Asociación de Cooperativas Arroceras del Ecuador*, peasant movement in rice zone

ACAL   *Asociación de Cooperativas Agrícolas del Litoral*, Leftish peasant movement active in rice zone, affiliated to FENOC

AID (also CLUSA, *Punto IV*) Agency for International Development

BNF   *Banco Nacional de Fomento*, the Government Development Bank

CESA   *Central Ecuatoriana de Servicios Agrícolas*, small consultancy organization made up of lawyers, engineers etc. linked to ACAL

CFP   *Confederación de Fuerzas Populares*, populist political movement led by Assad Bucaram on the Coast

ENAC   *Empresa Nacional de Almacemiento y Comercio*, Government wholesaling and marketing organization

ENPROVIT   *Empresa Nacional de Provisión y Transporte*, Government transport and marketing organization

FENACLE   *Federación Nacional de Campesinos Libres del Ecuador*, right-wing peasant movement on the Coast

FENACOOPARR   *Federación Nacional de Cooperativas Arroceras,* marketing organization representing rice 'cooperatives' on the Coast

FENOC *Federación de Campesinos*, leftish national peasant organization

FETAL *Federación de Trabajadores Agrícolas del Litoral*, communist led peasant organization

IERAC *Instituto Ecuatoriano de Reforma Agraria y Colonisación*, the Ecuadorian Land Reform Institute

JNP *Junta Nacional de Planificación*, the Government Planning Office

OCRA *Organisación Campesina de Reforma Agraria*, peasant 'cooperative' under the control of IERAC, in which land has not been finally handed over to the *campesinos*

ONAC *Oficina Nacional de Avaluación y Catastros*, the Government Land Valuation Office

PPEA *Programa de Promoción de Empresas Agrícolas*, Ministry of Agriculture programme for supervising a select number of rice cooperatives

Programa Nacional de Arroz (y maiz) the National Rice Programme

SIPPTAL *Sindicato de Productores y Trabajadores Agrícolas del Litoral*, nationalist landlord organization opposed to state intervention in agrarian sector

URCIMA *Unión Regional de Cooperativas Industriales de Mercadeo Arroceras*, break-away peasant movement, originally part of ACAL

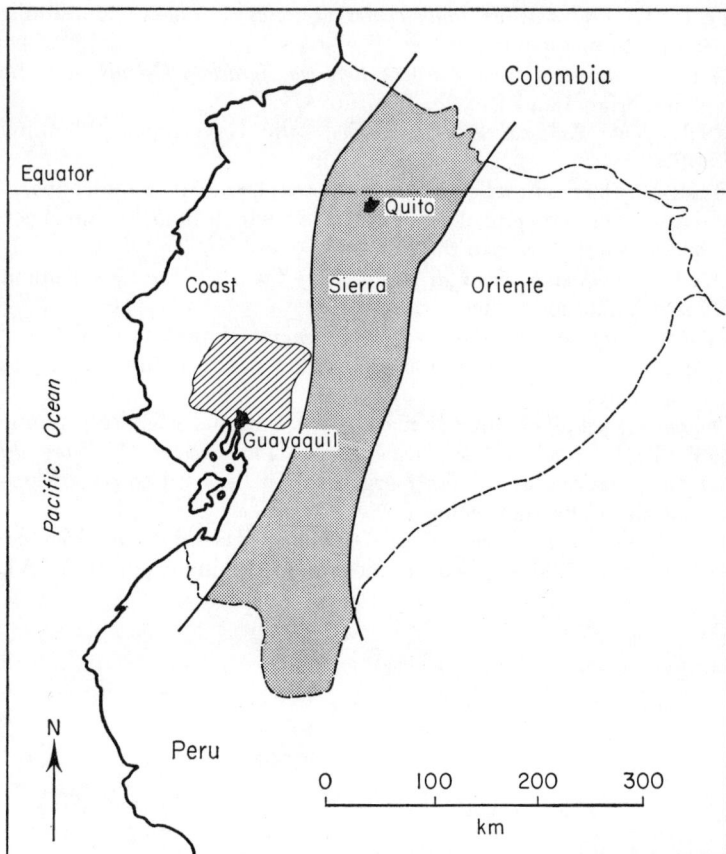

Colombia

Equator

Quito

Coast   Sierra   Oriente

Pacific Ocean

Guayaquil

N

Peru

0   100   200   300

km

Indicates the rice zone of the Guayas Basin

Indicates the Ecuadorian sierra

The Rice Zone of the Guayas River Basin

I

INTRODUCTION

This book focuses on a comparatively small geographical area of Latin America. It discusses the events which led to the abolition of tenancy relations (*precarismo*) among Ecuadorian Coastal rice producers in December 1970, and the agrarian reform which was carried out in the zone during the subsequent five years.[1] The rice zone was chosen for this study because it is the only area in which agrarian reform has been seriously attempted in Ecuador, and the principal area to benefit from oil revenues since 1972.

Although the historical and geographical focus of the study is a narrow one, most of the issues raised are not confined to one period of Ecuadorian history, or indeed to the history of any one developing country. The central theoretical focus is the relationship between the role of the state in developing countries and changes in the agrarian structure of those countries. This theme raises a number of questions which need to be considered from the outset. For example, how far can we explain changes in specific forms of land tenure in terms of global relations between social classes? Does the class physiognomy of the peasantry prior to reform, and in particular its structural relationship to other social classes, give an agrarian reform a specific character or imprint? If the availability of foreign exchange permits a developing country to undertake an agrarian reform without reliance on popular social forces, is that reform undertaken on behalf of landlords, a national bourgeoisie or the state itself? Is there a shared interest between landlords and urban bureaucrats in the implementation of such an agrarian reform?

Thus the book is addressed not only to a number of questions which have concerned scholars for many years, but also to questions which have received insufficient attention. The absence of radical political movements in Ecuador has meant that social scientists interested in other countries and regions have only rarely given it their attention. This study aims to rectify this situation. More specifically it examines the various factors which have contributed to one country's 'development ideology', and the ways that this ideology has been expressed in the behaviour of agrarian reform officials, *técnicos* and peasant leaders.

It is an important characteristic of some agrarian reforms that they do not come about as a result of pressure from below, although a government might rely on popular support for their implementation. This has been the case in Ecuador since 1970. Nevertheless this is not the only pressure for reform in Latin America. There is another important aspect of agrarian reform which should not be ignored. This is the effect of pressure from international bodies for an 'incrementalist' reform which places the emphasis on increasing agricultural production, even at the cost of alienating or displacing landlords who, within a region, still command considerable power. Chronic failures in rice production converted this possibility into a reality and, at the same time, led the state to play a more dynamic, interventionist role in the agricultural development of the Coastal region.

The history of agrarian reform in Ecuador can be usefully compared with that of neighbouring countries in Latin America. Unlike Mexico and Bolivia, both of which experienced a social revolution in which agrarian reform was a major goal of the rural masses, Ecuador remained relatively free from the forces let loose by agrarian capitalism in the one case and a mining economy in the other. There was no conflict as acute as that between the *haciendas* and peasant communities during the Porfiriato in Mexico, nor contending political forces like those in Bolivia after the disastrous Chaco War.[2] There was, in fact, no popular base from which pressure for an agrarian reform could be mounted.

It is also illuminating to compare recent Ecuadorian history with that of Peru, a country with which Ecuador shares a number of common features. Most analyses of the Peruvian agrarian reform since the military took power in 1968, have emphasized the inevitability of a radical, nationalist agrarian programme. By 1964 peasant unrest in the Highlands and the emergence of social classes committed to industrialization, had broken the back of landlordism in the Sierra. The agrarian reform, when it was eventually undertaken, was directed against foreign-owned interests rather than the weakened landlord class.[3] In Ecuador, as we shall see, the agrarian reform was partly the outcome of pressure from foreign interests. It would be misleading to claim that recent Ecuadorian military governments have taken no notice of what has happened in other Latin American countries, but some Ecuadorian commentators claim that these experiences do not 'constitute a point of reference for the civic authorities or the military in Ecuador'.[4]

The abolition of rice *precarismo* and the establishment of rice cooperatives on former estates, have not brought about a radical redistribution of land on the Ecuadorian Coast. The 'agrarian reform' has consisted in part of the manipulation of land titles and agricultural credit on the part of the state. This is not to say that social forces in the rice zone have remained dormant in the face of monolithic state interference. Since 1972, when revenues from oil first became a significant factor in Ecuadorian economic planning, the government has been able to offer a carrot as well as wield the whip in its relations with both landlords and former tenants. This has increased social differentiation. However, it is argued below that growing inequality in the rice zone is partly the result of uneven political pressures exerted by the *campesinos* themselves. At one remove the form taken by social inequality also reflects the aspirations of state *técnicos* to control agricultural development more closely than in the past. In doing this they are assisted by their possession of a new political resource— control over the use made of agricultural technology. This power to manipulate the benefits derived from the employment of new irrigation methods, and the close supervision of all aspects of agricultural production in the 'reformed' sector, has fundamentally altered the relations between landlords, peasants and the state. If we are to seek confirmation of major trends that have been identified in Latin American rural society, such as the 'proletarization' of the peasantry, we must begin by examining these changes in the control over resources. It is hoped that through the rigorous analysis of one specific situation, that of rice *precaristas* in Ecuador, we can learn more about the forces that are shaping comparable situations in other parts of Latin America today.

Before turning to the organization of the monograph, it is

necessary to say something further about the theoretical debates which have influenced the writing of it. Until the last decade or so relatively little attention was given to the relationship between the state and the agrarian structure of Latin American countries. One of the effects of the CIDA Reports on land tenure in Latin America was to cast the argument about land distribution and development in such a way that ongoing changes within the agrarian structure were often ignored, and the relations between urban social classes and the agricultural population hardly considered. It was recognized that unequal distribution of land contributed to low productivity in the agrarian sector and that agrarian reform policies reflected this inequality.[5] However, the growth of new social relations of production within agriculture and the development of highly efficient capitalist farming within the latifundist structure, were often ignored.

This emphasis on unequal distribution, which Lehmann has termed 'the Lorenz curve' approach, provided a static model of agrarian social relations.[6] It was the stability of the *latifundia* that received most attention. Some writers, such as Pearse and Stavenhagen, took their cue from Lenin in stressing the way in which the peasantry was being 'marginalized' and converted into a rural proletariat by the advance of capitalism into rural areas.[7] The large landholder, however, was rarely depicted as participating in a dynamic process of capitalist expansion; instead he was regarded as maintaining his control over the labour force through his ownership of land.

It was the contribution of the Neo-Marxists that they emphasized the interdependence of social relations in agriculture and in urban areas. In the writing of Frank, in particular, it was argued that relations of exploitation characterized apparently 'backward' geographical regions.[8] These ties of 'dependency' between 'satellite' and 'metropolitan' regions existed at the global level between countries, as well as within Latin American countries.[9] The form taken by *latifundia* agriculture was entirely consistent with, indeed rested upon, capitalist relations of production.[10]

With hindsight it is clear that some of the limitations of this Neo-Marxist analysis have produced a very fertile discussion about the nature of capitalist relations within agriculture. Economic anthropologists, influenced in particular by Althusser, have argued that it is possible to distinguish different modes of production within a given social formation.[11] Attention has been given to the way in which a 'surplus' is obtained from the peasantry, and the conditions under which this surplus has been appropriated. Discussion then centres on the effects of the capitalist mode of production on 'peasant' or 'sub-capitalist' modes of production. Some writers assume that the appropriation of the peasant's surplus is a condition for the expansion of industrial capitalism.[12] Others argue that the relative inefficiency of surplus appropriation ultimately leads to greater social differentiation among the peasantry on the lines suggested by Lenin.[13]

The discussion about class relations in agriculture has not only brought important theoretical and conceptual issues to light, it has also revealed interesting empirical comparisons.[14] The concern with the political conditions under which an agricultural surplus is created and transferred, has in turn led to a reconsideration of the role of the state. Rather than simply serving the interests of one particular class the state is now seen as acting autonomously within the process of capitalist expansion. The emphasis on structural relations within and between modes of production, which the 'Althusserian' analysis has provided, has even caused some scholars to argue that not enough attention is being paid to the part that social classes play in furthering underlying processes.[15]

This study of Coastal Ecuador shows that, among other things, social differentiation of the peasantry and unequal access to the state are partly the outcome of new forms of social consciousness. The 'proletarization' of the peasantry is not merely the structural outcome of the development of capitalism in agriculture, but the result of consciously sought ends. It is also suggested that the state can act to contain the interests of landlords that do not pursue 'modernizing' ends. Perhaps the view that was held prior to Frank's writing, that some landlords are not identifiable with urban bourgeois interests, is not quite as extraordinary as it appeared a few years ago. Further, although this study reinforces the view that advanced agricultural technology will often increase social differentiation, it also points to the need to examine the political implications of the control of technology.[16] These have been almost completely ignored.[17]

It will be objected by some that the discussion draws too eclectically on a number of theoretical analyses without containing a theoretical perspective of its own. It has been my aim to cast some light on existing theoretical concerns through considering what is unsatisfactory about them, rather than to write from one theoretical perspective. Readers can judge for themselves whether or not this is successful. I would merely reiterate that the case material and its interpretation are intended to raise important theoretical issues. These questions are discussed both *in situ*, where appropriate, and in the brief Conclusions.

The book is organized in the following way. First the background to the Coastal agrarian reform is provided in Chapter II by considering economic development and the Ecuadorian class structure at the national level, before looking at the contribution of the agricultural sector to Ecuador's overall development performance. It is emphasized that though the *latifundia* of the Sierra are not directly related to export markets they are by no means stagnant, and are constantly undergoing internal changes. The history of recent agrarian reform legislation is discussed, and the effects of this legislation in contributing to the 'marginalization' of much of the rural population. The hold of landlords on political power has also emasculated the tentative reforms that have been advocated since 1964. Finally, the antecedents of the current 'agrarian reform' ideology are identified.

The book then focuses in Chapter III on the evolution of social relations on the Coast. In this region the agrarian structure is more directly linked to the international economy, and this has given rise to a succession of 'agricultural frontiers' as new crops have been grown for world markets. The political expression of these export interests reached its zenith at the time of the 'Liberal Revolution' of 1896 under Eloy Alfaro, and the ascendancy of the *Banco Comercial* in Guayaquil. In the succeeding two or three decades the class structure of the coastal region took on most of the features it possesses today. The decline of cocoa fortunes in the 1920s, and the opening up of an 'internal frontier' by family farmers growing bananas, served to modify this structure. It is sometimes argued that the existence of an 'internal frontier' marked a 'democratization' of social relations on the Coast. However, this idea is found to be less convincing on close examination. The chapter ends with a description of the agrarian structure of the provinces of Guayas and Los Rios before 1970, the year which represents a watershed in social relations throughout the coastal region.

Discussion of the recent historical background to changes in the rice zone is followed, in Chapter IV, by a more detailed scrutiny of the system of rice tenancy or *precarismo*. The characteristics of landlord/tenant relations in the rice zone are analysed in the context of sharecropping arrangements in other Latin American societies. The most important aspect of the tenant's dependence on the landlord in the Ecuadorian rice zone is identified as his disadvantageous market situation, rather than obligations to perform labour services or the payment of rent to the landlord. The implications of this fact are discussed in later chapters.

The events contributing to the eventual abolition of rice *precarismo* are now discussed. In Chapter V it is argued that the principal objection to rice *precarismo* was that it prevented large scale investment and modernization in the zone, and hence precluded dramatic increases in production. It was these economic factors, rather than the vulnerability of the tenant, which persuaded the government to act. The immediate opportunity to do so was provided by a serious drought in 1968 and 1969 which threatened to destroy rice production on many estates. Pressures from technical assistance agencies to control the market for rice were paralleled at this time by experiments in setting up rice cooperatives. Finally, the decree abolishing 'precarious tenancy' in the rice zone, *Decreto 1001*, is compared with other agrarian reform legislation, and the immediate effects of its introduction are examined.

The abolition of *precarismo* accompanied the growth of peasant unrest in the rice zone. This is documented in Chapter VI which also discusses whether rice *precaristas* represented a social class with distinctive interests. Most of this chapter is devoted to specific case studies of peasant unrest on individual estates, and details are given of the kind of response this unrest provoked from landlords and the government. The articulation of landlord interests by one political group, SIPPTAL, is examined. Finally, the nature and objectives of the principal peasant federations are discussed. These are the secondary organizations supported by *campesinos* at the local level which represent the former tenants to the various state organizations responsible for implementing the reform. It is argued that, in the absence of a grass-roots consciousness of shared interests, the peasant federations are hamstrung by their dependence on the state, irrespective of their political complexion.

Chapter VII examines the process of agrarian reform in the rice zone since 1970. In addition to the 'political incorporation' of the *campesinos*, a process of social differentiation is distinguished which had led the major beneficiaries of the agrarian reform to increased collective dependence on the state. Figures for land distribution since 1970 are analysed and the redistribution of land titles, rather than a reduction in social inequality, is identified as the characteristic feature of the 'agrarian reform'. The fact that the adjudication of land is now linked to the provision of agricultural credit reinforces the dependency of the former tenants, and the failure to link the distribution of land to a more fundamental change in the balance of power between peasants and landlords. At the same time the state bureaucracy has been extended to the processing and marketing of rice, as well as the establishment of production cooperatives by the Ministry of Agriculture. The bureaucratic apparatus through which rice is marketed, the commercialization process, is seen as the necessary precondition for this kind of agrarian reform, and the means of achieving an increase in the marketed surplus.

Having analysed the agrarian reform process at the regional and national level, in Chapter VIII the focus is on the effects of agrarian reform in one rice cooperative. The problems facing this cooperative, 'Pancho Rule', are fairly typical of those faced by all but a few former estates in the reformed sector. First, differences in the private ownership of land and livestock within the cooperative affect each family's willingness to support corporate initiatives. Some groups expect to gain more than others from increasing the amount of communally-worked land, for example. Second, suspicion of the cooperative's leaders and the technical advisers with whom the members have close relations makes collective decision-making difficult. Although members express a belief in the value of greater unity, they do so for instrumental reasons rather than because of common feeling or common objectives. Unity is seen as a way of securing outside assistance. The divisions within the cooperative mirror divisions in the region as a whole, and the tense relations with development agencies at the local level vividly illustrate the ambivalence of *campesinos* towards state intervention throughout the rice zone. These themes are further considered in the Conclusion, where the wider significance of the processes described in previous chapters is finally assessed.

1. *Precarismo* was a form of leasehold tenure in which the tenant paid his rent in kind. It bears superficial similarity to *aparcería* or sharecropping. See Chapter IV below.

2. For Mexico see John Womack, *Zapata and the Mexican Revolution*, Penguin, 1972. For Bolivia see Dwight B. Heath, Charles Erasmus and Hans Buechler, *Land Reform and Social Revolution in Bolivia*, Praeger, New York, 1969.

3. Eric Hobsbawm, 'Peru: the "Peculiar" Revolution', *New York Review of Books*, 16 December 1971, pp. 33-4ff.
Fitzgerald has shown that the Peruvian 'Revolution' has done little to improve conditions in the urban 'informal' sector and among subsistence agriculturalists, E. V. Fitzgerald, 'The Political Economy of Peru 1968–75', *Development and Change*, vol. 7 (1976), pp. 7–33. The way in which the rural population of northern Peru attempted to push the agrarian reform in more radical directions is described by Colin Harding, 'Land Reform and Social Conflict in Peru', in Abraham F. Lowenthal (ed.), *The Peruvian Experiment*, Princeton University Press, 1975.

4. Baez remarks that: 'The experience of popular government in Chile, under Salvador Allende, the reformist exercise of Torres in Bolivia, and particularly the nationalist "model" of the Peruvian military, did not constitute a point of reference for the civil authorities or the military in Ecuador', R. Baez, 'Hacia un subdesarrollo "moderno"', in *Ecuador: pasado y presente*, Instituto de Investigaciones Económicas, Quito, p. 252.

5. It is not suggested that land concentration and political power are of little importance in Latin America, merely that such an analysis often ignores the way in which agricultural enterprises have changed. The importance of land concentration in Ecuador is asserted in Chapter II below. Cf. Keith Griffin, *Land Concentration and Rural Poverty*, Macmillan, 1976.

6. David Lehmann, 'Agrarian Structure: typology and paths of transformation in Latin America', *Peasants Seminar*, University of London, 11 June 1976.
The most useful summary of the CIDA Reports is S. Barraclough (ed.), *Agrarian Structure in Latin America*, D. C. Heath, 1973.

7. A. Pearse, 'Metropolis and Peasant: the expansion of the urban-industrial complex and the changing rural structure', in T. Shanin (ed.), *Peasants and Peasant Societies*, Penguin, 1971. R. Stavenhagen, 'Changing functions of the community in

underdeveloped countries', in H. Bernstein (ed.), *Underdevelopment and Development*, Penguin, 1973. V. I. Lenin, 'The Development of Capitalism in Russia', *Collected Works*, vol. 3, Lawrence and Wishart, London, 1972.

8. A. G. Frank, *Latin America: Underdevelopment or Revolution*, Monthly Review Press, New York, 1969. A. G. Frank, *Capitalism and Underdevelopment in Latin America*, Monthly Review Press, 1969; Penguin, 1972.

9. Among the best critiques of the Neo-Marxist approach are: Philip O'Brien, 'A Critique of Latin Theories of Dependency', in I. Oxaal *et al.*, *Beyond the Sociology of Development*, RKP, 1975, and David Booth, 'Andre Gunder Frank: an introduction and appreciation', in ibid. Cf. also, Aidan Foster-Carter, 'Neo-Marxist Approaches to Development and Underdevelopment', in Emanuel de Kadt and Gavin Williams (eds.), *Sociology and Development*, Tavistock, 1974.

10. For a cogent criticism of Frank cf. E. Laclau, 'Feudalism and Capitalism in Latin America', *New Left Review*, no. 67, May–June 1971.

11. L. Althusser and E. Balibar, *Reading Capital*, Pantheon Books, New York, 1970. C. Meillassoux, 'From reproduction: a Marxist approach to economic anthropology', *Economy and Society*, vol. 1, no. 1, 1972; W. Roseberry, 'Rent, Differentiation and the Development of Capitalism among Peasants', *American Anthropologist*, vol. 78, no. 1, 1976. A. Emmanuel (ed.), *Unequal Exchange*, New Left Books, 1972.

12. S. Amin and K. Vergopoulos, *La Question Paysanne et le Capitalisme*, Paris, Anthropos, 1974.

13. W. Roseberry, op. cit.

14. Juarez Brandao Lopes, 'Capitalist Development and Agrarian Structure in Brazil', paper given to the conference of the *Urban and Regional Studies Committee of the International Sociological Association*, Messina, Sicily, March 1976.

15. N. Mouzelis, 'Capitalism and the Development of Agriculture' (Review Article), *Journal of Peasant Studies*, vol. 3, no. 4, July 1976.

16. Keith Griffin, *The Political Economy of Agrarian Change*, Macmillan, 1974 and UNRISD, *Rural Cooperatives as Agents of Change*, Geneva, 1974. Both these publications—the fruits of a United Nations research project on the economic and social effects of the 'Green Revolution' technology—warn of the effects of this technology on the rural social structure.

17. An important exception is Ernest Feder, cf. for example, 'The New World Bank Programme for the Self-Liquidisation of the Third World Peasantry', *The Journal of Peasant Studies*, vol. 3, no. 3 April 1976.

II

AGRARIAN DEVELOPMENT IN ECUADOR

In this chapter the characteristics of Ecuadorian agrarian structure are examined in the context of economic development and the class structure at the national level.[1] As in other Latin American states, rural society in Ecuador is distinguished by the coexistence of areas of large landholdings (*latifundia*), which occupy most of the agricultural land, and smallholdings (*minifundia*), which support most of the rural population barely above subsistence level. Extensive cattle grazing on the highland *latifundia* accounts for both the poor economic performance of the agricultural sector, in providing insufficient agricultural produce for domestic consumption, and the inability of the *campesino* population to gain access to land themselves. It also explains the survival of a complex of patronage relations around the *hacienda* system which are prejudicial to the solidarity and well-being of the peasantry. These relations, which one report vividly describes as an 'institutional weft', limit the access of most of the rural population to urban benefits, as well as productive land.[2] An analysis of agrarian development policy begins, then, with the recognition that 'the agrarian structure both influences, and is influenced by, the social structure.[3]

The general empirical parameters of the *latifundia/minifundia* systems will first be established and the social relations arising out of land tenure discussed. We will then consider the disappointing history of agrarian reform in Ecuador. Agrarian reform has only been attempted in a desultory way during the last decade, in the face of strong landlord opposition, and without enthusiastic government support. The outcome has been that the agrarian structure remains substantially unchanged, and inequalities in rural society persist. Indeed, it is argued that the adjudication of land to former 'labour-tenants' under the 1964 Agrarian Reform Law, has served to reinforce social differentiation within the agrarian sector, by 'modernizing' production relations on the highland *latifundia* at the expense of inflating still further the numbers of *minifundistas* in the Sierra. The effort to establish modern capitalist farming, the 'marginalization' of much of the rural population, and the progressive decomposition of areas of *minifundia*, are themes to which we will return in later chapters.

ECONOMIC DEVELOPMENT AND THE CLASS STRUCTURE

The absence of any concerted pressure for agrarian reform in Ecuador is largely explained by the country's economic backwardness throughout the modern period. On the eve of the industrial expansion which the oil revenues promised, Ecuador remained one of the least industrialized Latin American countries. Perhaps of greater significance, the urban population was much less important than in neighbouring countries such as Colombia or Peru.[4]

Like many other countries in Latin America most of Ecuador's national territory is very thinly populated; the Oriente or eastern Amazonian region contained only 1·9 per cent of the population in 1969.[5] The bulk of the population live in the highland Sierra and lowland Coastal regions, both of which are characterized by the co-existence of *latifundia* and small peasant holdings (*minifundia*). In the Ecuadorian Sierra it is the *minifundia* which support the majority of families on arable land, while the large estates are devoted to cattle grazing or simply left fallow. The concentration of the Indian population on high-

Table 1. Percentage distribution of the economically active population between urban and rural areas (1962–80)

	Total population	Urban population	Rural population
	(100%)	%	%
1962	1,528,500	34·03	65·90
1965	1,649,800	34·79	65·21
1970	1,940,900	37·38	62·62
1975	2,297,600	40·30	59·70
1980	2,721,800	43·11	56·89

Sources: Censo Nacionales de Población 1950 and 1962, and as projected (1980) by the *Junta Nacional de Planificación.*

land *minifundia* found periodic release in seasonal migration to the Coast, where the migrants were employed in plantation work, cutting cane or harvesting bananas in areas such as Milagro and Pasaje.

During the 1950s migration from the Sierra to the Coast intensified. New colonization areas were opened up, such as Santo Domingo de los Colorados, and the city of Guayaquil expanded to cover the mangrove swamps at the mouth of the Guayas river. Four-fifths of the migrants during this decade moved to the provinces of Guayas, Los Rios and El Oro. It had been estimated that, if current trends continued, over 70 per cent of the population would be urban by 1990.[6]

Although the urbanization process came later in Ecuador than in most other Latin American states, its structural characteristics were very much the same as in other countries. Despite the fact that the net increase in population during the 1950s was roughly 3 per cent a year, only an insignificant part of this increase was absorbed by the industrial sector.[7] Thus in 1964 only 16 per cent of the labour force was employed in industry.[8] Even within this sector most employment was not in modern manufacturing industry but in artisan activities—only 1·7 per cent of the labour force was employed in manufacturing industry in 1964. At that time agriculture supported just under half of the labour force, and the service sector absorbed 36 per cent of the working population.[9]

Industrialization in Ecuador touched only a small minority of the population. Textile industry had developed in the Sierra in the early part of this century, but it was small in scale. In the 1920s there was some industrial expansion on the Coast, in cement production and food manufacturing, but it made an insignificant contribution to Gross Domestic Product. By 1968 over a third of all industrial manufacturing still consisted of food products, and only 7 per cent of manufacturing output was in heavy metals. Over 90 per cent of manufactured goods were for internal consumption.[10] The vast majority of factories were located in the provinces of Guayas and Pichincha, around Guayaquil and Quito respectively.[11]

The rapid increase in urban population, and the almost insignificant industrial base, made Ecuador a relatively poor country even by Latin American standards.[12] The increase in the *per capita* Gross National Product between 1950 and 1968 was about 5 per cent per annum, a rate which only just exceeded the rate of population increase. It should be added that *per capita* figures do not, of course, register inequality in the distribution of income between social classes. In 1968 a survey of the *Junta Nacional de Planificación* showed that almost 65 per cent of urban workers earned less than fifty U.S. dollars a month.[13] In one of the few attempts to represent the population in terms of social classes Torres suggested that in 1950 almost four-fifths of the population was 'lower-class'.[14] Hurtado was able to claim, ten years later, that the picture was substantially the same.[15]

There is considerable evidence that by the late 1960s Ecuador was more economically dependent on foreign capital investment than it had been ten years earlier. After 1965 the demand for bananas fell, particularly in North America, and the President, Velasco Ibarra, threatened to bring foreign interests under national control.[16] At the same time the bureaucracy was expanding in size, and civil servants' salaries were increased considerably.[17] Agustín Cueva dubbed this process, through which the enlarged bureaucracy employed the middle classes, 'the creation of a nuclei of technical-military decision making'.[18] This was also the period when foreign investment increased significantly, from 29·7 million U.S. dollars in 1961 to 78·9 million U.S. dollars in 1968.[19] Within a longer historical perspective this increase in foreign investment is even more marked. Between 1900 and 1959 only seventeen foreign-owned firms had operated in Ecuador; by 1975 there were a hundred and thirty-four.[20] This investment had not strengthened Ecuador's financial position in world trade, and by 1969 the balance of payments deficit stood at 81 million U.S. dollars.

This was the economic situation in 1971 when it was first announced that 'almost overnight Ecuador will be transformed from a "banana republic" into the second most important oil producer in the continent, after Venezuela'.[21] Within the next four years this rather startling conclusion seemed to be justified by the increase in export earnings from oil.[22] These earnings stimulated development efforts within the country which, unlike some other Latin American states, had never participated in 'import substitution' industrialization in the years during and after World War II. Ecuador entered its 'development phase' in the era of the multinational corporation, decades after most West European countries had successfully mounted their post-war economic recoveries.

This summary of recent economic development in Ecuador suggests a number of important factors to be considered in the discussion of agrarian reform. First, it is clear that pressures for agrarian reform were not mounted in Ecuador because a class of industrial entrepreneurs and an industrial working class had developed in the 1950s and 1960s. Left-wing political groups drew little or no popular support. Unlike Mexico, Venezuela or Chile urbanization had been belated in Ecuador and industry had been particularly slow to establish itself. Second, the exist-ence of traditional 'feudal' relations on the *haciendas* of the Sierra, and the shortage of regular wage employment in Coastal agriculture, made it possible for Coastal landlords to introduce *precarismo* in the rice zone and avail themselves of an im-poverished labour force. Third, throughout the 1960s Ecuador became more and more subject to foreign pressure to introduce reforms consistent with the Alliance for Progress. Unlike Peru, where agrarian reform was advocated as a way of keeping North American interests out of the country, in Ecuador agrarian reform was largely sponsored by North American interests, particularly the Agency for International Development. It is important to bear these facts in mind when considering the changes that have occurred in the agrarian structure of Ecuador during the last three decades.

LAND TENURE AND LAND DISTRIBUTION

Like many other Latin American countries, Ecuador is unable, under present circumstances, to produce enough food to feed its population. In 1967 it imported £7 million worth of agricultural produce; by 1970 this figure had risen to over £14 million, according to the Institute of Economic Research in Quito.[23] The very low rate of growth of agricultural production has served to depress internal demand for manufactured goods, while population increase has outstripped the capacity of both *latifundia* and *minifundia* to meet domestic food needs. The malaise of the agricultural sector is not new: in 1961 ECLA commented on the low capital investment in agriculture, the low productivity of labour and the imbalance between land and labour, all of which were largely attributable to the land tenure system. It commented that 'the high degree of concentration of agricultural holdings, combined with their unequal size distribution' was responsible for the low levels of productivity in agriculture.[24] Almost ten years later the Commission for the Development of the Guayas Basin (CEDEGE) similarly stated that the rural sector was characterized by 'inadequate and anachronistic systems of land tenure and labour relations . . . an unjust distribution of income . . . and a lack of social mobility'.[25]

According to the last complete Agricultural Census (1954), most of the population engaged in agricultural production were landowners. Without distinguishing between large estates and small holdings, both types of 'landowner' were found to work 68 per cent of farm units and 81·5 per cent of agricultural land. By comparison 'tenants', both in cash and in kind (share-croppers), worked only 9 per cent of farm units and 8 per cent of the land area (see Table 2). The most significant differences,

Table 2. Land distribution by type of tenure, 1954

| Type of Tenure | Farm Units | | Land Area | |
	Number of farms	%	1,000 ha	%
Owners	233,900	67·9	4,889·4	81·5
Renters	17,039	4·9	426·2	7·1
Sharecroppers	13,336	3·9	64·7	1·1
Huasipungeros	19,747	4·7	60·8	1·0
Comuneros	5,778	1·7	25·7	0·4
Other simple leaseholders	23,783	6·9	202·0	3·4
Other mixed types	30,652	9·0	330·9	5·5
Total	344,234	100·0	5,999·7	100·0

Source: *Primer Censo Agropecuario Nacional—1954*, Tabla no. 4, pp. 25–6.

as we would expect, are those between different categories of land ownership (as set out in Table 3). Given the monopolization of land by relatively few landowning families, perhaps it is

Table 3. Land distribution by size of farm, 1954 and 1968

Size of Farm (ha)	Farm Units				Area			
	1954		1968		1954		1968	
	Number	%	Number	%	1,000 ha	%	1,000 ha	%
Less than 1·0	92,387	26·8	106,273	32·6	46·0	0·8	93·0	1·3
1·0– 4·9	159,299	46·3	264,074	41·7	386·2	6·4	615·6	8·9
5·0– 9·9	36,250	10·5	68,527	10·8	271·5	4·5	466·3	6·7
10·0–19·9	21,400	6·2	36,228	5·7	294·3	4·9	485·6	7·0
20·0–49·9	19,415	5·6	32,746	5·2	591·5	9·9	1018·3	14·7
50·0–99·9	8,327	2·4	15,555	2·5	547·2	9·1	976·7	14·1
100·0–499·9	5,787	1·7	8,467	1·3	1,156·3	19·3	1,647·9	23·8
500·0–999·9	664	0·2	922	0·1	464·7	7·7	634·6	9·1
1,000 and more	705	0·2	426	0·1	2,242·0	37·4	999·6	14·4
Total	344,234	100·0	633,218	100·0	5,999·7	100·0	6,937·5	100·0

Note: data for 1954 and 1968 are not entirely comparable because of difference in geographic coverage.
Sources: Primer Censo Agropecuario Nacional—1954, Tabla no. 3, p. 7; Encuesta Agropecuaria Nacional—1968, Cuadro no. 1, p. 1.

not surprising that leaving land unproductive is, under some circumstances, a rational course of action for a landlord to take.[26] A redistribution of the factors of production among the rural population as a whole would, however, yield higher aggregate production, and bring more land into use.

During the 1960s, in particular, increasing numbers of *campesinos* left the land and settled in urban areas (see Table 1). This migrant population accounts for the high rate of growth of the urban population (4·7 per cent) compared with the smaller net increase of population in rural areas (2·7 per cent). This reduction in the relative size of the agricultural population, however, was not matched by increased agricultural production such as that experienced in developed countries during their industrialization. In 1972, the net increase in agricultural production exceeded the net increase in population by less than 1 per cent per annum.[27] The same source points out that the agricultural sector still accounted for over half the economically active population in that year, and almost 90 per cent of the goods destined for domestic consumption.[28] It was thus possible to conclude that 'the *latifundia* and the *minifundia* are the structural cause of the crisis in the production of foodstuffs that the country is suffering from, and which manifests itself in price rises and huge food imports'.[29]

The distribution of agricultural land in Ecuador was even more unequal than that of most of the countries studied by CIDA in the 1960s. Of the seven countries studied, Ecuador had the highest percentage (89·9 per cent) of farm units classified as 'sub-family' units.[30] At the other end of the scale the 1954 Census showed that barely 1 per cent of the total number of farms occupied almost 57 per cent of the agricultural land (Table 3). This land was largely devoted to extensive pastoral farming in the Sierra.

Inequality in land ownership, a fact firmly established by the 1954 Agricultural Census, was confirmed by the Sample Census of 1968. In the intervening years an Agrarian Reform Law, the first in Ecuadorian history, had been passed. It had already been noted that investment in agriculture, both private and public, was very much less than in either commerce or industry, despite the economy's heavy dependence on agricultural production.[31] This lack of investment, among other factors, was given as the main reason why Ecuador would benefit from agrarian reform, providing that land redistribution was combined with technical and financial assistance to small producers.[32]

The distribution of land in Ecuador as a whole should also be considered in relation to differences between the coastal and sierra population (see Table 4). In recent years movements of population have served to alter the social composition of the

Table 4. Percentage distribution of the population by regions*

	Total population	Sierra population	Coastal population
	(100%)	%	%
1950	3,202,757	58·0	40·5
1962	4,476,007	50·7	47·6
1969	5,973,300	49·8	48·2

*The Oriente and Galapagos Islands have been excluded from this Table.
Sources: Censos 1950 and 1962 and as projected (1969) by the Junta Nacional de Planificación.

urban and rural populations in both regions of the country. Most remarkably, the Coastal port of Guayaquil has grown in size to a city of over a million inhabitants. Traditionally Coastal political interests were the only ones associated with foreign trade, and combined this activity with the production on Coastal plantations of cash crops for export markets. By contrast, the Sierra landowners contributed little to export production, and represented the more traditional conservative influence in the country.

What has distinguished the Coast from the Sierra, however, is not an absence of *latifundia* on the Coast, but the differences in the organization of production between large estates in both regions. In the Sierra most of the Indian population had been 'tied' to the estate by debts of labour service, or lived at subsistence levels on independent *minifundia*. In practice the highland *campesino* population migrated regularly to the Coast, sometimes on a seasonal basis. There was also permanent settlement. On the Coast the majority of *campesinos* are either free wage labourers or tenant farmers producing crops for export.[33]

Most Coastal crop production, like that of cocoa, which formed the basis for Ecuador's boom in the late nineteenth and early twentieth centuries, is founded upon the plantation, using a more advanced technology than that of the highland *hacienda*.[34] The absence of sufficient labour for plantation work also stimulated employers to provide better working conditions and better wages than those found in the Sierra.[35]

Since Alfaro's Liberal Revolution in 1895, when Coastal interests asserted themselves at the national political level, the landowning classes in both Sierra and Coast have been broadly in alignment in their opposition to a redistributive agrarian reform. Today the two regions may constitute 'two super-imposed worlds', as the title of a recent book has put it; but these two worlds do not reflect incompatible class interests.[36] Since, as we have seen, the implications of land distribution, and the forms of land tenure, extend beyond the economic considerations discussed above, it is necessary to consider the nature of social relations on the *latifundia* of the Sierra in more detail, before examining the record of agrarian reform.

SOCIAL RELATIONS ON THE 'HACIENDA'

A cursory glance at the way an Ecuadorian *hacienda* is organized might leave one with the impression that social relations have changed little since colonial times. This view would be seriously misleading. It is a merit of the CIDA study, published in 1965, that in its analysis of social relations on the *hacienda*, it emphasizes the way in which estates are shedding many of their traditional features. Having acknowledged the dynamism within the 'modern' estate it is essential, nevertheless, to account, too, for the remarkable historical continuity of social relations in the Sierra.

As elsewhere in Andean Latin America, the economic and social relations between *latifundia* and the *campesino* population are essentially symbiotic. In the Andean countries, the existence of a large indigenous population at the time of the Conquest, introduced an ethnic component into this relationship from the outset. The Indian population was concentrated in peasant communities, whose lands were periodically threatened by the expansion of the *hacienda* system. At the same time the inhabitants of these communities were drawn upon to make up workforces, for use in the mines and agricultural enterprises of the Spanish population. Through the institution of the *mita* an obligation was placed upon Indian settlements to supply a certain proportion of their labour force, on a rota basis, for work of different kinds.

Parallel and complementary to the institution of the *mita* was the institution of labour-service, which 'refers to the contrived bondage of an individual' rather than assigning a group to the obligatory performance of labour.[37] In return for the usufruct to a piece of land on the estate, the *campesino* was expected to undertake so many days of labour service on the *hacienda*. As elsewhere in the Andean countries the severity of the labour obligation, and the bargaining position of the peasant in relation to that of the landlord, depended on the availability of labour and the intensity of production on the estate. On occasions the Indian population had to be coerced directly into this role; on other occasions inducements could be used to make this role relatively more attractive. Consequently, the degree of rigour with which labour-service was enforced, and the number of opportunities for employment off the estate, conditioned the freedom of movement of the *hacienda* dependants.[38] Normally, however, the landlord was a patron in the widest sense, and the *campesino* who worked on the estate was dependent on the goodwill of the landlord as well as being heavily 'indebted' to him.

The institution of the '*huasipungo*', the plot of land binding the 'serf' to the estate, was the Ecuadorian equivalent of a system found throughout Andean Latin America.[39] The conditions under which the *huasipungero* existed on the estate, were probably no worse than those in the Indian communities which bordered the *hacienda*. Both sections of the Indian population, those on the estate and those in the communities or *minifundia*, were inhibited structurally by the existence of the *latifundia* system, and the demands it made on both land and labour. Where they differed was in the degree to which they could seal themselves off from the penetration of *criollo* values, as well as economic pressures. Ethnic 'boundaries' encircled the Indian community for reasons of self-protection rather than cultural myopia. This fact alone should make one suspicious of rhetorical demands for the 'integration' of the *minifundia,* such as those which have accompanied most political strategies of agrarian reform in Ecuador.

In the original edition of the CIDA Report, and in subsequent publications, Baraona established a typology of highland estate systems undergoing internal changes.[40] These systems are distinguished by the relative importance of three factors in the *hacienda* enterprise: the landlord's capacity to extract rent from *campesinos* operating their own 'enterprises' on his land (cash-tenants and sharecroppers); the assistance given by the *campesino* in the functioning of the landlord's enterprise (the *huasipungero*); and what he terms the 'manorial power' of the landlord over groups that often live outside the *hacienda* (such as the *yanapa*). The appropriateness of the term 'manorial' for expressing these relations can be disputed.[41] There is, nevertheless, some merit in distinguishing between the roles performed by the landlord, as well as the *campesino,* not merely in the interest of analytical clarity, but also because the way in which these roles are combined is changing markedly in many parts of the Ecuadorian Sierra. Similarly, for the peasant, the nature of the 'structural binds' which link him to the market derive in some degree from the precise tenurial relationships in which he plays a part.[42]

In practice the types of social relation depicted by Baraona might all be found on the same estate, and the actual way in which roles are interpreted varies widely. The types of *hacienda* system that Baraona distinguishes—'infra-traditional', 'traditional in disintegration', 'common traditional' and 'emerging modern'—correspond to 'ideal types' in the Weberian sense rather than empirical categories.[43] What Baraona identifies through his typology is the successful penetration of capitalist working relations on the *hacienda,* the employment of new technologies, and the substitution of wage-labour for traditional forms of servitude. As Barraclough has said, commenting on Baraona's report, until such time as the dominance of the *hacienda* is ended in the Sierra, 'even the transference of *huasipungos* has simply meant that some people change their position within the same invariable institutional framework'.[44]

AGRARIAN REFORM (I) 1964-1970

Agrarian reform first became a political issue in Ecuador in the 1960 Presidential election campaign. Until then few politicians had been willing to espouse the cause of the *campesino* population, whose own attempts at political organization met with ruthless opposition, particularly in the Sierra.[45] An organized labour movement scarcely existed even on the Coast, where most of the population came to support populist politicians, notably Asaad Bucaram, leader of the *Confederación de Fuerzas Populares* (C.F.P.). In the Sierra almost half a century had passed since the abolition of imprisonment for debts had removed the legal basis for the forced conscription of the Indian population, the *concertaje*.[46]

By the early 1950s, however, particularly following the publication of the 1954 Agrarian Census, the accumulation of evidence on the landholding structure persuaded some of those concerned with Ecuador's 'development' that agrarian reform was necessary if industrialization was to be achieved. There followed a series of publications dealing with the structural problems of Ecuadorian agriculture, and the deficiencies of the rural social structure.[47] In May 1954 the newly created National Planning Organization (*Junta Nacional de Planificación*) prepared a report advocating agrarian reform, which helped to provide the impetus for the foundation of the embryo Agrarian Reform Institute, the *Instituto Nacional de Colonización*, in 1957. In the following year the *Instituto* carried out a pilot project for the colonization of Santo Domingo de Los Colorados, an area of land on the Coast, sixty miles west of Quito.

The election of Velasco Ibarra to the Presidency in 1960 brought promises of agrarian reform for the first time; but when Velasco appointed a commission to study the agrarian problem he encountered concerted opposition from landholding interests. His successor, Carlos Julio Arosemena, who at one point declared himself sympathetic to the Castro government in Havana, agreed to enact an agrarian reform by executive decree, but he was deposed by a military coup in July 1963. It was left to the military government to introduce Ecuador's first

Agrarian Reform Law in 1964, and to establish the Agrarian Reform Institute (IERAC).

The Agrarian Reform Law of 1964 was referred to by the military government at the time as 'the cornerstone on which to build a new, harmonious, just and dynamic Ecuador'.[48] Inspired, like other agrarian reforms in Latin America of the same period, by the Charter of the Alliance for Progress drawn up in *Punta del Este*, Uruguay, the 1964 Law aimed to reform the agrarian structure through the consent of all the interested parties. The ideological inspiration for the Law was the 'modernization' of Ecuadorian agriculture through the displacement of 'feudal' tenurial institutions and the establishment of modern business farming. The main provision of the Law was the abolition of so-called 'precarious' systems of land tenure (*precarismo*), notably the *huasipungo* system and its equivalent in the province of Loja, the *arrimado*. Otherwise, except for a small number of estates owned by the Church which were handed over to IERAC, there were few clauses directed at the large landowners in the Sierra. A 'ceiling' was established which was supposed to constitute the maximum legal limit of landholding, 2,500 ha on the Coast and 800 ha in the Sierra, plus 1,000 ha of pasture land in either region; but this was never enforced. In addition a system was worked out through which landlords whose lands were affected by the Reform, would receive compensation in the form of agrarian reform bonds issued by IERAC.

Landlord opposition, even to the moderate provisions of the 1964 Law, made its enforcement difficult. This opposition was particularly successful given the lack of enthusiasm for the Law in government circles. The need to provide funds with which to compensate landowners, combined with other financial problems at the time, forced the government to impose new import duties, and these in turn aroused the opposition of Coastal trading interests.[49] Even prior to the publication of the Law the landlords' organization, the *Cámara de Agricultura*, stated its opposition to any attempt to redistribute land, declaring that 'the only solution was to look for increased production, which will automatically bring improvements in living standards'.[50] Twelve years later, and after a succession of similar statements from the *Cámaras*, the magazine *Nueva* commented that it was 'laughable that the most backward and inept organization (in Ecuador) sought protection in technical arguments to defend its privileges'.[51]

Most commentators on the 1964 Agrarian Reform Law are agreed that it 'aimed to establish the dominance of capitalist development within Ecuadorian agriculture'.[52] This was to be secured, apparently, with the active participation of the land-lords themselves. The liberal credentials of the Reform were obvious. As José Moncada commented:

What is certain is that the Agrarian Reform Law . . . constituted an instrument for inspiring absolute respect for private landed property, by securing the intervention of the 'reformed' sector in the reform itself.[53]

The CIDA Report had noted that the language of the Law was much more 'developmentalist' than 'redistributive', although it was conceded that it had important political implications.[54] Not everyone agreed with the Ecuadorian Communist Party leader, Pedro Saad, that restrictions on the size of landed property were 'the first fundamental objective' of an agrarian reform; but most commentators concurred in the belief that under the provisions of the Law 'not one large property could be affected'.[55]

Broadly speaking, the 1964 Law conforms to what Antonio García, the Colombian sociologist, has described as a 'marginal agrarian reform'. Such a reform has three main functions, according to García: to preserve the *latifundia* under the aegis of a liberal State, to deny to the *campesinos* any say in the way the reform is carried out, and to establish a capitalist land market through investment in existing large enterprises.[56] Judged by these criteria the Reform might be considered a success, al-though for more than a decade after the Law was passed even the capitalist landowning interests who might have been expected to support the principles of the reform, have judged it a failure.

Whatever the ideological inspiration for the 1964 Agrarian Reform Law, and the shortcomings of its provisions, much more might have been achieved by implementing the reform vigor-ously from the beginning. The failures of the succeeding years can partly be attributed to the fact that *campesino* support was never enlisted in the implementation of the Law. Noting the pressure put on its Legislative supporters by the *Cámaras de Agricultura*, the CIDA Report compared this unfavourably with the 'absence of any discussion of ideas originating from the *campesinos*'.[57] The strategy of the Agrarian Reform was to avoid confrontation with landlords, something 'which would occur if the *campesinos* took the initiative in occupying land . . . as they had done elsewhere in Latin America'.[58] *Campesino* participation in the carrying out of the reform was as alien to the spirit of the Law as *campesino* participation in the framing of the Law itself. Unlike other agrarian reforms in Latin America, such as those in Bolivia and in Mexico, this Law had not been the result of pressure from below.[59]

The second major impediment to the successful implementation of the 1964 Law, was the financial and political vulnerability of the Land Reform Institute, IERAC. From the beginning IERAC did not receive the financial resources which were necessary, if the Law was to be properly enforced. Between 1964 and mid-1970 a succession of governments did little 'but pay lip service to the desirability of an effective agrarian reform'.[60] At the beginning of the period the budget allocated to IERAC was more generous than it subsequently became; over £2 million being spent between 1964 and the end of 1966. From 1966 until 1969 the budget was cut drastically, and the organization suffered from a change of Director, on average, once every seven months.[61] Within the public sector most government departments were suffering from expenditure cuts, and only the *Junta Nacional de Planificación*, which had no direct operational role, supported the idea of agrarian reform.[62]

The crises which constantly recurred in the hierarchy of IERAC were partly a response to fluctuating budgets and partly the result of intrigues by political appointees, many of whom had no enthusiasm for agrarian reform.[63] In the Sierra *campesino* attempts at mobilization were easily thwarted; only on the Coast did land invasions pose a real threat to landlord interests after 1967. The abolition of the *huasipungo* system, where it still existed, was sometimes undertaken with the support, indeed the connivance, of the landlords themselves. In these cases landlords welcomed the opportunity to rid themselves of 'tenants' whose labour was not as useful as that of free wage-labourers.

Five years after the 1964 Law was introduced it was calculated that, at the current rate at which land was being handed over to former *huasipungeros*, it would be one hundred and seventy years before all the *precaristas* in Ecuador were in possession of land.[64] At this time there were an estimated 176,000 such tenants throughout the country. Of these an estimated 21,000 *huasipungeros* were calculated to have benefited through the Reform.[65] The estimates of the Land Reform Institute itself, put the figure at 23,485 *huasipungeros* and *arrimados* in possession of titles to land by 1973.[66] What is certain is that the number of smallholdings increased by very much more than this during the same period; largely because of the sale of plots to *campesinos* by landlords.[67]

The implementation of the 1963 Agrarian Reform Law was not simply unenthusiastic; it was also the occasion for many abuses on the part of landlords and IERAC technical personnel. Although the Law prohibited the division of parcels once adjudicated, the 'land famine' was such that many parcels were subdivided.[68] This meant that plots of 3 ha, for example, were divided two or three more times. Subdivision of holdings thus weakened the *campesino's* position *vis-à-vis* the landlord. In the southern province of Loja landlords sold much of the land which the *arrimados* should have received, to middlemen, in an attempt to circumvent the reform. Amongst the *arrimados*, those who could count on favours from the landlord received the best parcels of land.[69] Many 'beneficiaries' had to work for wages in an attempt to pay for the land they received. In other cases the landlords, hoping to elude the officials from IERAC, claimed that the proposed beneficiaries had never been *arrimados*, or had failed to complete the ten years service without which the former labour-tenant could not receive the plot without payment.[70] For these reasons, the Law was not even successful in meeting its limited objectives. Moreover, the manner in which the Law was evaded makes any systematic attempt to retrace what actually happened extremely difficult. By 1970, certainly, the implementation of the Reform had lost rather than gained momentum, and general disillusionment with IERAC had increased on all sides.

AGRARIAN REFORM (II) 1970–1975

In 1970 Velasco Ibarra, then President for the fifth time, made efforts to centralize the Ecuadorian agrarian reform, on what was taken to be the 'Peruvian Model'. Considerable interest was shown in the agrarian reform being carried out in Peru, particularly in the Peruvian claim that the 'Revolution' that was occurring in that country pointed towards a middle way between Communism and capitalism.[71] Such a perspective had some appeal for Velasco Ibarra, and in conscious imitation of the Peruvian military's experience, he placed IERAC under the control of the Ministry of Agriculture. Whatever its intention the effect of this measure was almost the opposite of that in Peru:

Whereas in the progressive Peruvian regime, this bureaucratic structure gave the law the full force of support by the regime, in Ecuador it debilitated the Land Reform Institute by delivering it to the control of the agrarian elite interests dominating the Ministry of Agriculture, and prevented the President from direct action.[72]

This interpretation can be challenged for, as Blankstein and Zuvekas suggest, what really counts in an agrarian reform is the support given to a programme 'not its location in the bureaucracy'.[73] However, the fact that in this case the bureaucracy concerned was so opposed to agrarian reform certainly cannot be discounted. As will be demonstrated in later chapters, the policy of the Ministry of Agriculture towards the *campesino* population of the Coast compares unfavourably even with other departments of the State.

In the period between 1970 and 1973 little progress was made in adjudicating land under the existing Agrarian Reform Law. Most of IERAC's activity was confined to colonization zones, particularly in the Oriente. Here 19,000 peasant families were settled on 709,000 ha of land by 1973; this represented almost as many families, and three times as much land, as was adjudicated to the *campesinos* under the agrarian reform proper.[74] As elsewhere in Latin America, colonization was promoted as an alternative to land redistribution in areas of population pressure.

The politics of agrarian reform in the early 1970s, and especially after oil revenues became significant in 1972, was dominated by recurring rumours of an imminent and radical new Agrarian Reform Law. Eventually, in April 1972, Velasco Ibarra was deposed and a military government came to power. In July 1972 after only a few months of the military regime, a document purporting to come from IERAC, and advocating more sweeping changes in policy, was 'leaked' to the press. This caused alarm among Coastal landlords, who threatened to stop paying taxes on their land if the proposals were implemented.[75] The government replied that the document was not official, but merely the first draft of a working-party report. This denial had little effect in assuaging the fears of landowners or the expectations of peasants. Indeed, the *Federación Nacional de Campesinos* (FENOC) took the opportunity to demand radical proposals immediately.[76] There were also voices raised in support of a more radical agrarian reform, from within the IERAC hierarchy. The Regional Director of IERAC on the Coast, Fernandez Chaves, spoke at a rally of *campesinos* in more forthright terms than was customary:

We are bound by a Law that prevents us from developing our more dynamic aspirations . . . it is necessary that we do so if we are to meet the needs of the *campesino* masses. A Ministry of Agrarian Reform must be created in order to comply with the objectives of the Agrarian Reform.[77]

Almost a year later, in June 1973, the alarm was raised again. This time a report was leaked that important changes were on the way, while the new Minister of Agriculture, Guillermo Maldonado was discussing the subject with the interested parties.[78] Nothing happened, however, until the removal of Maldonado soon after the proclamation of the new Agrarian Reform Law on the 15th October. It has been assumed that Maldonado was removed from office as the result of landlord pressure, because he was said to favour a more vigorous implementation of the Law.[79]

The anticipation of a more radical Agrarian Reform Law was entirely consistent with the view espoused by the military government itself on assuming office in 1972. At that time the military had made similar utterances to those that had followed their previous assumption of power:

. . . an Agrarian Reform will be undertaken that is real and effective in such a way that we will see the disappearance of unjust forms of land tenure, the failure to take advantage of natural resources, the human degradation that exists in the countryside and the poor returns from backward systems of agricultural production.[80]

Furthermore, for the first time in Ecuadorian history the possession of significant foreign exchange from the sale of oil made the prospect of an 'agrarian reform' a real possibility. This reform could be financed without a major redistribution of wealth or power. Such a reform could utilize sophisticated technology, where it was appropriate, and through infra- structural improvements make a contribution to solving the deficit in domestic food production.

Doubts had been raised about the likelihood of such measures. The *Junta de Planificación* had warned against the prospect of oil revenues being used to pay for growing food imports. This 'would eventually mean a progressive destruction of agricultural production for internal consumption'.[81] This view was shared by the Communist Party leader, Pedro Saad, who feared that the oil revenues would give the existing agrarian structure a new lease of life.[82] Such motives were certainly in the minds of the landlords themselves, who stepped up the pressure for more government loans and credits.[83] These would be used for buying tractors from abroad, although in the absence of infrastructural changes, mechanization would be of little benefit to either small producers or consumers.

The text of the 1973 Agrarian Reform Law differed only in its emphasis from that of 1964. It stated that the government would play an increasingly active part in encouraging large landlords to introduce new methods of agricultural production, and to bring more underutilized land under the plough. The main objectives of the reform were to introduce internal changes in an enterprise through a mixture of private and public invest- ment, and to abolish once and for all the spectre of 'feudal' forms of land tenure. These provisions, which had already characterized the prosecution of the agrarian reform in the Coastal rice zone, were extended to the whole country.

Firstly, the 1973 Law allowed the State to select zones in which the 'transformation of the productive system' could be undertaken by means of the concentration of public and private investment and the application of modern technology.[84] This was alluded to in the first Article of the Law, as 'a new social system of market enterprises'.[85] Two years after the 1973 Agrarian Reform Law, the government issued a clarification of its original position, when a new '*Ley de Fomento Agropecuario*' was being contemplated. This statement confirms that the government's main aim was 'to give the agriculturist the role, not merely of landowner, but of a modern entrepreneur'.[86]

Secondly, the 1973 Law provided for no 'ceiling' on land-holding, like that of 1964. This met with landlord support, and Ruben Chiriboga, the President of the *Cámara de Agricultura*, stated that any such legislation was looked upon favourably by landlords, since 'it respects ... property which is worked properly whatever its extension'.[87] All that was required was that landowners respected the 'social function of property', which the State had a duty to enforce.[88] This phrase had cropped up continually in Ecuadorian legislation since the early 1960s, and had become almost the hallmark of liberal agrarian reform measures. The failure to conform with the 'social function of property' gave the State the right to intervene in the agrarian structure, even at the risk of contravening the right of the individual to own land. In practice this meant that where it could be proved that the landlord was not cultivating at least 80 per cent of his land it could be expropriated.[89]

It was clear, then, that the 1973 Law was not directed at the maldistribution of land, but rather the form that agricultural enterprises took. Article 23 of the Law stated that any land owned by a proprietor who did not administer it directly, was eligible for expropriation.[90] Those who used the labour of *precaristas* were not working their land directly, and could expect IERAC to intervene on behalf of the tenants. Such *precaristas* were defined as 'any peasants who work land that does not belong to them, and pay for its use with money, produce, work or services'.[91] This would appear to include cash-tenants (*arrendatarios*), many of whom worked on modern enterprises, like those in the province of El Oro. However, the following article of the Law, specifically excluded from the definition of *precarista* any tenants who worked land which IERAC judged to be in conformity with 'the social functions of property'.[92]

In practice the Law was aimed at those landlords who had proved to be least able, or willing, to modernize their estimates on the lines advocated by the government. Where it could be proved that 'precarious forms of tenure' existed, and *campesino* organizations had some degree of official recognition, 'agricultural cooperatives' were to be formed. To this effect the 1973 Law officially established *Organisaciones Campesinas Provisionales de Reforma Agraria* (OCRAs) or 'pre-cooperatives' which would 'promote among members the exploitation in common, of the land'.[93] The implications of organizing production cooperatives in this way, are examined in a later chapter.

By the time the 1973 Agrarian Reform Law was issued the oil revenues were already making possible an estimated ten-fold increase in publicly-financed agricultural development.[94] This was the process that the President, Rodriguez Lara, had referred to as '*La siembra del petróleo*' (the sowing of oil), an expression which was soon taken up by peasant organizations on the Coast. The intention of the 1973 Law was to promote internal changes in estates which would make them more productive, and less liable to the charge that their owners worked land inefficiently or did not work it at all. It was rather disingenuous of the Ecuadorian Communist Party to claim, then, that the Law could be interpreted as a means to redistribution.[95] The important thing was that it could be implemented without being interpreted as a means to redistribution. What the military government intended was to establish a much larger capitalist sector within agriculture, which in chosen areas of the country would be subject to much more urban bureaucratic control. Any benefits to tenants working under systems of *precarismo* were thus incidental to the main objective of the Law.

THE CRISIS OF THE 'MINIFUNDIA'

Although nominally intended to liquidate 'feudal' forms of land tenure, the principal effect of the 1964 Agrarian Reform Law, as we have seen, was to add to the proliferation of smallholdings in the Sierra. By 1973 it was abundantly clear that no redistributive land reform was likely, at least in the short term, and that the main efforts of the military would be expended in efforts to 'modernize' agricultural production on the *latifundia*. The nature of the crisis developing in areas of *minifundia* in the years following the first Agrarian Reform Law, needs to be analysed before the full significance of this '*desarrollista*' strategy in the agricultural sector can be appreciated.[96]

After eleven years of 'agrarian reform' it has been estimated that the Ecuadorian Sierra supports over 1,850,000 *campesinos* and their families on approximately 1,236,000 ha of land. The average density of population engaged in agriculture is thus roughly 150 *campesinos* to the square kilometre. In many places ratios exceed 500 to the square kilometre, however.[97] It is clear that any attempt to 'integrate' the *minifundia* spatially into a 'reformed' estate sector would rest on the displacement of over one million people.[98] Such efforts would also meet with some opposition from those ex-*huasipungeros* and their families who were either adjudicated land under the Agrarian Reform Law, or who have bought land from latifundists. Perhaps two hundred thousand people, cultivating an average of three hectares each family, make up this stratum of ex-tenants.

In the years between 1964 and 1973 it became clear that the proliferation of *minifundia* could not provide a solution to the declining fortunes of the *campesinos* of the Sierra. From the Agricultural Census figures for 1954 and 1968 it can be calculated that the numbers of *minifundistas* of different kinds cultivating less than one hectare of land, had increased from 93,000 to 206,000.[99] By 1968, well over a million people in the Sierra were scraping a living from barely one hectare of land. The contribution of the Agrarian Reform Law of 1964 had been to reinforce existing fragmentation, and population pressure on land. Land had been sold to peasant families by landlords. It had also accelerated 'the immense flight of capital from rural areas, as the money that *campesinos* handed over to landlords was invested in the urban economy, where returns were better'.[100] This stimulus to industrial investment was one of the goals of the architects of the agrarian reform policy.

At the same time the Agrarian Reform Law of 1964 did not

contribute to a raising of *campesino* consciousness in ways that the government could exploit in its dealings with landowning interests. The adjudication of small parcels of land had only served to intensify the individualism of the *campesino*, and to make the formation of genuine agricultural cooperatives more difficult.[101] As Jaime Galarza, a constant critic of both civilian and military governments, had maintained 'the possession of land had become a joke, and the freedom of action (of *campesinos*) was a complete illusion'.[102]

On the basis of their own dubious calculations the landowners in the *Cámara de Agricultura* argued that the only solution to the 'surplus population' in the Sierra was the immediate large-scale colonization of the Oriente jungle.[103] The subdivision of large landholdings in the Sierra would only 'provide a parcel of land four hectares in size for each resettled *campesino* family'.[104] The alternative for the impoverished rural population of the country, who still made up 70 per cent of the 'marginalized' sector according to the Institute of Economic Research, was thus either a settlement in the jungle or in the festering *suburbios* (squatter settlements) of Guayaquil.[105]

The paradox of agrarian reform policy in Eucador is that although little was attempted, and still less achieved, the advocates of agrarian reform have constantly been on the defensive. The changes following the Agrarian Reform Law of 1964 added to the proliferation of *minifundia*, and did nothing to remove the pressure of population upon land. At the same time moral encouragement and, after 1972, financial inducements were provided for the latifundist landlord who was prepared to 'modernize' his holding. As we have seen, this 'modernization' process consisted of conformity to an imaginary 'social function of property'. In cruder but more realistic terms this meant the employment of wage labourers rather than tenants. So far as the ex-*huasipungero* was concerned there were few advantages in exchanging the status of '*precarista*' for that of wage-labourer. The flight from the land, and the increased reliance on wages earned on Coastal plantations or modern estates in the Sierra, were related structurally to the emphasis on capitalist farming. The desperate plight of the majority of the Sierra population does not, as Andrew Pearse recognizes, imply stagnation. Rather 'it suggests a dynamic process of attrition as the peasantry desperately looks for new livelihood opportunities and passes into the later stages of resource-ratio decline'.[106] In the following chapters the process through which tenurial relations have been changed, and modern agricultural enterprises formed, is examined in relation to a part of the Ecuadorian Coast where the changes in the agrarian structure foreshadow the momentum of change in the wider society.

1. 'Agrarian structure' refers to the political, economic and social aspects of agricultural production and land use. 'Land tenure' refers to the rights and obligations governing the ownership and control of land; a somewhat narrower concept.

2. Comisión de Estudios para el Desarrollo de la Cuenca del Rio Guayas (CEDEGE), *Tenencia de la Tierra y Reforma Agraria—un estudio socio-económico y legal*, 1970a, T. Ingledow and Associates Ltd/Guayasconsult, Guayaquil, P. B1.

3. Jose Ignacio Albuja, *Estructura Agraria y Estructura Social*, Universidad Católica, Quito, 1964, p. 17.

4. In 1970 the Ecuadorian population was expected to be 37 per cent urban and 63 per cent rural. The comparable estimates for Colombia were 46 per cent urban and 54 per cent rural, and for Peru they were 53 per cent urban and 47 per cent rural. S. Barraclough and A. Domike, 'Agrarian Structure in Seven Latin American Countries', *L TC Reprint No. 25*, Land Tenure Center, University of Wisconsin, Madison, November 1966

5. Estimate of the *Junta Nacional de Planificación* (1969).

6. Estimate of the *JNP*, quoted in O. Hurtado, *Dos Mundos Superpuestos*, Quito, 1971, p. 87.

7. Net population increase was 2·9 per cent *per annum* in 1950. In 1960 it was 3·2 per cent. *Plan General de Desarrollo*, JNP, Quito, 1963.

8. JNP—*Banco Central* figures, 1964.

9. Ibid.

10. JNP figure for 1965. Three years later the United Nations commented: 'Ecuador still had to import almost all its supplies of equipment and intermediate products and, as in many other Latin American countries, the substitution process was hampered by the narrowness of the domestic market.' *Economic Survey of Latin America 1966*, United Nations New York, 1968, p. 146.

11. *Anuario Estadistica*, Quito, 1968.

12. Ecuador's *per capita* GNP in 1967 was 190 U.S. dollars. This was less than every South American country other than Haiti and Bolivia, *The Times*, London, 29.9.69, p. 11.

13. JNP, survey, 1968, Quito.

14. Reinaldo Torres Caicedo, *Los Estratos Socioeconómicos del Ecuador*, JNP, Quito, 1960.

15. O. Hurtado, op. cit., p. 98.

16. Réne Baez, 'Hacia un subdesarrollo "moderno"', in *Ecuador: pasado y presente*, Instituto de Investigaciones Económicas, Quito, 1976, p. 252.

17. Between 1960 and 1962 salaries in the public sector increased by 8·1 per cent. Between 1964 and 1966 they increased by 23·5 per cent, *Estadísticas Económicas*, JNP, Quito, 1967.

18. A. Cueva, 'La crisis de los años "60"', in *Ecuador: pasado y presente*, op. cit., p. 238.

19. R. Baez, op. cit., p. 250.

20. Of these 134 firms, 110 had been established since 1967. Guillermo Navarro, *La Concentración de Capitales en el Ecuador*, Universidad Central, Quito, 1975.

21. *New York Times*, 18 July 1971.

22. In 1971 Ecuadorian exports were valued at 242·9 million U.S. dollars. Figures for subsequent years were: (1972) 323·2 million, (1973) 575·1 million, (1974) 1,050·0 million

23. Instituto de Investigaciones Económicas, *Visión de Ecuador*, Universidad Central, Quito, 1975, p. 15.

24. Economic Bulletin for Latin America. 'Productivity of the Agricultural Sector in Ecuador', *Economic Commission for Latin America (ECLA)*, vol. vi, no. 2, p. 69.

25. CEDEGE, 1970a, op. cit., p. B12.

26. A Neo-Classical interpretation of landlord decision making is offered by Anthony Bottomley, 'Monopolistic Rent Determination in Underdeveloped Rural Areas', *Kyklos*, vol. xix, 1966, pp. 106–17.

17. *Visión*, op. cit., p. 13.

28. Ibid., p. 14.

29. Ibid., p. 15.

30. That is, units unable to support one family at subsistence levels. Comite Interamericano de Desarrolla Agricola (CIDA), *Tenencia de la Tierra y Desarrollo Socio-Económico del Sector Agrícola, Ecuador*, Washington D. C., 1965.

31. Juan Casals, 'Ecuador: la Estructura Agraria', in Oscar Delgado (ed.), *Reformas Agrarias en la América Latina*, Fondo de Cultura Económico, Mexico, 1965, p. 680.

32. Ibid., p. 684.

33. Central Ecuatoriana de Servicios Agrícolas (CESA), *Una Experienca en Desarrollo Rural*, Quito, 1974, p. 14.

34. Significantly, the Coastal tenants with lowest status until recently, were also producing for the domestic market. These were the rice tenants (*precaristas*) whose change in status is examined in subsequent chapters.

35. CESA, 1974, op. cit., p. 14.

36. Osvaldo Hurtado, *Dos Mundos Superpuestos*, Instituto Ecuatoriano para el Desarrollo Social (INEDES), Quito, 1971.

37. Andrew Pearse, *The Latin American Peasant*, Frank Cass, London, 1975, p. 27.

38. The power of the *hacendado* to control the movement of labour has usually, been exaggerated. This is discussed by Juan Martinez-Alier, 'Landowners and Peasants in the Central Sierra of Peru', paper delivered to the Symposium on 'Landlord and Peasant in Latin America and the Caribbean', University of Cambridge, 1972.

39. Cf. Piedad Costales, *El Huasipungo*, Quito, 1962; Manuel M. Marzal, 'El Indio y la Tierra en el Ecuador', *América Indigena*, enero 1963; Jorge Icaza's remarkable novel, *Huasipungo*, Buenos Aires, Editorial Losada, 1953; Hugo Burgos Guevara, *Relaciones Interétnicas en Riobamba*, Mexico, 1970. For the most complete bibliography on Ecuador, including the ethnographic literature, see R. J. Bromley, *Bibliografía del Ecuador: Ciencias Sociales, Económicas y Geograficas*, Junta de Planifacación, Quito, 1970.

40. CIDA, op. cit., and Solon Barraclough, *Agrarian Structure in Latin America*, D. C. Heath, 1973, p. 201, a summary of all seven CIDA reports.

41. Cf. Cristóbal Kay, 1971, *Comparative Development of the European Manorial System and the Latin American Hacienda System*, University of Sussex, D.Phil. thesis.

42. B. Galjart, 'Peasant cooperation, consciousness and solidarity', *Development and Change*, vol. vi, no. 4, October 1975.

43. Max Weber, *The Methodology of the Social Sciences*, Glencoe, 1949, p. 90.

44. Barraclough, op. cit. p. 213.

45. Muriel Crespi, 'Changing power relations: the rise of peasant unions on traditional Ecuadorian *haciendas*', *Cuadernos Americanos*, vol. 44, no, 4, October 1971.

46. Marzal, op. cit., p. 14.

47. Jose C. Cárdenas, 'Reforma Agraria y Desarrollo Económico en el Ecuador', *El Trimestre Económico*, Julio-Septiembre 1954, pp. 304–25; Juan Casals, 'La Estructura Agraria del Ecuador', *Revista Interamericana de Ciencias Sociales*, 1963.

48. *Ley de Reforma Agraria y Colonización*, Decreto No. 1480, *Registro Oficial*, 23.7.64, p. 1.

49. This at least is the argument of Leslie Ann Brownrigg, 'Interest Groups in Regime Changes in Ecuador', *Inter-American Economic Affairs*, vol. 28, no. 1, 1974, p. 9.

50. *Cámara de Agricultura, Primera Zona*, 17.12.63.

51. *Nueva*, Quito, no. 19 May 1975, p. 13.

52. Proceedings of the *Primer Congreso de Estudiantes de Ciencias Agrícolas del Ecuador*, University of Guayaquil, March 1972, p. 103.

53. José Moncada, *Pasado y presente de la Planifacación en el Ecuador*, Quito, 1973, p. 24.

54. CIDA, op. cit., p. 497.

55. Pedro Saad, *La Realidad Agropecuaria del Ecuador*, Ediciones Claridad, Guayaquil, 1972, pp. 31 and 32.

56. A. Garcia, *Reforma Agraria y Economia Empresarial en América Latina*, Santiago, 1967, p. 28.

57. CIDA, op. cit., p. 495.

58. Ibid., p. 500.

59. CESA, op. cit., p. 16.

60. Charles S. Blankstein and Clarence Zuvekas Jr, 'Agrarian Reform in Ecuador', The Land Tenure Center, University of Wisconsin, Madison, 1974, p. 16. A version of this paper was also published in *Economic Development and Cultural Change*, vol. 22 October 1973, pp. 73–94.

61. Marcelo Ortiz, *El Cooperativismo, un Mito de la Democracia Representativa*, Universidad Central, Quito, 1970, p. 175.

62. Blankstein and Zuvekas, op. cit., 16.

63. Ibid., p. 18.

64. Ortiz, op. cit., p. 128.

65. CESA, op. cit., p. 19.

66. IERAC, *Estadísticas de las Adjudicaciones Legalizadas en Reforma Agraria y Colonización*, Quito, 1973, p. 7.

67. CESA, op. cit., p. 19.

68. Piedad y Alfredo Costales, *Historia Social del Ecuador: Reforma Agraria*, vol. 4, Casa de la Cultura, Quito, 1971, p. 214.

69. Jaime Galarza Zavala, *Los Campesinos dd Loja y Zamora*, Universidad Central, 1973, p. 216.

70. Ibid., pp. 203–25 *passim*.

71. For example, articles in *Mensajero*, January and October 1974, and in *Nueva*, June and July 1975.

72. Brownrigg, op. cit., p. 11.

73. Blankstein and Zuvekas, op. cit., p. 21.

74. IERAC, 'Estadisticas . . .', op. cit., pp. 6 and 7.

75. *El Universo*, Guayaquil, 4.8.72 and 6.8.72.

76. *El Comercio*, Quito, 12.8.72.

77. Reported by Eduardo Morel in *Mensajero*, July 1973, p. 15.

78. *Nueva*, December 1974, p. 51.

79. Ibid., p. 51.

80. *Filosofía y Plan de Acción del Gobierno Revolucionario y Nacionalista del Ecuador*, 10 March 1972.

81. Junta Nacional de Planificación, *Lineamientos fundamentales del plan integral de transformacion y desarrollo*, Quito, 1972.

82. Pedro Saad, 'Nueva Ley de Reforma Agraria del Ecuador', *Documentos IX Congreso P. C. E.*, November 1973, p. 179.

83. *Nueva*, December 1974, p. 53.

84. *Ley de Reforma Agraria*, Registro Oficial no. 410, 15.10.73, Article 3.

85. Ibid., Article 1.

86. *El Comercio*, Quito, 2.7.75.

87. *Nueva*, February 1975, p. 59.

88. *Ley de Reforma Agraria*, 1973 op. cit., Article 2.

89. Ibid., Article 25, paragraph one.

90. Ibid., Article 23.

91. Ibid., Article 34.

92. Ibid., Article 35.

93. Ibid., Article 58, paragraph five.

94. Government sources, reported in *El Universo*, 21.7.75.

95. Saad, 1973, op. cit., *passim*.

96. The term 'desarrollista' I take from Guillermo Navarro, *La Concentración de Capitales en el Ecuador*, Universidad Central, Quito, 1975, p. 102.

97. Emilio Bonifaz, 'La Población Marginada de la Sierra Ecuatoriana', *Ecuador: población y crisis*, CCIE, Quito, 1975, p. 34.

98. Ibid., p. 34.

99. *Primer Censo Agropecuario Nacional 1954* and *Encuesta Agropecuario Nacional 1968*. The 1974 Agricultural Census, due to appear in 1976, is expected to reveal increased numbers.

100. CESA, op. cit., p. 19.

101. Ortiz, op. cit., p. 91.

102. Galarza, 1973, op. cit., p. 247.

103. *Mensajero*, July 1973, p. 14.

104. Ibid., p. 15.

105. *Visión*, op. cit., p. 15.

106. Pearse, op. cit., p. 190.

III

THE EVOLUTION OF COASTAL SOCIETY

The social institutions of the highland *latifundia* have their roots in the *encomienda* system established by the conquistadores, and the functioning of the *hacienda* has to be seen against the historical context of the colonial period. In contrast coastal social relations are the product of nineteenth and twentieth century conditions, particularly the expansion in world trade which led Ecuador, like most Latin American states, to specialize in the production of one or more of the tropical crops.[1] Agricultural production on the Coast was geared to foreign markets, and cycles in the demand for particular crops brought with them different land tenure systems and labour markets. Today rural society in the coastal region reflects a 'diversity of land tenure systems, each of which has its origins in the processes of land occupation'.[2] The result is what Baraona described in the CIDA Report, as 'successive agricultural frontiers, the oldest of which retain traditional qualities that we cannot observe in the more recent'.[3]

Until the export of bananas became an important source of revenue after the Second World War, the pattern of landholding associated with successive export 'booms' was that of tropical *latifundia* as elsewhere on the Pacific Litoral. As in Brazil, 'the new export agriculture was . . . modelled on the large unit, it achieved a basic solidarity with the established *latifundio*'.[4] The banana boom, however, marked the beginning of what has been termed a 'democratization' process within coastal society, as middle-class professional people came to own land on the newly settled 'frontier'. This 'frontier' extended northwards and eastwards from the traditional cocoa estates of the Guayas Basin.[5] The evidence from agricultural censuses is that this much vaunted 'democratization' made little difference to the concentration of landownership in the coastal region as a whole. However, it undoubtedly had profound effects on rural labour markets; accelerating migration from some areas and widening the employment choices open to the coastal *campesino* (*montuvio*). The *campesino* on the Coast had long enjoyed a reputation for independence and freedom from 'feudal' forms of domination. These characteristics were attributed to his participation in a succession of agricultural 'booms'. However, in the 1950s and 1960s the *montuvio* experienced even greater geographical mobility than in the past. *Montuvios* were drawn to the city of Guayaquil as migrants; but at the same time agricultural colonization extended to parts of the coastal hinterland which had never been occupied before. Here the unusual availability of land was a variable that modified the apparent monopolization of power by large landowners in the region.

THE LIBERAL REVOLUTION OF 1896
AND THE COCOA BOOM

Cocoa was exported from Guayaquil in the colonial period and in the early nineteenth century it had a limited market in Europe.[6] Most early accounts of the Ecuadorian Coast, however, suggest that cocoa was only one of a number of tropical crops in the region. Villavicencio mentions that cotton, sugar cane and tobacco were all widely grown in the provinces of Guayas and Los Rios.[7] This was in 1860. Later rubber was produced in commercial quantities, until the initiative passed to Brazil later in the century. Following the brief rubber boom, Ecuador began exporting 'tagua' nuts from the province of Manabí and a dye from the plant '*orchilla colorante*'. None of these products provided the basis for commercial consolidation, however, and the upturns in demand for them were short-lived.

The more settled area of the Guayas Basin, where cocoa and rice were later to be cultivated, was 'little inhabited and little cultivated', according to Wolf in the 1880s.[8] The climate of the area was oppressive particularly during the 'rainy season' between December and March, when flooding made anything but the rearing of livestock difficult. Cocoa was already an important crop by the turn of the century, but its cultivation was confined to the drier areas and the river banks.[9] Foreign travellers, like Edward Whymper in 1879, found that communications on the Coast were primitive, and deplored the difficulty with which mule-trains journeyed from Guayaquil to Quito.[10] The monsoon climate was suitable for the cultivation of rice, but little seems to have been grown. Of the forty-two estates in the Daule area in 1908 only two cultivated rice at all. The most important activities were cattle raising, cocoa and coffee cultivation, and the making of *aguardiente* from sugar grown in the area.[11]

Towards the end of the nineteenth century Ecuador began exporting considerable quantities of cocoa, and the amount of land devoted to the crop increased until the 1920s. During most of this period Ecuador was the world's largest exporter of cocoa, a lead that it subsequently lost to Brazil and the Gold Coast, although even during the height of the cocoa boom many producers did not grow cocoa to the exclusion of all other crops.[12]

The cocoa boom differed from previous speculative adventures principally in providing the first real stimulus to the tropical colonization of the coastal region, which spread northwards from Guayaquil to cover the central and southern parts of the Guayas Basin by the 1920s.[13] It seems appropriate that cocoa, which was named the *'pepa de oro'* ('golden bean'), attracted labour into zones which had previously been sparsely populated, almost in the style of a classical 'gold rush'. It also summoned up entreprenurial talents and energies, in a way that had no precedent in Ecuadorian history. In De la Cuadra's words 'it was soon proposed to convert the *zona montuvia* into one immense cocoa farm, just as Cuba was being converted into an immense sugar factory'.[14]

Except in the area known as the 'Arriba District', along the middle Babahoyo River and its tributaries, cocoa estates were widely dispersed, and cocoa was usually grown in conjunction with other crops. The commercial potential opened up by its cultivation acted as a magnet for absentee landlords, bringing them back to their estates, in some cases from overseas.[15] This in turn stimulated the commercial and banking sector of Guayaquil, which rapidly became an important port and business centre. Foreign observers who were otherwise critical of Ecuador conceded that Guayaquil had economic significance. The North American William Eleroy Curtis remarked that Guayaquil was 'the only town in Ecuador worth speaking of from a commercial point of view'.[16] He added that there was 'a considerable business done (there), some of the merchants carry stocks of imported goods valued at half a million dollars, with an annual trade of double that amount'.[17] Gradually the business interests associated with the export of cocoa developed a political and economic ideology inspired by 'laissez-faire', seeing in Ecuador's agricultural specialization the means to lucrative self-advancement. Such liberal sentiments drew popular support on the Coast, and gave the region a political identity *vis-à-vis* the dominant conservative interests of the sierra.

The political structure of Ecuador was characterized by almost continuous *caudillismo*, in which government performance depended upon the personal qualities of individual dictators or presidents. From the early 1860s Gabriel García Moreno ruled Ecuador ruthlessly but was responsible for a number of notable achievements in the fields of communication and technical progress.[18] In the succeeding two decades, after García Moreno's death in 1875, the coastal business and landowning interests grew in strength. Under the leadership of Eloy Alfaro, Liberalism became the political expression of this new commercial class and captured the support of the masses as well as the export bourgeoisie. The rural population made up *montoneras*, or popular militias, which supported Alfaro in the hope of receiving plots of land when the 'Liberal Revolution' succeeded.[19] This success came in 1896, and the 'Revolution' was institutionalized by Alfaro's successor, Leonidas Plaza, during Ecuador's period of greatest commercial prosperity in the early years of this century.

The supremacy of Liberal political interests was marked by the military victory of 1896, when Alfaro's troops arrived in Quito. This victory for liberalism confirmed the economic ascendancy of the *Banco Comercial y Agrícola de Guayaquil*, which was founded in 1894. The anti-clerical tendencies of coastal landowners, and later colonization, had reduced to insignificance the power exercised by the Church in the region.[20] Power lay with the export interests and in the early stages of the cocoa boom these were indistinguishable from the landholding class of the region.[21] The period between 1900 and 1913, however, saw a four-fold increase in the provision of credit to cocoa producers and with it a specialization of functions within the financial community. According to one interpretation, this period 'saw the concentration of wealth . . . in the hands of different fractions of the bourgeoisie'.[22] This process of economic consolidation and class solidarity was only possible because the economic interests of the State and the *Banco Comercial* were looked upon as inseparable. Between 1913 and 1917 the *Banco Comercial* increased its financial interest in external trade from 17 per cent to 71 per cent of total export credit. By the latter date the coastal export interests constituted the dominant social class and had achieved its objective which was, according to Moreano, 'the control of external trade, monetary circulation, credit mechanisms and the budgetary apparatus of the state'.[23] From 1916 to 1925 the coastal interests representing the vast bulk of commercial activity in the country dominated national politics, through the controlling hand of the *Banco Comercial*.

THE COCOA SLUMP AND THE JULY REVOLUTION OF 1925

The period between 1880 and 1920 marked a rise in the fortunes of the coastal export interests, and the diminishing influence of *serrano* landowners on national policy. It has been suggested that these years saw the transition from a preponderantly 'feudal mode of production' to a 'capitalist' one, but such an interpretation is too sweeping.[24] Detailed examination of coastal social structure during this period reveals important shifts in the balance of social forces, and the first stirrings of group consciousness among much of the rural population. The *montuvio*, according to Agustín Cueva, was acquiring a 'class physiognomy', although the origins of this process can be distinguished in an earlier period.[25]

Coastal labour had always exhibited greater independence of the landlords than the largely Indian population of the Sierra. This gave rise to an exaggerated regional pride, which can be seen in the Press and other documents of the period. Quintana and Palacios describe the *montuvio* as:

An independent character, with a love of liberty and an extraordinary sensitivity yet rebelliousness towards despotic impositions. This distinguishes the people of the Littoral, preventing them from being slaves, or virtual slaves, like the Indian population of the Sierra.[26]

Such perspectives on the 'characteristics' of a region's population are not altogether free from ethnocentrism.[27] Nevertheless, the view which the *montuvio* took of himself as well as of other groups, cannot be entirely ignored. In the estimation of most Ecuadorians he was an independent and outgoing individual.

The comparative 'independence' of the coastal population should not be explained simply in economic terms, though it would be wrong to underestimate the importance of market forces generally on the people of the region. Since the abolition of *concertaje* the demand for labour, particularly during the 'peak' periods of sowing and harvesting, had given the *montuvio* some bargaining power in relation to the landlord.[28] The scarcity of population on the coast 'made it difficult to establish semi-feudal social relations', and in order to attract people to the region from the Sierra 'it was necessary to offer them better conditions of work and wages in cash'.[29] As Cueva has pointed out, capitalist social relations existed even when coastal exports consisted solely of products derived from the forests, like timber, furs and rubber.[30] Wage labour, however, was not introduced 'until the plantation owners, growing cocoa and coffee, had to attract labour to work for them'.[31] By the early 1960s, when the CIDA Report was published, an estimated 52 per cent of the agricultural population of the coast was made up of wage-labourers.[32]

During the period of the cocoa boom wage-labourers were not the only social class to make its appearance on the coast. Many small producers were tenants, so called '*finqueros*', like those in Milagro described in the CIDA Report.[33] Similar land tenure systems existed for other crops of longer growing cycle, too, such as bananas and coffee. These were cultivated under the system of '*redención*'. The sowing of the crop, and the care of the plants, were the responsibility of the tenant who paid the landlord for the use of his land. Under the system of *redención*, however, the tenant did not market the crop himself; rather, the landlord stepped in to 'redeem' the plants just prior to the harvest, paying the tenant a sum of money for each plant.[34] This system, which was particularly disliked by the *finqueros*, was one in which 'the landlord used the land solely to obtain rent, playing a passive role in relation to production'.[35] For the tenant, then, institutions like the *redención* merely 'substituted robbery for slavery'.[36]

Tenant cultivators, like the cocoa *finquero*, often employed labour themselves, and this shaped their attitudes not only to the *rentier* landlord but to the wage-labourers beneath them in the social hierarchy. Some writers have interpreted the status of the *finquero* as an 'intermediate' one which provided the landlord with the labour of the *campesino* family as well as peasant entrepreneurship. The *finquero* participated in this system in the hope of one day becoming a landowner himself.[37] As José de la Cuadra observed, 'this is the ambition of the *finquero*, and in accomplishing it he will sacrifice whatever is necessary'.[38] The most usual sacrifice was the acceptance of the landlord's patronage 'which made an ally of the tenant'. De la Cuadra thus locates the tenant 'between the exploited labourer and the exploiting landlord, occupying a middle position, but disposed to unite his interests with those of the dominant class'.[39]

The cocoa boom was longer-lived than previous periods of commercial prosperity, but ultimately cocoa was equally vulnerable to both changes in world demand and crop diseases. Production reached its peak in 1914 when 47,200 tons of cocoa were exported, but within a decade production had been cut to a third of this magnitude.[40] The change had come about partly as a result of the ravages of 'Witch's Broom' and 'Monilla' diseases, and partly because of a contraction in demand.[41] The population of the declining cocoa estates shifted to the cities in large numbers.[42] The cocoa slump also led to the conversion of the interior of many cocoa estates into areas of rice production. As Palacios and Quintana commented, 'it became customary to permit annual sowings, principally of rice, but at an excessively high annual rental'.[43] The cocoa tenant and wage labourer were thus transformed, in many instances, to an even more onerous existence as rice *precaristas*. At the same time the highly labour intensive nature of rice production, especially under 'transplanting' systems of cultivation, 'helped to absorb most of the surplus population that was unable to find work after the crisis of the 1920s'.[44]

The process which began with the slump in cocoa production did not lead directly to an expansion in rice production however. The conversion of part of the labour force employed on the cocoa estates into rice producers, spanned several decades, and many ex-cocoa *finqueros* migrated to the city. Some large estates were bought by the banks, or passed to them as the landlords' creditors.[45] Others were divided into parcels of about 10 ha and sold to former tenants, usually after the tenants had claimed the land as their own.[46] Thus the economic crisis also stimulated peasant entrepreneurship on the Coast. Sometimes the estates were simply left physically to disintegrate.[47] After a period of time, and following the parcellization of some estates, they were bought by foreign companies who consolidated the smallholdings that had been formed.[48] These companies were credited by coastal landlords with offering better conditions to their work-force, and thus making it difficult for Ecuadorian landowners to attract labour.[49] This competition for labour probably forced many Ecuadorian landlords to live on their estates and supervise production more carefully. Certainly commentators at the time detected a lower rate of absenteeism among proprietors of smaller plantations than had been the case in the 1880s and 1890s.[50] Overall, the slump years saw a growing complexity in the forms of land tenure employed on nationally-owned estates, and a strengthening of foreign-owned estates.

In the light of subsequent developments, one of the most significant effects of the cocoa slump was increased group 'consciousness' among *campesinos* on the coast, although the degree of 'class consciousness' was limited. De la Cuadra, noting the way in which *montuvios* resisted dismissal from the estates, had commented on the lack of unity with which they reacted to the change in their economic fortunes.[51] On thirteen cocoa estates cited by Albornoz, the labour force was reduced by two-thirds within the space of three years.[52] Discontent was also pronounced among small producers, who could not obtain financial assistance from the banks.[53] This was so great in some areas that 'peasants took up arms and formed the classical *"montoneras"* to fight the landowners', just as forty years previously they had fought with the landlords for Alfaro's cause. In reply the government formed 'hunting brigades' in Guayas and Los Rios, to contain the rural protest. There had been mounting evidence of disaffection for some time. Between 1908 and 1927 there were a series of strikes on the coast, particularly on the railroads and cocoa estates.[54] At one time, in 1922, the coastal port of Guayaquil was described as 'paralysed by street demonstrations . . . until it looked as if it was composed of nothing but the proletarian masses'.[55]

The July Revolution of 1925 signified the reassertion of nationalist conservative politics at the national level. The coastal banking 'plutocracy' was blamed for the widespread social protest and the general economic malaise in which the country found itself. The army, which was largely made up of *serranos*, rebelled, and politics came under the control once more of non-Liberal interests. The 'anti-oligarchical' character of coastal Liberalism had rested on the support of the rural and urban masses, but the slump in demand for cocoa had contributed to their alienation from Liberal politics and undermined their automatic support of the landowning class. Since 1925 political success in Ecuador has consisted of culling support from both regions of the country. This has been achieved through the espousal of populist policies which are capable of attracting widespread, if shallow, popular support. The analysis of the political consequences of these changes does not directly concern us.[56] What is immediately relevant is the fragmented nature of coastal society following the demise of the cocoa estates, and the increasing role played by foreign-owned plantations. Finally the dispersal of the population, and its settlement on the 'frontier' opened up by banana cultivation, was to provide coastal society with a 'middle-class' ingredient that was absent during the years of the cocoa boom.

THE CREATION OF AN INTERNAL FRONTIER

The slump in cocoa production contributed, as we have seen, to the weakening of coastal interests at the national level. At the same time the break-up of the cocoa estates produced a plurality of social relations on the Coast. The structural changes in the economy, which found their political expression in the July

Revolution of 1925, also brought unemployment and reprisals from landlords for many *montuvios*. It was not until after the Second World War that Ecuador was to experience a boom comparable to that of cocoa. This time it was social changes associated with banana production which altered the face of coastal society (see Table 5).

Table 5. Exports of agricultural products from Ecuador

Products	1955		1962		1969	
			(millions of U.S. dollars)			
		%		%		%
Bananas	36·8	41·0	88·8	60·6	65·6	43·1
Cocoa	18·7	20·8	15·9	10·9	24·5	16·1
Coffee	23·1	25·7	21·0	14·5	26·6	17·6
Others	5·9	6·6	11·2	7·7	4·1	2·7
Total	84·5	94·1	136·1	93·7	120·8	79·5

Source: *Banco Central del Ecuador*, as published in O. Hurtado, *Dos Mundos Superpuestos* (INEDES), Quito, 1971.

The CIDA Report documents two areas of the Coast where bananas were being grown in the early 1960s, each of which has distinctive characteristics. These were the province of El Oro in the south and the newer colonization zone around Santo Domingo. In the southern province of El Oro bananas were being grown on irrigated land under relatively advanced technical conditions. The development of this area, largely by people from the southern Sierra, took place later than in the Guayas Basin, but before Santo Domingo. Banana plantations occupied 25,000 hectares of irrigated land in 1962. In this year an estimated 50 per cent of the land devoted to banana cultivation in El Oro was owned by four families.[57] The rest of the land was divided up among owners and tenants of small and medium size holdings—the average size was about 20 ha by 1971.[58] At the time of the CIDA Report 60 per cent of these small and medium size holdings were being worked by cash tenants.[59] Nevertheless, the Report commented on the absence of 'precarious' tenure relations in the area, and the fact that minifundism did not 'exhibit such grave characteristics as in other regions of the country'.[60]

The second banana zone to be considered in the CIDA Report was that around Santo Domingo de los Colorados to the north of the Guayas Basin which had not been colonized until the 1950s and 1960s. The commercial production of bananas had begun in the Babahoyo-Naranjal area of the Guayas Basin in the late 1940s and the area under cultivation stretched northwards to Quevedo and Santo Domingo within the space of a decade. The variety of banana grown in this area, the 'Gros Michel', suffered from a number of diseases which were eventually kept in check by government-organized spraying from the air. However, difficulties in the cultivation of the 'Gros Michel' led to another variety, the 'Cavendish', being introduced later to the drier irrigated soils of El Oro (see Table 6). The climate

Table 6. Banana plantations in Ecuador (1971)

Provinces	'Gross Michel'		'Cavendish'		Total	
	Number	Hectares	Number	Hectares	Number	Hectares
Guayas	11	323	239	16,507	250	16,830
Manabí	5	123	15	495	20	618
Esmeraldas	136	3,506	1	4	137	3,510
Los Rios	796	35,306	171	8,950	967	44,246
El Oro	6	179	1,217	25,438	1,224	25,617
Pichincha	98	5,114	22	351	120	5,465
Cotopaxi	71	2,611	20	510	91	3,121
Canar	—	—	56	2,071	56	2,071
Azuay	—	—	2	49	2	49
Total	1,124	47,162	1,743	54,375	2,867	101,537

Source: Programa Nacional del Banana, Guayaquil Económico, Instituto de Investigaciones Económicas y Políticas, Universidad de Guayaquil, 1971.

and their distance from a port made Quevedo and Santo Domingo 'frontier' zones, which were settled by people from other parts of the Coast and particularly urban middle class families.

The movement of people into these northern 'frontier' zones has often been interpreted as part of a 'democratization' process, which replaced the coastal *latifundia* with family farming.[61] Herrera Vásconez, in his study of banana producers, states that 'this middle class element has produced a real democratization

Table 7. Distribution of banana plantations by size of holding (1963)

Size of plantation	Holdings		Area	
	Number	%	Hectares	%
less than 25 ha	871	47·88	11,024	10·89
26 to 100 ha	740	40·69	38,559	38·10
101 to 500 ha	192	10·55	36,606	36·17
501 to 1000 ha	11	0·60	7,701	7·61
more than 1000 ha	5	0·28	7,313	7·23
Total	1,819	100·00	101,203	100·00

Source: Cesar Herrera Vásconez, El Cultivo del Banana en el Ecuador (1963), unpublished MS prepared for Junta Nacional de Planificación.

... there is no longer the association between traditional *hacendados*, distinguished by birth and fortune, and their work force ...'.[62] There is some empirical evidence to support this contention, particularly if we look at the modal type of farm. In 1965, 87 per cent of farm units cultivating bananas were under 100 ha in size.[63] Throughout the country the average size of banana holdings was as little as 50 ha in 1971.[64] However, these figures mask the fact that large units (over 100 ha) occupy about half the land devoted to banana cultivation, many of them in the provinces of Guayas and Los Rios.[65]

The 'frontier' which is supposed to have democratized rural society was not made up of the conjunction of *latifundia* and *minifundia* as elsewhere in Ecuador. Further analysis of the groups which have colonized this frontier, reveals that many were of urban middle class origin. CIDA found that of the 71 settlers in one part of Santo Domingo, only 31 had been agriculturalists prior to the colonization of the zone. Among the people of urban origin only a third lived on their holdings, most of which were run by an 'administrator'.[66] Spontaneous colonization had certainly attracted poorer people from Manabí, and the Sierra, but the beneficiaries of 'official' colonization schemes were usually retired servicemen and professionals.[67] Colonization represented a form of investment for the urban middle class.

Between 1948 and 1954 the amount of land opened up to the cultivation of bananas increased tenfold to about 150,000 ha.[68] Problems connected with disease and marketing have tended to counteract the 'redistributive' effects of frontier colonization since this period. Because of the necessity to negotiate with the international companies which buy the crop, many owners are forced to be absent from their holdings for at least two days a week.[69] This foothold gain by urban middle class groups has served to push out their weaker competitors. The CIDA Report summed up this tendency in these words:

The option to ascend the social ladder for the middle-class man, who today might be a landowner, has been qualitatively more significant than the opportunity offered the wage earner or agricultural labourer who remains linked to the new class of proprietors.[70]

CIDA also found that conditions on family farms were often poor for the resident workers, who were given less protection than on large foreign-owned plantations.

It is important to note that the holding of the small producer, particularly when he was solely dependent on it, was less technologically advanced than that of the larger producer, and more vulnerable to plant diseases.[71] The small producer was less able to respond to technical innovations, and could not diversify into other crops as easily as the larger producer.[72] This problem may be aggravated in the long term. The CIDA Report showed that in El Oro province the tenants wanted to specialize in banana production, while their owners from whom they leased the land wanted to diversify.[73] In the more traditional northern zone small producers are under pressure from the international companies which control the export trade, and impose a 'quota' on the amount they are prepared to buy from producers. This effectively reduces the prices the producers receive.[74] Finally, the fact that banana production has been maintained in recent years has not helped the producers, partly because 'export availabilities have expanded more rapidly than import demand'.[75]

The expansion of the agricultural frontier associated with banana production has not had the effect that was anticipated by some commentators in the early 1960s. The majority of banana plantations are, it is true, much smaller than either the livestock *hacienda* of the sierra, or the cocoa plantations of an earlier period. However, the economic vulnerability of small banana producers, and their inability to benefit from economies of scale and technical advances, as well as the control of the exporting companies, have weighted the balance of advantages in favour of larger producers.[76]

The migration northwards within the Guayas Basin has not diminished social tensions in areas of greater population density. As we have seen, many former cocoa *finqueros* were absorbed into production on the interior of estates, where rice was increasingly grown. Here, 'they cultivated a product for domestic consumption under onerous conditions, in areas peripheral to export production'.[77] In some respects their situation was worse as rice *precaristas* than it had been as cocoa tenants, whose contract with the landowner was for several years, corresponding to the longer maturation of the plant. During the cocoa boom years the tenant had been able to exercise some pressure on the landlord, and there was a real opportunity to become an owner in his own right.[78] As a rice producer his opportunity of becoming a landowner receded considerably.

Apart from the migrant population which participated in the colonization of the banana zones, others left the rural areas for the city. This pattern of migration to Guayaquil has been left almost uncharted.[79] Not surprisingly the omission has produced a number of generalizations about the 'alienation' of the urban poor, that have yet to be supported by empirical evidence.[80] What is relatively clear, however, is the scale of migration to Guayaquil. By 1975, the population of the city stood at more than a million, at least 60 per cent of which was made up of first generation immigrants.[81] Among men over 45 only 28 per cent had been born in Guayaquil, and among women of the same age only 20 per cent.[82] The growth in the size of Guayaquil thus accompanied the demise of the cocoa estates, and the increase in rice production on many of these estates. The choice for most *montuvios* in the 1950s and 1960s was between employment as a rice *precarista* in the humid swamps of the Guayas Basin, migration to the newly opened banana zone, or participation in the 'informal sector' of Guayaquil, among some of the most appalling squatter settlements in Latin America.

LAND DISTRIBUTION IN THE RICE ZONE
BEFORE 1970

In the preceding sections of this chapter we looked at the underlying processes of agrarian change on the Coast. Two such processes were identified. First the slump in cocoa production led
to the break-up of estates, although not necessarily to the benefit
of the former tenants.[83] Secondly, the colonization of the
interior of the coast by migrant families of banana producers
also contributed to the social heterogeneity of the region. The
beneficiaries, however, were usually middle class urban groups.
Neither of these processes served to diminish the weak market
position of the small producers, and within two or three decades
the vacuum left by the cocoa slump was filled by the increased
production of rice in the interior of the cocoa estates. In this
concluding section the general pattern of land distribution in
the rice zone is examined against the background of land distribution on the Coast as a whole.

There are various sources of information on the way land was
owned and worked before 1970, the year which marked the
beginning of the coastal agrarian reform. The most comprehensive data is that presented in the first agrarian census (1954)
and the succeeding 'sample' census for 1968.[84] These censuses
are the principal sources for the analysis presented in this section. There are, however, two other sources of information for
the rice producing provinces of Guayas and Los Rios, which are
particularly useful. These are the studies of the Commission for
the Development of the Guayas Basin (CEDEGE), and the
study undertaken for CESA of the production and marketing of
rice.[85]

The unequal distribution of land on the coast before rice
production became important is evident from the 1954 Agricultural Census. For convenience the agricultural holdings (*explo-
taciones*) depicted in the census can be organized into three
strata: those which were less than 10 ha in size, those which
were between 10 and 100 ha and those which were over 100 ha.
From Table 8 we can see that although there are thirteen times
as many units in the 'smallest' stratum 'A', the amount of land

occupied by these holdings is only a ninth of that occupied by the large holdings (stratum 'C').

Fortunately, the 1954 Agricultural Census also provides figures for the amount of cultivated land in units of different sizes. Thus we can compare the way in which the land in different landholding strata was utilized. A comparison of these figures shows that on the largest estates less than a third of the land was cultivated, while on the smallest holdings over 80 per cent of the land was cultivated (Table 9). Clearly on the Coast, as well as in the Sierra, most of the land on the *latifundia* was left fallow or used for grazing cattle, rather than used for the production of crops for export or domestic markets.

Finally, we can consider the proportion of agricultural units worked by tenants, and compare this with the proportion worked by owner-occupiers (Table 10). This reveals that, taking the Coast as a whole, tenants were a small minority, although they were more numerous on small holdings than on large. The early significance of tenancy in the rice zone, however, is suggested by figures for the rice producing provinces of Los Rios and Guayas (Table 11). If we discount holdings which were of a 'mixed' type, or which employed other forms of land tenure (10,000 units altogether), the remaining 21,000 holdings were more often owner-occupied than tenanted. Nevertheless, among the stratum of smallest landholdings (stratum 'A') there were more tenants than owners. It is clear from these figures that the rice producing areas of the Coast were untypical of the Coast as a whole, in that many more holdings were likely to be worked by tenants.[86]

The differences in production on large and small holdings devoted to the cultivation of rice, was also determined in the 1954 Census. At that time each stratum was cultivating about the same aggregate amount of land and producing about the same amount of rice (see Table 12). However, there were fourteen times as many holdings in the 'smallest' stratum as in the 'largest' stratum. The distribution of land actually cultivated was markedly unequal. Furthermore, the extent to which the land was left uncultivated on 'rice' estates emerges clearly from the fact that the average amount of land cultivated with rice on estates of over 100 ha was only 16 ha.

Table 8. Landholding according to strata 1954 (Coast)

	No. of holdings	Hectares
Stratum 'A' (under 10 ha)	53,000	200,000
Stratum 'B' (11 to 100 ha)	27,000	850,000
Stratum 'C' (more than 100 ha	4,000	1,950,000
Total	85,000	3,000,000

Source: Censo Agropecuario Nacional 1954.

Table 9. Land cultivation according to strata 1954 (Coast)

	Landholding (ha)	Land cultivated (ha)
Stratum 'A' (under 10 ha)	200,000	167,000
Stratum 'B' (11 to 100 ha)	850,000	472,000
Stratum 'C' (more than 100 ha)	1,950,000	590,000
Total	3,000,000	1,229,000

Source: Censo Agropecuario Nacional 1954.

Table 10. Tenanted and owned holdings according to strata 1954 (Coast)

	Tenanted holdings	Owned holdings
Stratum 'A' (under 10 ha)	19,000	34,000
Stratum 'B' (11 to 100 ha)	5,000	22,000
Stratum 'C' (more than 100 ha)	200	3,800
Total	24,200	59,800

Source: Censo Agropecuario Nacional 1954.

Table 11. Tenanted and owned holdings in Guayas and Los Rios* 1954

	Tenanted holdings	Owned holdings
Stratum 'A' (under 10 ha)	7,000	6,000
Stratum 'B' (11 to 100 ha)	1,000	5,000
Stratum 'C' (more than 100 ha)	70	2,000
Total	8,070	13,000

*Excluding 'mixed' tenure holdings.
Source: Censo Agropecuario Nacional 1954.

Table 12. Distribution of land under rice cultivation* 1954

	No. of holdings	Hectares	Production (metric cwt.)
Stratum 'A' (under 10 ha)	14,000	19,000	500,000
Stratum 'B' (11 to 100 ha)	7,000	18,000	460,000
Stratum 'C' (more than 100 ha)	1,000	16,000	490,000
Total	22,000	53,000	1,450,000

* 'Winter' season only.
Source: Censo Agropecuario Nacional 1954. .

Table 13. Distribution of land under rice cultivation* 1968

	No. of holdings	Hectares	Production (metric cwt.)
Stratum 'A' (under 10 ha)	78,000	100,000	700,000
Stratum 'B' (11 to 100 ha)	20,000	74,000	840,000
Stratum 'C' (more than 100 ha)	2,000	105,000	1,600,000
Total	100,000	279,000	3,140,000

*'Winter' season only.
Source: Encuesta Agropecuaria Nacional 1968.

The data for landholding and production in 1954 can be use-fully compared with that for 1968, when a 'sample' Agricultural Census was conducted.[87] The information in this Census reveals an accelerating process of socioeconomic differentiation in the rice areas, compared with the situation fifteen years earlier. The total amount of land cultivated by each stratum had increased enormously in magnitude, although the distribution of land between strata was no more unequal (Table 13). Differentiation can be said to have occurred, however, because the number of small-holdings had risen dramatically in the intervening period. There were now almost forty times as many small-holdings as large ones, and the average size of the smallest stratum of hold-ings had dropped from 1·5 ha to just over 1 ha.

A comparison of the 1968 and 1954 census figures also reveals dramatic changes in production on different size holdings. Whereas in 1954 both stratum 'A' and stratum 'C' produced about the same amount of rice on the same amount of land, by

1968 the largest holdings were producing over three times as much rice as the smallest holdings on the same amount of land as the smallest holdings. The changes in the intervening years had not only reduced the size and inflated the number of small landholdings, there had also been a shift in the proportion of rice production contributed by each stratum in favour of the largest landholdings. These holdings were becoming more productive while the smallest holdings, the majority of which were tenanted, were apparently producing only 50 per cent more rice on five times as much land.[88] In terms of productivity per hectare it is worth noting that there had been a marked decline over the preceding fourteen years.

Table 14. Babahoyo: ownership of land 1965

Size of holding	No. of owners	%	Extension (ha)	%
less than 20 ha	757	58·0	6,506	6·4
20 to 99·9 ha	372	28·5	16,668	16·3
100 to 499·9 ha	143	11·0	23,233	30·5
more than 500 ha	34	2·5	47,868	46·8
Total	1,306	100·0	102,275	100·0

Source: CIDA 1965, p. 328

Table 15. Daule–Peripa: ownership of land 1970

Size of holding	No. of holdings	%	Extension (ha)	%
less than 25 ha	2,288	94·3	6,460	20·4
25 to 100 ha	89	3·7	4,340	13·7
100 to 500 ha	41	1·7	8,137	25·6
more than 500 ha	7	0·3	12,770	40·3
Total	2,425	100·0	31,707	100·0

Source: Proyecto de Propósito Multiple Guayas, Resumen de los Estudios Realizados, CEDEGE, vol. 1, 1975.

These figures for the rice producing zone as a whole can be usefully compared with those for one of CEDEGE's 'project areas', Daule-Peripa (Table 15). In this area only 18 per cent of the agriculturists were owners, and 60 per cent were described as 'precaristas'. The 'owners' controlled 75 per cent of the land, compared with 11 per cent controlled by the tenants.[89] The amount of land owned by large owners was particularly important in this area; only 1·5 per cent of the proprietors owned over half the land devoted to rice production.

By 1968 there were fifty-one rice estates of over a thousand hectares, which the Agricultural Census chose to classify as single holdings. There was also an increasing number of very small holdings, which were usually located on large estates but worked by tenants. The former stratum of holdings was becoming increasingly mechanized and productive; the latter was merely absorbing population at a very low technological level. The ease with which the production of rice can keep pace with population expansion in South East Asia has been eloquently documented.[90] What appears to distinguish this area of the Ecuadorian Coast from rice producing areas like Java, however, is the existence of very large rice estates, growing rice under technically advanced conditions. Rice estates in Ecuador have not merely absorbed population expansion; they have also contributed towards growing inequality between different sections of the rural population.

1. As Celso Furtado has written: 'The century between the 1820s and the outbreak of the First World War saw the establishment of an international division of labour and the shaping of a world economic system. The economic activities of a growing proportion of the world's population became interdependent elements of an integrated complex'. Celso Furtado, *Economic Development of Latin America*, Cambridge University Press, 1970, p. 29.

2. CIDA, op. cit., p. 407.

3. Ibid., p. 407.

4. Furtado, op. cit., p. 26.

5. Cesar Herrera Vásconez, *El Cultivo del Banano en el Ecuador*. Report presented to the *Junta Nacional de Planificación* (1963, unpublished), p. 184.

6. Ricketts to Canning, 27 December 1826, in R. A. Humphreys (ed.), *British Consular Reports on the Trade and Politics of Latin America 1824–1826*, London, 1940, p. 184.

7. X. Villavicencio, *Geografía del Ecuador*, Quito, 1860, p. 462.

8. Teodoro Wolf, *Geografía y Geología del Ecuador*, Leipzig, 1892, p. 115.

9. Ibid., p. 142.

10. 'Although republican Ecuadorians have done much levelling, and amongst other things have abolished titles of nobility, they have omitted to level their roads, and cling with curious tenacity to the pompous title of this primitive trade.' Edward Whymper, *Travels amongst the Great Andes of the Equator*, ed. Eric Shipton, Charles Knight, London, 1972, p. 5.

11. Today the Daule area is important for its rice production. Emiliano Caicedo, *El Canton Daule en la Exposición Internacional de Quito*, Guayaquil, 1908, p. 15.

12. Ivar Erneholm, *Cocoa Production of South America: historical development and present geographical distribution*, Gothenburg, 1948. See also James B. Rover, 'Ecuador Cocoa', *Tropical Agriculture*, vol. 3, no. 3, 1926, pp. 46–7 and vol. 3, no. 4, pp. 68–9.

13. Michael T. Hamerly, *A Social and Economic History of the City and District of Guayaquil during the Late Colonial and Independence Periods*, Gainsville, Florida, unpublished Ph.D. thesis, 1970, pp. 137–66 *passim*. *Historia social y económica de la antigua provincia de Guayaquil 1763–1842*, Guayaquil, 1973.

14. José De la Cuadra, 'El Montuvio Ecuatoriano' (1937), in *Obras Completas de José de la Cuadra*, Casa de la Cultura, Quito, 1958, p. 872.

15. 'Compatriots, or the children of compatriots, whose nationality was Ecuadorian, but who had never before trodden the soil of our country, installed themselves with resignation in our wooden houses, drove off the mosquitos and breathed the warm air of the Coast.' De la Cuadra, op. cit., p. 875.

16. William Eleroy Curtis, *The Capitals of Spanish America*, Praeger, New York, 1969, p. 303.

17. Ibid., p. 303.

18. The construction of the Guayaquil-Quito railway was begun, roads were built and schools were founded. However, national unity was only bought at the price of alienating those who did not agree with the religious despotism that García Morena tried to establish. Cf. Oscar Efren Reyes, *Breve Historia General del Ecuador*, vol. 2 (1809–1940), Quito, 1942.

19. Alfaro himself related how, during the battle of Gatazo, a soldier of peasant origin had been spurred by the ardour of the moment to say that he was 'fighting for his liberty', and to request his freedom from the *concertaje*. 'La tierra, viejo conflicto nacional', *Nueva*, no. 19, May 1975, p. 9.

20. Oswaldo Albornoz notes that by 1947, of the 133 *latifundia* owned by the Church in Ecuador, only two were located on the Coast. *Historia de la acción clerical en el Ecuador*, Ediciones Espejo, Quito, 1963, p. 226.

21. Alberto Moreno Cornejo, *Ecuador, Capitalismo y Dependencia*, Quito, 1973, vol. 1, p. 35.

22. Alejandro Moreano, 'Capitalismo y lucha de clases en la primera mitad del siglo XX', in *Ecuador: pasado y presente*, Instituto de Investigaciones Económicas, Universidad Central, Quito, 1975, p. 147.

23. Ibid., p. 148.

24. Moreno writes that, 'the Liberals took power with popular support principally through the *montoneras* . . . taking the initiative in the definitive step for Ecuador, from a preponderantly feudal mode of production to a capitalist one'. Moreno, op. cit., p. 36. He does not, however, show how each mode of production was constituted or consider their interrelationship in different historical periods.

25. 'In effect, on the Coast, at the same time as the integration of a bourgeoisie made up of plantation owners, large merchants and bankers, and a nucleus of petty-bourgeois made up of medium size traders . . . *campesino* groups were also acquiring a class physiognomy, composed not of "serfs" as in the Sierra, but of agricultural labourers or self-employed workers . . . and the appearance of the first "subproletarian" groups, formed as a result of the port activities in Guayaquil.' Cueva, op. cit., p. 11.

26. M. E. Quintana M. and L. A. Palacios O., *Monografía y Album de los Rios*, Quito, 1937, p. 21.

27. This fact is well illustrated by Whitten, who notes that the black population of north-west Ecuador use the term '*montuvio*' as one of abuse, applied exclusively to

coastal Whites. N. E. Whitten Jr., *Black Frontiersmen, A South American Case*, Schenkman, Cambridge, Mass., 1974. p. 179.

28. Quintana and Palacios, op. cit., p.22.
29. CESA, 1974, op. cit., p. 14.
30. Cueva, op. cit., p. 9.
31. Ibid., p. 10.
32. CIDA, 1965, op. cit., p. 16.
33. Ibid., pp. 382–90 *passim*.
34. Hurtado, 1971, op. cit., p. 33.
35. CIDA, 1965, op. cit., p. 385.
36. Quintana and Palacios, op. cit., p. 23.
37. Albuja, op. cit., p. 129.
38. De la Cuadra, op. cit., p. 899.
39. Ibid., p. 899.
40. *Area Handbook for Ecuador*, the American University, Washington D.C. 1966, p. 352.
41. Erneholm, op. cit., pp. 76–92.
42. In view of the fact that many had been working on coastal plantations Moreno's assertion that those who migrated to the city were 'leaving behind feudal relations of production' is inaccurate. Moreno, op. cit., p. 42.
43. Quintana and Palacios, op. cit., p. 116.
44. CESA, 1974, op. cit., p. 14.
45. Quintana and Palacios, op. cit., p. 116.
46. CIDA, pp. 382–90 *passim*, and *Area Handbook*, op. cit., p. 353.
47. Quintana and Palacios, op. cit., p. 116.
48. De la Cuadra, op. cit., p. 895.
49. Ibid., p. 905.
50. Albuja, op. cit., p. 113.
52. De la Cuadra, op. cit., p. 874.
52. Oswaldo Albornoz, *Del Crimen de El Ejido a la Revolución del 9 de Julio, 1925*, Ediciones Claridad, Guayaquil, 1969, p. 61.
53. Ibid., p. 67.
54. Ibid., p. 110.
55. Oscar Efren Reyes, *Breve Historia General del Ecuador*, Ediciones Fray Jodoco Riche, 1960, p. 727.
56. Cf. Lilo Linke, *Ecuador, Country of Contrasts*, O.U.P., 1967; George Maier, *The Ecuadorian Presidential Election of June 2nd 1968: an Analysis*, Washington D.C., Institute for the Comparative Study of Political Systems, 1969; Peter Pyne, 'The Politics of Instability in Ecuador', *Journal of Latin American Studies*, vol. 7, part 1, May 1975; Cueva, op. cit., pp. 81–112 *passim*.
57. CIDA, op. cit., p. 400.
58. See Table 6 this chapter.
59. CIDA, op. cit., p. 406.
60. Ibid., p. 406.
61. For example: 'the production of bananas, coffee and rice . . . has changed the situation considerably (on the Coast) as agricultural units are democratised and profits are distributed among more people'. Juan Casals, op. cit., p. 47.
62. Herrera, op. cit., quoted by Albuja, op. cit., p. 46.
63. *Area Handbook*, op. cit., p. 351; cf. also Table 7 this chapter.
64. See Table 6 this chapter.
65. See Table 7 this chapter.
66. CIDA, op. cit., p. 381.

67. The dilemma of poor migrants from the province of Manabí, is depicted in the play by Simón Corral, *El Cuento de Don Mateo* (Casa de la Culture, Guayaquil), 1967.

68. *Area Handbook*, op. cit., p. 351.

69. CIDA, op. cit., p. 413.

70. Ibid., p. 415.

71. Anne Collin Delavaud, 'La Banane et la Colonisation de la Côte Centrale Equatorienne', paper presented to the Symposium on Regions and Regionalism, International Congress of Americanists, Mexico, September 1974, p. 40.

72. Ibid., p. 41.

73. CIDA, op. cit., pp. 392–406.

74. Alfredo Vera Arrata, *Historia de un Triste Banano*, Imprenta Abad, Guayaquil, 1972.

75. Between 1961 and 1965, Ecuador produced an average of 1,202,000 tons of bananas a year. This increased to 1,267,000 between 1966 and 1970. By 1972 the annual production stood at 1,400,000 tons. *Commodity Review and Outlook*, F.A.O., 1972/3.

76. The CIDA Report predicted these changes a decade ago; and recommended the diversification of agricultural production on 'cooperatives' formed by small producers. CIDA, op. cit., p. 416.

77. CESA, 1974, op. cit., p. 14.

78. De la Cuadra, op. cit., p. 905.

79. An exception is *El Estrato Popular Urbano*, Junto Nacional de Planificación, 1973.

80. Cf. for example, chapter two of Javier Espinosa Zevallos, *La Introducción de la Sociología en el Ecuador*, Casa de la Cultura, Guayaquil, 1972

81. Moreover, most of those who were not themselves migrants were children of migrants. *El Estrato*, op. cit., p. 95.

82. Ibid., p. 103.

83. The CIDA Report, in the section on Babahoyo, commented that large landowners in the area had willingly sold off a small proportion of the land on their estates. This was undertaken so that the price of the land should remain high, and most of the sales were to people other than cocoa *finqueros*. CIDA, op. cit., p. 328.

84. Censo, 1954, op. cit., and Encuesta, 1968, op. cit.,

85. *Tenencia de la Tierre*, op. cit.; also, *Babahoyo Irrigation Project Feasibility Report*, T. Ingledow and Associates, Guayasconsult, CEDEGE, January 1970; *Zones One*, *Prefeasibility Report*, T. Ingledow and Associates, CEDEGE, February 1970; *Proyecto de Propósito Multiple Guayas, Subzona IIIA, Resumen de los Estudios Realizados*, vol. 1, March 1975, CEDEGE, Guayaquil; *Informe de la Encuesta sobre la comercialización por el campesino de la Costa*, CESA, Guayaquil, 1971.

86. It should be added that official statistics tend to disguise the true number of tenants, especially in the rice zone where landlords often denied employing *precaristas*. See Chapter IV, p. 64 below.

87. The *Encuesta*, 1968 did not include information on types of land tenure by crop, like the *Censo*, 1954.

88. This unlikely statistic confirms that it is extremely difficult to assess the production of rice on small holdings, from the quantities that were marketed. Cf. *Informe de la Encuesta Sobre la Comercialización por el Campesino de la Costa*, CESA, 1971, Quito.

89. *Proyecto*, CEDEGE, op. cit., p. 25.

90. Clifford Geertz, *Agricultural Involution*, University of California Press, 1971.

IV

THE SYSTEM OF RICE *PRECARISMO*

In previous chapters we have considered the history of agrarian reform in Ecuador, and the social forces which are represented in the present agrarian structure of the coastal region. It was established that rice production took place on former cocoa estates, which had suffered from the depredations of the cocoa slump in the 1920s. The system of land tenure in the rice zone known as *precarismo*, shows similarities with some sharecropping systems.[1] In this chapter the nature of rice *precarismo* is discussed in more detail, both in terms of the social relations of production which existed on the estate, and the effect of these relations on the way in which rice was processed and sold (the commercialization process). Before considering the specific form that *precarismo* took among rice producers in Ecuador, however, it is necessary to make some general remarks about the characteristics of sharecropping systems and the explanations that have been offered for the existence of such systems.

THE CHARACTERISTICS OF SHARECROPPING AND SIMILAR TENANCY SYSTEMS

The discussion of sharecropping in Latin America has suffered from a number of conceptual and analytical confusions. The most common of these is that which equates 'feudal' type relations such as those between landlord and peasant in the Ecuadorian Sierra, with share-tenancy in areas of export crop production.[2] In the latter case it is unusual to find the tenant performing labour services for the landlord, his labour being confined to the cultivation of a plot of land over which he has some degree of entrepreneurial control. The 'true' sharecropper is also much more closely linked to the market than the highland Indian paying labour service, and relatively free from the landlord's extra-economic coercion. The relations of production found in sharecropping systems in Ecuador are those of the landowning classes associated with exporting interests. If we wish to understand why certain forms of land tenure occur in some parts of a country, and other forms of tenure in another region, there are a number of possible explanations. A conventional economic approach to this question emphasizes either technological determinism or 'factor' endowments in an area. The necessity to preserve the social position or political influence of the landlord class is of secondary importance.[3] Indeed, purely technical reasons have been advanced for the existence of share-tenancy, principal among them the variation in crop yields and the costs of supervising the labour force.[4] Other scholars, such as Martinez-Alier, have attempted to show that if, in the absence of mechanization, economic factors alone are considered, it is the alleged trend towards the increased use of wage-labour which needs to be explained, rather than the survival of share-cropping.[5]

The essence of sharecropping is the agreement which tenant and landlord make about what to produce, what each contribute to the production process and how production should be divided. That there is an 'agreement' between landlord and tenant, however, does not mean that each party to the contract is free from constraint. The tenant's ability to influence the outcome of the contract is obviously much less than that of the landowner.[6] Nevertheless, in any discussion of sharecropping some weight must be attached to the bargaining power of the tenant, and if the tenant possesses the capacity to organize or there is the threat of a land reform, this bargaining power can be considerable. Martinez-Alier, in his analysis of landlord decisions concerning the employment of sharecroppers, argues that these non-economic factors upset the landlord's purely economic logic.[7]

Variations in the degree of entrepreneurial control exercised by the tenant are important on several counts. Tenants who exercise considerable entrepreneurial control are usually most resistant to the payment of any rent at all. The *rentier* landlord is exposed to the allegation that he makes a living from the monopolization of landholding, rather than exhibiting 'enterprise' like an entrepreneur. According to some writers, share-cropping is a source of stability which offers the tenant an interest in agricultural production and more independence of action than he would possess as a wage-labourer.[8] Nevertheless, conferring entrepreneurship on an individual without providing for the ownership of land obviously makes land itself the object of contention.

It is a characteristic of sharecropping systems in areas of export crop production that dependence on the market is at least as important as dependence on the landlord. Like the agricultural labourer on a plantation, the sharecropper is ultimately vulnerable to the impact of external depressions in export crop prices.[9] This risk is, of course, often shared with the landowner. But the utilization of entrepreneurial skills, which the labourer cannot exercise, does not elevate the social status of the sharecropper.[10] In many cases wage labourers are aware of the fact that the tenant's income is less than their own. Unlike most labourers the sharecropper is often able to produce food for his own consumption, and the cultivation of subsistence crops is often an inducement to sharecroppers to settle a 'frontier' region as among coffee growers in Southern Brazil.[11] In other circumstances, however, tenants 'have little or no choice in the selection of what to plant, methods of cultivation, harvesting or marketing of the crop'.[12]

Sharecropping can come into existence under a number of different circumstances. But wherever it exists it possesses certain advantages for the landlord. By employing family labour at less than the ruling wage paid to the rural proletariat, it compensates for the low capital investment in the estate.[13] By allowing the landlord to alter the proportions of the crop which the tenant pays him in rent, it allows the landlord flexibility in the face of market changes.[14] Finally, sharecropping also utilizes what has been described as 'the excess of entrepreneurship in the peasant economy'.[15]

THE SOCIAL RELATIONS OF PRODUCTION UNDER RICE 'PRECARISMO'

Most of the landlords interviewed by CEDEGE in the Guayas Basin would not admit to employing *precaristas*.[16] This was despite abundant evidence that this form of tenancy was common in the rice zone. One survey by CESA of 34 estates located throughout the zone indicated that nine out of ten workers on these estates were *precaristas*.[17] The widespread use of leasehold-tenancy is also suggested by the fact that holdings in the rice zone far outnumbered landowners. A study of the Daule area undertaken by CEDEGE in 1969 suggested that 56 large land-owners were in charge of 631 holdings, while in Babahoyo 57 owners controlled 449 separate holdings. Even allowing for some small proprietors, the conclusion was that '*precarismo* was the principal method of working the land'.[18] The same study also found that 88 per cent of the informants, from all sizes of landholding, were prepared to admit that '*precarismo* was com-mon in the area'. The most reluctant to admit the prevalence of *precarismo* were the largest landowners.[19] Even the records of the *Cámara de Agricultura* on the Coast, an organization of land-owners particularly sensitive to the issue, show that over two-thirds of holdings in the Daule area were worked by tenants.[20]

The way that rice estates were managed before 1970, depended very much on the size of the holding. CEDEGE found that of the ten largest landowners in the Babahoyo area only one was permanently resident on his estate.[21] The other estates were under the day-to-day control of an administrator appointed by the landlord. The absence of the landowner from the estate is partly explained by the fact that 70 per cent of the estates over 500 ha in size were considered by their owners to be of less importance than their non-agricultural activities.[22] On smaller estates the landlord's livelihood was much more likely to be solely dependent on agriculture.

According to Baraona and Delgado the collection of rent was less important than the payment of interest on the credit given to the *precarista*.[23] Under normal circumstances the *precarista* gave the landlord between three and four metric hundredweight of rice in husk for each *cuadra* of land cultivated by the tenant.[24] Since production averaged between 30 and 40 metric hundred-weight a *cuadra*, this amount represented about one-tenth of his production.[25] This estimate, by Baraona and Delgado, is con-firmed by other sources, notably Hurtado and Ojeda.[26] Once subsistence needs had been met, and the rental payment made, the 'surplus' was marketed through intermediaries. However, the *precarista* also had to repay, with interest, those inter-mediaries who had lent him credit.

Production was undertaken entirely by the tenant, who sup-plied the necessary tools and draught animals. Normally these consisted of a sickle, a machete and a horse or mule. The tenant levelled the land, removed the foliage that was growing wild, and prepared the plot for sowing. (This constituted the *desmonte*, after which the tenant was described as a *desmontero*.) These operations were performed in November or December, before the rains arrived. With the commencement of the 'wet season' in January, the crop was sown and later in the season it was usually transplanted. During the growing season there was weeding to be done, and harvesting in May and June, when the rains had subsided.[27] During the harvest even the poorest tenants employed outside labour on their holdings. Very few *precaristas* were able to grow a second crop later in the year.[28]

The amount of land worked by *precaristas* varied widely. The CESA study suggests that the 'poorest' tenants cultivated one-twentieth of the amount of land cultivated by the 'richest', although these examples clearly represent the extremes.[29] The average holding was usually between three and eight hectares.[30] In some areas like Daule, the average size holding was much larger, and throughout the Guayas Basin the amount of land cultivated varied depending on the availability of water. With-out proper irrigation rice production is dependent on variations in rainfall alone.

In comparison with most sharecropping systems a rent of one-tenth of the total production is very small. Nevertheless, accord-ing to the calculation of Baraona and Delgado, 'it enabled the owner to recover the total value of his land (at market prices) within one year'.[31] This is largely attributable to the low value of land on rice estates.[32] These calculations were based on land valuations of the government's valuation office (ONAC) for large estates of more than 1,500 ha. Baraona and Delgado admit that smaller estates, on which land was more highly valued. could not use *precaristas* quite so profitably. On such estates it would take two or three years to recover the value of the land.[33] Not surprisingly, interviews with *precaristas* indicated that 'they were aware that through the exploitation of their labour they had already paid several times over for the land they had worked'.[34]

The rent extracted from the *precarista* by the landlord did not merely consist of rice 'in husk' however. The tenant also paid for the use of water pumps, when they were available, adding another two to four metric cwt. to the rent for each *cuadra* of land.[35] In addition many landlords, though not all, insisted that the tenant paid his rent in 'dehusked' rice. This meant that the landlord obtained more than one-tenth of production. According to Galarza each *precarista* handed over about 180 to 200 pounds of rice as the equivalent of 100 pounds of dehusked rice, when the correct figure would have been about 150 pounds.[36] This enabled the landlords to obtain an income, in 1962, of about eight million *sucres* (£170,000).[37] Considering the artificially low value attached to land at the time, this income from being a *rentier* landlord made it an attractive proposition to employ *precaristas*.

An alternative way of calculating the economic advantages of employing tenants is suggested by Baraona and Delgado. They compare the opportunity cost of employing tenants in place of wage-labourers on rice estates. They calculate that at an hourly rate the income of a *precarista* in 1970 was about half their 'market value' of 5,760 *sucres* p.a. (*c.* £120 p.a.). This market value corresponded to the wage that would be received by a casual wage-labourer for working six hours a day for 240 days. They point out that a permanent wage-labourer could expect to earn about 7,200 sucres a year (£150).[38] Clearly, whether one calculates the landlord's return on the basis of the value attached to the land, or in terms of alternative ways of employing labour, the system of rice *precarismo* had considerable advantages for the landlord.

The advantages of employing tenants were not merely economic, however. What has been described as 'the illusion that he was overtaking the income of a labourer', as well as the necessity to provide so much of his crop in rent, forced the tenant to maximize the efforts he put into production. In doing so he also 'liberated the *hacienda* from the necessity to provide an administrative and supervisory apparatus'.[39] This in turn enabled the landlord to be absent from his estate, which was left in the hands of a bailiff or *mayordomo*.

PATRONAGE AND THE COMMERCIALIZATION PROCESS

The rice which the *precarista* paid to the landlord was only the first of several obligations which he had to meet before his crop could be sold. In return for loans from the owners of rice-mills (*piladoras*) and money-lenders (*fomentadores*) the tenant was obliged to repay the debts he had contracted at high rates of interest. In most cases he sold his crop immediately it had been harvested, so that he could pay off these debts. However, in 37 per cent of the cases studied by CESA the crop was actually sold in anticipation of the harvest.[40] The money-lender who had advanced a loan could then expect to receive about 5 per cent interest monthly, equivalent to 60 per cent interest if spread over the entire year.[41] For the tenant this meant that about 28 per cent of his cash income from selling rice was spent in paying interest on loans he had contracted to private dealers.[42]

The advance sale of the crop bore a similarity to the system of *redención* found amongst producers of crops of longer growing cycle, like coffee and cocoa. Usually the tenant sold the crop to the landlord, or to a rice-mill, if not to a dealer. Most rice-mills were owned by landlords, and the three roles were quite commonly played by one man, or members of the same family. In some circumstances this monopolization of control over the commercialization process meant that landlords-cum-dealers could charge rates of interest as high as 10 per cent per month to tenants.[43] It also enabled the landlord to 'create more subtle bonds (with the tenant) such as gratitude and godparent ties . . . which, in effect, were born of the "protection" which was offered the tenant if he fell foul of the law, or needed medical assistance, or transport . . .'.[44] The multiplicity of cross-cutting ties which bound tenant to landlord made it difficult for the *precarista* to free himself from debt, as well as reinforced his moral obligations to his patron.

According to the leader of the Ecuadorian Communist Party, Pedro Saad, money-lenders bought the rice that the tenant produced at less than the cost of production, which contributed towards an accumulation of debts from one year to the next.[45] Money-lenders were not the only sources of credit, however. CEDEGE found that of the *precaristas* who obtained credit, 33 per cent obtained it from the rice-mills, another 33 per cent from dealers (*comerciantes*) and 26 per cent from money-lenders.[46] In their survey CESA found that in over half the cases they examined *precaristas* used one or more of these sources of credit. Their sample of informants, however, was already collaborating with their organization, and thus was better placed to use official sources of credit.[47] CEDEGE's more representative sample revealed that only 8 per cent of tenants in the rice zone obtained credit from the banks in 1971.[48] In the majority of cases informants were found to 'prefer credit from official sources if it were available'. It was not available, according to the tenants themselves, 'because they did not possess a title to land'.[49] This belief was obviously well founded. Ojeda and his colleagues comment that 'the lack of titles to land, and the need for rental contracts of at least eight years, impeded the *campesino's* access to official sources of credit'.[50]

The control exercised over the tenant by the money-lender and the landlord was matched by that of the *piladora* owner. Unable to obtain credit from official sources, the *precarista* was also unable to sell his rice to anybody but the local rice-mill owner.[51] Baraona and Delgado estimate that most rice-mills bought about 200 to 240 pounds of unmilled rice from tenants for each 100 pounds of milled rice that passed through their hands. This meant that for every 200 pounds of rice the private mill-owner received between 15 and 55 pounds more than the officially-controlled 'Piladora Modelo',[52] Galarza claims that the mills were even more exacting; paying for only 200 pounds of rice for each 100 pounds that was milled.[53] Another private source suggests that 'the most unscrupulous rice-mill owners were able to recoup the capital cost of their mills within a space of three years'.[54] Most rice-mill owners and dealers gave 'over-production' as the reason for the low price the *campesinos* were paid for their rice. This ignores the fact that rice was hoarded by dealers and middlemen after good harvests, until the retail price improved, and in good years even exported at a considerable profit.

The geographical isolation of the *precarista* also contributed towards his dependence on the landowner and his market vulnerability. He could get a better price for his crop by transporting it to Guayaquil to be sold. However, he rarely possessed private transport, and roads were bad. During much of the year the rivers were flooded, roads were unpassable and communication was necessarily by canoe. Nevertheless, on average the *precarista* had to travel eight kilometres to sell his crop to an intermediary or mill-owner.[55] Dealers who were not known to a landowner, or whom he disliked, were forbidden from entering an estate to buy rice.[56] The monopolization of power in the hands of the landlords was thus most effectively seen in the control exerted over the commercialization of the product.

THE STRUCTURAL CHARACTERISTICS OF RICE 'PRECARISMO'

The full significance of a system of land tenure is not confined to the relations between landlord and tenant on an estate. In this chapter we have examined the nature of rice *precarismo* and the economic and social advantages it offered landlords. Explanations for the existence of *precarismo* in the rice zone are not difficult to find. As in similar systems of land tenure elsewhere, rice *precarismo* provided the landlord with excellent returns on his land despite a lack of investment in improved agricultural methods. Labour was plentiful, and its employment within a 'peasant mode of production' enabled the landlord to benefit from the tenant's entrepreneurial efforts as well as the longer hours he spent in the field. Within the production process it was the tenant who took most of the risks, not the landlord, and the tenant's identification with the enterprise made supervision unnecessary. Rice *precarismo* also provided the landlord with control of the commercialization process, by monopolizing the available market outlets for the product. As the owners of rice-mills, landlords were able to appropriate a significant part of the agricultural production of the zone. Looking beyond the production process itself to the system of commercialization which served to trap the *precarista*, CEDEGE commented that 'nothing short of a change in the "mode of production" is necessary before *desmonteros* can become socially integrated'. This social integration would 'not be brought about automatically by the simple transference of a plot of land'.[57]

There are a number of other variables which need to be considered before we can evaluate the full significance of rice *precarismo*. We have established that the form of *precarismo* practised in the rice zone bears little relationship to so-called 'feudal' forms of tenure elsewhere in Latin America. Rice *precarismo* had been introduced within the lifetime of most tenants, to meet the needs of absentee landlords who were unwilling to shoulder the risks of rice production with a paucity of capital. Although the payment of rent in kind was an important part of the system which these landlords introduced, it was by no means as onerous for the tenant as his dependence on the market which the landlord controlled. The absence of proper irrigation techniques and of chemical herbicides provided a brake on the production possibilities offered under *precarismo*. Nevertheless, the enormous profits earned by landlords and mill-owners were regarded as an impediment to an increased marketable surplus, at reduced prices. It was a desire to rectify this situation, rather than concern for the exploitation of the tenant, which eventually persuaded the Ecuadorian government to abolish rice *precarismo*.[58]

1. The term *'precarismo'* means, literally, 'precarious tenancy'. Rice *precarismo* is not a sharecropping system. The rent paid by the tenant was a fixed amount, rather than a 'share'. It was also much less than under classic 'sharecropping' conditions. For example, cf. A. W. Johnson, *Sharecroppers of the Sertão*, Stanford University Press, 1971 for an excellent treatment of the relations between landlords and sharecroppers, in this case the *moradores* of the Brazilian north-east. The term' sharecropper' (*aparcero*) is, however, used of rice *precaristas* by Baraona and Delgado, R. Baraona and O. Delgado, *El Proyecto de Reforma Agraria en la region arrocera del Ecuador*, F.A.O., Santiago, 1972, Chapter 1. However, a more correct description would be 'leasehold tenancy in which the rent is paid in kind'. The landlord shared none of the risks of production and was rarely resident on the estate. The tenant was a fully fledged entrepreneur and owned the meagre equipment that was employed in production.

2. The confusion is identified and discussed by J. Martinez-Alier, 'Peasants and labourers in Southern Spain, Cuba and Highland Peru', *Journal of Peasant Studies*, vol. 1, no. 2, January 1974, p. 135.

3. Martin T. Katzman, 'The Brazilian Frontier in Comparative Perspective', *Comparative Studies in Society and History*, vol. 17, no. 3, July 1975, p. 273.

4. Steven N. S. Cheung, *The Theory of Share Tenancy*, University of Chicago Press, 1970.

5. Martinez-Alier, op. cit., p. 137.

6. *Inventory of Information Basic to the Planning of Agricultural Development in Latin America*, C.I.D.A., 1963, p. 57.

7. Martinez-Alier, op. cit., p. 135.

8. Albuja, op. cit., p. 129.

9. *Reforma Agraria y Desarrollo Económico en el Ecuador*, Banco Central del Ecuador, Quito, 1960, p. 19.

10. Thomas C. Greaves, 'The Andean Rural Proletarians', *Anthropological Quarterly*, vol. 45, no. 2, 1972.

11. G. Beckford, *Persistent Poverty, Underdevelopment in Plantation Economies of the Third World*, O.U.P., New York, 1972, p. 95.

12. Beckford, ibid., p. 283.

13. Erasmus describes a part of north-west Mexico where 'sharecropping takes place on contiguous *ejido* land when there is an absence of capital', Charles J. Erasmus, 'Agrarian Reform versus Land Reform: three Latin American countries', in Dwight B. Heath (ed.), *Contemporary Cultures and Societies of Latin America*, 1974, 2nd edition, p. 147; cf. also the section on *yanaconaje* in northern Peru in *Tenencia de la tierra y Desarrollo Socio-Económico del sector Agrícola*, Peru, CIDA, 1966.

14. Feder provides the example of the transition to tenant farming in the Brazilian north-east when sugar prices fell. Later, when prices rose again, land-owners evicted workers and forced them to destroy their permanent crops. E. Feder, *The Rape of the Peasantry*, Anchor Books, New York, 1971, p. 116.

15. Beckford, op. cit., p. 180.

16. CEDEGE, 1970, op. cit., p. 40.

17. *Informe de la Encuesta sobre la Comercialización por el Campesino de la Costa*, CESA, 1971, p. 116

18. CEDEGE, op. cit., pp. 72 and 73.

19. CEDEGE, ibid., p. 40.

20. Register of landholding Cámara de Agricultura, 2nd Zone Guayaquil.

21. CEDEGE, op. cit., p. 37.

22. Ibid., p. 42.

23. Delgado and Baraona, op. cit., p. 2. Many of their calculations appear to be unreliable and I have ignored them in this chapter. Their general analysis is accurate enough.

24. 1 *cuadra* = 0·76 ha.

25. Delgado and Baraona, op. cit., p. 2.

26. Hurtado, op. cit., p. 32 and Ojeda, L., *Dominación Política en la Cuenca del Guayas*, MS, Quito, p. 26.

27. CESA, 1971, op. cit., p. 22.

28. This second crop (*arroz de verano*) was grown between August and October.

29. CESA, 1971, op. cit., p. 14.

30. According to Hurtado the average was 7 ha (Hurtado, op. cit., p. 32). In my view the estimate of CESA, that it was about 4 ha, is more accurate (CESA, 1971, op. cit., pp. 13. and 14).

31. Baraona and Delgado, op. cit., p. 3.

32. Clarence Zuvekas Jr., 'Agrarian Reform in Ecuador's Guayas River Basin', *Land Economics*, vol. 52, no. 3, August 1976. The low market price for land prompted attempts to find buyers from within the *campesino* population: see Chapter V,

page 82 below. The existence of high profits and a low market price for land is attributed, by Zuvekas, to an unwillingness to buy land in the rice zone for fear of peasant land invasions.

33. Ibid., p. 3.
34. Ibid., p. 3.
35. Ibid., p. 2.
36. Jaime Galarza, *El Yugo Feudal, Visión del Campo Ecuatoriano*, Quito, 1962, p. 51.
37. Ibid., p. 52.
38. Baraona and Delgado, op. cit., p. 5.
39. Ibid., p. 5.
40. CESA, 1971, op. cit., p. 28.
41. If interest is compounded it is more than 60 per cent p.a. Baraona and Delgado, op. cit., p. 4.
42. CESA, 1971, op. cit., pp. 28–30.
43. Ojeda, op. cit., p. 21.
44. Ibid., p. 21.
45. Pedro Saad, 'La Reforma Agraria', *Revista Bandera Roja*, no. 1.
46. CEDEGE, 1970, op. cit., p. 56.
47. CESA, 1971, op. cit., p. 34.
48. CEDEGE, 1970, op. cit., p. 56.
49. Ibid., pp. 56–9.
50. Ojeda, op. cit., p. 21.
51. The 'Piladora Modelo', owned by the *Banco Nacional de Fomento*, bought about a quarter of total rice production at officially controlled prices.
52. Baraona and Delgado, op. cit., p. 4.
53. Galarza, 1962, op. cit., p. 53.
54. Miguel Salazar Barragán, of the *Asociación Nacional de Industriales Arrozeras* (ANIA), personal communication (28.5.75).
55. CESA, 1971, op. cit., p. 26.
56. Galarza, 1962. op, cit., p. 54.
57. CEDEGE, 1970, op. cit., p. 50.
58. In July 1946 the Government sought to 'liberalize' tenancy agreements between landlords and tenants apparently in the hope of stimulating investment. The main effect of the decree was to enable landlords to obtain higher rents, and to provide the support of the law for any landowner who wanted to dismiss his tenant. *El Universo*, Guayaquil, 31.7.46 and 2.8.46.

V

THE ABOLITION OF RICE *PRECARISMO*

The eventual abolition of rice *precarismo*, in December 1970, can be attributed to a number of factors. In the short term the government of José Maria Velasco Ibarra faced an immediate production crisis, as the effects of drought exacerbated social relations on the rice estates, and hastened the abandonment of rice cultivation by many landlords. The unwillingness of land-owners to invest in improved production, in levelling and irrigating the land and improving marketing arrangements, provided an excuse for government intervention in the rice zone. The technical possibilities of increasing rice production in the Guayas Basin were enormous, provided that the area was developed in an integrated way.[1] Awareness of these possibilities was increasing all the time, particularly as a result of the early investigations of the Commission for the Development of the Guayas Basin (CEDEGE), dating from the end of 1967.

At the same time popular opposition to the system of rice *precarismo* had increased in the zone, and was actively encouraged by the North American Agency for International Development (AID). *Campesino* resistance to dismissal from the estates was greater than many landlords had anticipated, and the tenant's cause was now being championed by foreign as well as national interests. The examples of improved production on privately owned estates where advanced agricultural technology was employed, and the early successes of a few rice cooperatives, combined to convince the government that a change in the system of land tenure was both desirable and possible. In the next chapter the relations between peasant organizations and the Ecuadorian State are examined more fully. In this chapter the decree which abolished rice *precarismo* (*Decreto 1001*) is analysed against the background of the economic circumstances of the time, and the ideological influences which were brought to bear on the government.

THE CRISIS IN RICE PRODUCTION

According to ECLA, during the mid-1950s Ecuador's rice production per hectare was about half that of Colombia, and less than a third of Argentina's.[2] Within a decade yields per hectare had improved, although production failed to keep abreast of demand (see Table 16). The quantity of rice produced, as well

Table 16. Rice production in Ecuador 1965–1975*

1965	157,000	1971	243,000
1966	185,000	1972	189,000
1967	173,000	1973	228,000
1968	288,000	1974	93,000†
1969	161,000	1975	335,000†
1970	147,000		

*Source: United Nations Statistical Yearbook (1974).
†Source: Bank of London and South America Review, April 1976, vol. x, no. 4.

as the amount of land dedicated to its cultivation, increased gradually until 1966, when production stood at just over 330,000 metric tons. The desirability of increasing rice consumption in much of Latin America has been emphasized in many international publications.[3] Clearly production had not yet reached a level where increased consumption, through the substitution of rice for other elements in the popular diet, was at all feasible.

During the 1960s many landowners in the Guayas Basin began converting their estates into 'mixed' holdings, on which cattle became increasingly important.[4] This process was even more marked after two years of drought, in 1967 and 1968, which resulted in production per hectare falling by 50 per cent.[5] Already in September 1968, there were discussions about the measures that would have to be taken to avoid speculation, if, as expected, the supply of rice fell dramatically.[6] The impending crisis even led the landlords to call for State intervention 'to ensure the supply', arguing at the same time that such intervention should not 'prevent a loss of incentive in the private sector and prevent the free development of market forces'.[7]

Finally, the government asserted that it was justified in intervening, because 'an equilibrium between the supply and demand for rice is doubly necessary, as it is the foodstuff of greatest importance to the nation'.[8]

By November 1968 it was feared that at least half the rice crop had been lost because of the drought.[9] There were already rumours of speculation and the clandestine exportation of rice to Peru, while rice was imported from Italy to help make up the deficit in domestic production.[10] The Guayaquil newspaper *El Telégrafo* claimed that middlemen and mill-owners were profiting from the shortages, which were in no way benefiting the 'poor *montuvio*'.[11] On the first of January 1969 the government agreed to the importation of 500,000 metric hundredweight of rice, which was the equivalent of a quarter of the total production that had entered the rice-mills after the previous harvest.[12] An employee of the *Comisión Nacional de Arroz* was quoted as saying that neither he, nor anybody else, knew who was responsible for the hoarding and speculation which had accompanied the shortages.[13]

Although the harvest improved the situation later in 1969, the early months were marked by the ejection of *precaristas* from rice estates and continued conflicts in Guayaquil. There were a number of violent incidents between retailers and the police, as a result of the government's attempts to reduce speculation and control prices.[14] Lorries taking rice from Guayaquil were 'captured' by the police, and efforts were made to prevent rice leaving the country. Eventually the U.S.A. agreed to sell rice to Ecuador, amid accusations that even government ministers were implicated in large-scale speculative activities.[15] This moment was chosen for the introduction of a new government-approved contract between landlords and rice *precaristas*, which had been prepared as long ago as 1965. This contract let landlords obtain credit from the *Banco Nacional de Fomento* on behalf of their tenants, in the 'hope that this would obviate the use of *fomentadores*' (money-lenders).[16] Its effect was only to increase the tenant's dependence on the landlord.

Although harvests improved in 1969 and 1970, tension between landlords and tenants increased. The shortages during

1968 and 1969 had impressed on the government the need to control the distribution and sale of rice, in the interests of preserving public order in Guayaquil as well as in the country-side. In the period following the drought peasant organization also began in earnest, as further, more radical, agrarian reform measures were anticipated. The prospect of increasingly re-calcitrant tenants on their estates served to harden the attitudes of landlords, who met peasant resistance with further dismissals.

TECHNICAL OBJECTIONS TO RICE 'PRECARISMO'

It has been suggested that the decision to intervene in the marketing of rice was eventually forced on the government by the scandals and social conflicts which had followed shortages in 1968 and 1969. Any government intervention necessarily struck at the landlords, who controlled the commercialization as well as the production of rice. The government was assisted in its resolve to act by the mounting evidence of the productive potential of the Guayas Basin, whose full development was frustrated by the lack of proper irrigation.[17] This evidence was reported, after 1967, in the studies of the *Comisión de Estudios para el Desarrollo de la Cuenca del Rio Guayas* (CEDEGE).

The first study of CEDEGE's was financed through a grant from the Canadian Government channelled through the International Development Bank (I.D.B.) of 1,250,000 Canadian dollars. This study, a pilot project, considered the advantages of irrigating 11,500 ha of land to the east of Babahoyo. The report which established the feasibility of the project, was published in January 1970, although work on the project did not commence until October 1974.[18] The early investigations made it clear that if CEDEGE was to undertake development work in the area its role would have to be more than merely technical. Indeed, the success of technical improvements de-pended on changes in social and legal relationships. The right to use water supplies, for example, was one of several technical considerations which CEDEGE felt required legislation.[19] It had also become apparent to the *técnicos* serving with the organization that any infrastructural improvements would increase the value of land ten or twenty times over. This enormous appreciation in the value of land should be to the 'public benefit' and not merely that of existing landowners.[20] Such projects would be difficult to undertake without a 'revision in the system of land tenure in the project area'. Finally, it was suggested that the banks 'would not provide finance for the *latifundia* in the area without making sure that landowners operating with *precaristas* made better use of their land and natural resources'.[21]

The studies of CEDEGE represented a new element in the prolonged discussions about Ecuadorian agrarian reform and land tenure. For the first time a prestigious organization, with considerable financial and technical expertise, was prepared to advocate sweeping changes in the agrarian structure for technical as well as humanitarian reasons. The first comprehensive and well documented study of the Guayas Basin had given forceful expression to this new approach:

> ... the type of agrarian structure found in Ecuador is not only morally indefensible, but also counter-productive to economic development. It is therefore necessary to abolish all those landed interests that intervene between those who cultivate the land and the government, giving parity to all the rights that govern the use of land in such a way that we achieve a separation between the social hierarchy and the control of land.[22]

Such sentiments could be expected to inflame landlords employing tenants in the Babahoyo region. Accordingly, CEDEGE staff were cautious in the approach they made to landlords, placing the emphasis on the benefits landowners themselves could expect from irrigation works:

Establishment of a sound legal, organizational and social framework within which the project can operate will remove many constraints ... the owners have long established rights and collectively, strong political influence. Attempts to interfere with their rights, in particular by reducing property sizes to a point where they derive no benefit from irrigation, would encounter strong opposition. However, the potential increase in project area productivity is so great that the opportunity exists for substantial reductions in their property sizes. Additionally, opportunities will be created in other project-related activities such as the provision of agricultural equipment and in processing, marketing and transportation ... Many large property owners have already moved into commerce and the professions, and delegate the farm operation to managers. Thus, the possibility of compensation in other areas exists ... an equitable solution to the problem of large properties must, therefore, be found ....[23]

Despite the efforts made to reassure landlord opinion concerning its role, the activities of CEDEGE provoked considerable opposition from landlords. A young Ecuadorian sociologist, Lautarano Ojeda, and his colleagues, conducting research in the area, were able to identify a group of large landowners who took advantage of public confusion about CEDEGE's work. These landowners 'had conducted their campaign with considerable efficiency'. The result was that, in the words of a local schoolteacher, 'nobody knew what CEDEGE wanted to do in the area, nor how it was proposing to do it'.[24] It was alleged that CEDEGE had proceeded 'in an authoritarian way, which made little attempt to enlist the support of the social classes which would benefit from the project, who were still under the control of landlords ...'.[25] Another informant stated that CEDEGE employees 'had failed to talk to the people of the area in language they understood ... the peasants here do not know what a "cheque" is, let alone what is meant by "an Agrarian Reform bond"'.[26]

The opposition mounted by landlords was concentrated on a number of factors. They resisted the idea of being compensated for their land with agrarian reform bonds, which they claimed were worthless. They insisted on the valuation of their estates being undertaken by the government's evaluation office, the *Oficina Nacional de Avaluación y Catastros* (O.N.A.C.). It had been proposed by CEDEGE that landlords should be compensated according to the valuation contained in the municipal *catastros* for 1966.[27] Landlords also complained about not being eligible for credit from the *Banco Nacional de Fomento* while the future of the area was in dispute.[28]

Despite the local opposition to the Babahoyo project CEDEGE was given special powers to develop the area under a decree, *Decreto 70*, which was issued in February 1971. The terms of this decree foresaw the active cooperation of CEDEGE, the Land Reform Institute (IERAC) and the *Banco Nacional de Fomento*. The priorities for land adjudication would be assessed on social as well as technical grounds, and IERAC would be put in charge of this process.[29] In preparing a case for an executive decree, CEDEGE officials had emphasized to the President that any experience gained in the area would be invaluable for later agrarian reform policy.[30] The Babahoyo area was looked upon as a 'pilot project' for agrarian reform in the coastal region as a whole. In the press, however, efforts were made to reassure landlords about CEDEGE's role, and the powers conferred on the organization by *Decreto 70*. On 3 February 1971, the headline in *El Universo* emphasized that 'the development of the Guayas Basin is no cause for alarm', and the following day the view was expressed that 'contrary to speculation, private property and free enterprise have not been threatened'.[31] This did little to placate feelings in the area. There were accusations that CEDEGE was squandering money by spending nearly two million pounds on preliminary studies.[32] Furthermore, work was to commence on the Babahoyo project despite the fact that the report on the second 'priority zone', Daule-Peripa, had still not been published.[33]

CEDEGE played a prominent part in the setting up of rice cooperatives in the Babahoyo area. In May 1969 there were sixteen 'cooperatives' and 'pre-cooperatives', all of which were organized by AID.[34] These early cooperatives were established on land which had been sold to the tenants by landowners. By 1975 there were twenty-four cooperatives in the area, cultivating 13,000 ha of land, most of which was still in the process of being adjudicated to the former tenants under the agrarian reform. This represented only six per cent of the land under rice cultivation in Ecuador. These ex-tenants received over £520,000 worth of agricultural credit from the *Banco Nacional de Fomento*.[35] In 1973 CEDEGE's figures were improved by a grant of 20,000,000 U.S. dollars from the IBD, for the partial financing of the Babahoyo project.[36] Progress on the Daule-Peripa project was also stepped up. Eventually the large landowners in the Babahoyo area were offered 23,000,000 U.S. dollars in Agrarian Reform bonds for their land, under an agreement signed between IERAC and CEDEGE in February 1974.[37] It is too early to know what the outcome of this offer will be as lawyers employed by the landlords are still disputing the legality of the bonds they have been offered. Ten years earlier, however, it would have been inconceivable that any offer of this sort should have been made.

THE DISSEMINATION OF A 'COOPERATIVE' IDEOLOGY

The history of rice cooperatives in the Guayas Basin began with the efforts of the Agency for International Development to organize tenants in the mid-1960s.[38] These efforts followed the passing of the 1964 Agrarian Reform Law, and the agreement which was entered into between AID and the Ministry of Social Provision in 1966.[39] It was understood that the role of AID should be confined to providing technical assistance and finding sources of finance in the early stages of the cooperatives' development. By February 1969, when the International Director of CLUSA (the Cooperative Leagues of the United States) made a visit to Ecuador, there were six rice cooperatives in the Guayas Basin.[40] The programme under which they had been established was described at that time as a 'joint one', the responsibility being shared by the Cooperative Bank and *Punto IV*, the technical arm of AID.[41] A bank loan of £5,000 had been negotiated on behalf of one of the first rice cooperatives, 'La Carmela', which had been formed as the result of a dispute between the landowner and tenants in which AID took the part of the *precaristas*.[42]

According to Ojeda and his colleagues, there were four principal reasons why AID became involved in the organization of rice cooperatives. The first reason was that the landlords in the area were unwilling to invest in infrastructural improvements. Secondly, AID recognized that improvements in production necessitated improved varieties of rice as well as more advanced systems of cultivation. Thirdly, it was clear that *precaristas* could not obtain credit from the banks, even the *Banco Nacional de Fomento*, without the possession of land titles. Finally, the commercialization of rice was in the hands of landowners who were unwilling to countenance more efficient marketing and storage methods.[43] These factors influenced AID in assisting the organization of cooperatives, and in pressing on the government the necessity of a land reform that gave the tenants titles to the land they worked.

The early interest of AID in the formation of cooperatives was not universally welcomed. In 1962 Jaime Galarza had maintained that:

... the imperialist penetration of agriculture is today being effected by CLUSA, the Andean Mission of the International Labour Organisation (ILO) and the Four 'F' Clubs ... these orientate production towards imperialist interests and remove the peasant, particularly the young, from revolutionary action ...[44]

The effects of AID activities were undeniable, even if the motives of the organization were in dispute. One of the early advocates of cooperatives in the rice zone, who worked closely with AID and CLUSA, was Gustavo Riofrio. He later became the head of the *Federación Nacional de Cooperativas Arroceras* (FENACOOPARR) a Federation of rice cooperatives which was brought into being in 1970, under the influence of AID. Still later Riofrio left FENACOOPARR to become Under-Secretary at the Ministry of Agriculture. In charting the history of the cooperative movement in Ecuador, Hurtado and Herudek comment that ...

... all the services provided by FENACOOPARR, that have constituted such an important contribution to the development of the rice cooperative movement, have in large measure been financed with resources from AID, and have utilized the technical assistance of CLUSA.[45]

The single most important contribution of AID, however, was not the actual organization of *precaristas* into cooperatives. This would have occurred eventually under the terms of *Decreto 1001*, even if AID had not taken the part of the *precaristas*. More significant was the plan under which land would be transferred to the tenants, through the active intervention of the banking sector. This plan, known as 'Land Sale Guaranty', was officially launched in 1970 as a way of resolving the disputes between landlords and tenants without violence or the confiscation of land.[46] In an article about the operation of 'Land Sale Guaranty', Blankstein and Zuvekas draw attention to the originality of the programme under which this transference of land would take place. Their defence of this programme, the *Programa de Promoción de Empresas Agrícolas*, is worth quoting at length:

The program provides a mechanism to guarantee the extension of credit by participating financial institutions to *campesino* cooperatives purchasing land in voluntary transactions . . . The theory is to make it possible for *campesinos* capable of managing an agricultural enterprise to buy land and to obtain the working capital and technical assistance necessary to farm the land effectively, and generate the income necessary to pay for the land. The transaction is voluntary. Interviews with potential land sellers in the area of operation demonstrate that there are a sufficient number of individuals in the target area who would be prepared to sell at reasonable prices . . . The reasons for their unwillingness to sell may vary from one landowner to another, but generally the major reasons are the uncertainties of the political life of the country, the threat of land invasions, and the desire on the part of individuals to convert land into liquid assets.[47]

It is clear from this description that 'Land Sale Guaranty' itself was not considered revolutionary in the political sense. Rather, it represented a way of displacing landlords who were unwilling to modernize their estates, without recourse to the confiscation of land. The plan, if implemented, would defuse conflict between landlords and their tenants, and provide the opportunity for dramatic improvements in production. Furthermore, the plan was looked upon by its authors as a catalyst, which would 'have the effect of increasing the pressures for a broader-based, traditional agrarian reform program'.[48]

The 'Land Sale Guaranty' programme was advocated because it was thought that many landowners would be prepared to part with land if it were not so undervalued. *Precaristas* themselves could not afford to buy the land they worked, and landowners could not 'afford' to sell when land was so cheap. Blankstein and Zuvekas anticipated the possibility that the programme might inflate land prices if implemented.[49] If this happened they believed the solution lay in lengthening the period within which the former tenants paid for the land.[50] It was also conceded that 'the program aims initially at the most capable element of the *campesinos* in the target area', but they added that 'field experience indicates that even those below the top level will not have much difficulty in raising the required down payment'.[51]

In his account of contemporary agrarian reforms in Latin America, the Colombian sociologist, Antonio García, argues that 'the only cooperatives that have achieved the massive mobilization of technical and financial resources, have been cooperatives of commercialization, following a North American type of organization'.[52] Such cooperatives have three main characteristics. Through vertical linkages they bring about an 'association' of small and large producers; they limit their activities to marketing without challenging the structure of property or other agricultural enterprises. Such cooperatives serve to deflect interest away from agrarian reform. Despite the liberal intentions of its architects, or perhaps because of them, this description of García's approximates quite closely to the rice cooperatives which were established by AID in the 1960s, and advocated under the 'Land Sale Guaranty' programme.

In its own appraisal of the 'Land Sale Guaranty' programme AID has claimed limited success. It notes that 'the possession of land has improved morale, attitudes and behaviour' and that the former tenant now has access to other official institutions.[53] The same document states that although the programme had 'no measurable effect on Ecuador's economic self-sufficiency production had increased in the participating cooperatives'.[54] The authors of the scheme had also been right in assuming that 'the small farm units would be sufficiently profitable to allow *campesinos* to repay the bank loans', and comment favourably on the fact that 'some cooperatives have become employers of rural labour'.[55]

In 1972, when the military took power in Ecuador, the *Programa de Promoción ed Empresas Agrícolas* was taken under the wing of the Ministry of Agriculture, where it is located today. It was felt at the time that a programme like that of 'Land Sale Guaranty' was too conservative to be consistent with the 'nationalist and revolutionary' goals of the military. However, one of the originators of the plan has since commented that 'earlier efforts at structuring development finance to support cooperative needs appear to have borne fruit'.[56] In the light of subsequent developments, which are described in chapter 7 below, this is a very modest claim. The efforts of AID to establish cooperatives in the Guayas Basin were of considerable importance in persuading the government to abolish rice *precarismo* in 1970. Furthermore, the pattern of relations which AID helped to establish between the *campesinos* and the official bodies in charge of the agrarian reform, survived the apparent demise of AID itself, and continue to influence the relations between social classes and their organizations on the Ecuadorian Coast.

THE SIGNIFICANCE OF 'DECRETO 1001'

In comparison with most Ecuadorian agrarian legislation *Decreto 1001*, which formally abolished rice *precarismo*, was both innovatory and successful. This decree also covered a land-tenure situation which had received almost no recognition in law. Before 1970 the situation of the coastal tenant had been virtually ignored, by politicians and commentators alike. Commenting on the absence of information about Coastal *precarismo*, Marcel Ortiz noted that little was known about population pressure on the Coast 'despite the fact that the legal position of Coastal tenants is worse than that of the *huasipungero*, as they have no protection under the Agrarian Reform Law'.[57] He adds that although there was more land in the hands of *precaristas* on the Coast, and social conflicts there were more serious, there were still no reliable statistics about the area. The Agrarian Reform Law of 1964 devoted only five paragraphs to Coastal *precarismo*, and even the CIDA Report discussed the Coastal region in eighty-eight out of a total of five hundred pages.[58] Commentators on the Ecuadorian agrarian structure invariably made the same omission. Piedad and Alfredo Costales in the fourth volume of their authoritative *Historia social del Ecuador*, which is devoted to the agrarian situation, dismiss Coastal *precarismo* in only two paragraphs.[59]

Three years after the proclamation of *Decreto 1001* something of its significance had been grasped. One writer described the decree as 'simple and effective ... producing a miracle by simultaneously guaranteeing the ex-*precarista* the right to occupy

land and increasing significantly the production of rice . . .
for the first time something like an agrarian reform was put
into motion'.[60] Hurtado and Herudek had already referred to
Decreto 1001 as having heralded 'a very significant structural
change in the large rice *haciendas* of the river Guayas, which
have now passed into the hands of *campesinos* in significant
numbers'.[61] These expressions of enthusiasm for *Decreto 1001*
were shared by most *campesino* organizations, which five years
later campaigned for its prolongation.[62] Characteristic of the
landlord reaction is the response of one man who told Ojeda
that, 'since *Decreto 1001* the *precaristas* want to work the land
without paying rent . . . Velasco is mad'.[63] Finally, the views of
many *técnicos* who were not attached to either side are illustrated
by a remark of a FENACOOPARR official that I overheard,
that concerned a landowner who had sold a third of his estate to
his former tenants, and developed the rest of his land with the
money he received from them. 'There you are,' said the FENA-
COOPARR man, 'if all landlords had acted like that there
would be no need for *Decreto 1001.*'

The introduction of *Decreto 1001* in December 1970 was
preceded by a general decree, *Decreto 373*, which was issued
three months earlier. This decree had the effect of abolishing
all forms of 'precarious tenure', including those which had been
excluded from the 1964 Agrarian Reform Law. According to
one commentator *Decreto 373* was 'inspired by the principle of
free enterprise', and sought to increase the number of small
producers (*minifundistas*) throughout the country.[64] The effect
of the decree, if implemented, would be to increase the 'marginalization' of the former tenant 'while the landlord retained
the best land on his estate'.[65] Since titles to land were issued to
individuals, any cooperatives that were formed would quickly
disintegrate in the face of heightened individualism. Furthermore, tenants would be forced to sell their produce individually,
and 'would thus maintain the present chain of intermediaries
that cooperatives were meant to eliminate'.[66]

In view of the probable effects of the implementation of
Decreto 373, perhaps it is fortunate that the landlord's reaction
to its proclamation was so violent that it provoked a more
radical measure, *Decreto 1001*. At the beginning of December

1970, it was clear that landlords had reacted to *Decreto 373* by refusing to cultivate rice, and ejecting tenants from their estates. The Minister of Production, alarmed by the consequences of this revolt, hinted that he was considering more effective measures to deal with landlord disaffection.[67] The following day 'mobile teams of IERAC officials went into action in the province of Guayas, to make sure that the Law abolishing *precarismo* was properly enforced'.[68] The landlords pleaded for the suspension of *Decreto 373*, arguing that they would not otherwise be able to give tenants seeds and advance credit to them. Constantino Endara in *El Universo* commented that 'the majority of these landowners are the last defenders of the old order that has allowed them to retain their privileges and feudal rights'.[69]

The prospect of widespread and open confrontation between landlords and tenants increased daily, even after the fifteenth of December when *Decreto 1001* was issued. Gustavo Riofrio, the head of FENACOOPARR, was interviewed by the press, and warned that 'blood will flow the moment the peasants are expelled from the land they have worked for generations'.[70] By the beginning of January there were thirty mobile brigades made up of *técnicos* from IERAC, trying to implement the reform in the rice zone.[71] Despite the official view that 'most landlords were cooperating with these mobile teams', it was soon reported that 'thousands of hectares were being abandoned because of the application of *Decreto 1001*'.[72] The Regional Director of IERAC, Ernesto Campoverde, claimed that although there had been difficulties in applying the decrees, these difficulties had gradually been overcome. The important point about *Decreto 1001* in his view was that it prevented the complete abandonment of rice cultivation by giving IERAC the power to expropriate the estate of anyone who employed *precaristas*.[73]

An evaluation of the provisions of *Decreto 1001* reveals that in a number of important respects it cannot be interpreted as radical agrarian reform legislation. Firstly, the issuing of land titles is not the same thing as the redistribution of land, but rather a means of increasing land tenure security.[74] As Thome remarks, 'the lack of secure rights on the land is often a disincentive to increased production'.[75] As we have seen the main objective of Ecuadorian legislation was the encouragement of capitalist relations in agriculture. It was held that changes in the organization of landholding were a prerequisite for increased production. This is asserted in the first article of *Decreto 1001*, where it is argued that the land dedicated to the cultivation of rice is a public utility and that it is essential that production be increased.[76] Within the paradigm established by Antonio García for assessing agrarian reforms these changes would probably be designated as a 'marginal agrarian reform'.[77]

Secondly, even within the terms of *Decreto 1001* there are opportunities for landlords and tenants to come to a private agreement about the ownership of land, provided IERAC gives its assent.[78] Thirdly, it was clearly understood that the tenants who received titles for the land they worked, would pay for the land in annual payments spread over ten years (article 6). The principle of payment for the land has been resisted by several of the peasant organizations that have been formed in the rice zone, and is clearly contrary to the spirit of a radical agrarian reform.[79] The efforts that have been made to convince landlords that they still have an important role to play in agricultural development, especially by employing wage-labour on the land they retained, make it clear that a major transference of power to the peasantry was not contemplated.

There are a number of respects, however, in which *Decreto 1001* represents an important innovation in Ecuadorian agrarian legislation. First of all, article two of the decree authorized IERAC officials to intervene on any estate where *precarismo* was suspected, although tenants were also free to petition for IERAC's intervention if they chose to. IERAC also had the power to take over the control of any land which had been cultivated with rice, even if it was not currently being used for that purpose. This clause made it difficult for landlords to evade the law by dismissing tenants from their estates. As Galo Lara observed, this right to requisition land not actively being cultivated by tenants, did not exist under *Decreto 373* or the 1964 Agrarian Reform Law.[80]

The second major innovation contained in the decree was the support it gave for the setting up of cooperatives. Article 10 of the decree stated that, 'the beneficiaries of land adjudication

will form associations of producers', the exact nature of which
was not described. However, the Minister of Production was
given the authority to form '*empresas de economía mixta*' ('mixed
enterprises') in areas which were deemed to be suitable. This
clause provides evidence of the Ecuadorian government's
intention to play a much larger part in the organization of the
'reformed sector' than had hitherto been the case. Ideologically
it proved to be the progenitor of the Agrarian Reform Law of
1973, and the creation of '*empresas agrícolas*' in areas particularly
well favoured in terms of natural resources.

The third significant innovation marked by *Decreto 1001* was
the direct relationship it established between the adjudication
of land and receiving credit from the *Banco Nacional de Fomento*.
Article 9 stated that the bank would 'make the necessary funds
available (to tenants) on the basis of the certificates issued by
IERAC'. In practice tenants did not even have to wait for titles
to receive credit for their crop, they merely had to show that
they would cooperate with IERAC in the carrying out of the
reform, and the setting up of a cooperative. This provision
widened the role of the *Banco Nacional de Fomento* considerably.
Landlords were, by comparison, subjected to even more
effective sanctions. Opposition to the law was punishable by
fines up to the value of the land on their estate that was worked
by *precaristas* (article 8). Since rice production was considered
'a case of collective social benefit', expropriation was not
merely 'justified' it was a 'necessity'.[81]

A week after it was issued, further clarifications were made to
Decreto 1001. It was announced that it applied to all rice *precaristas* who had worked the land for at least three years con-
tinuously. If they worked several plots of land they had the
right to obtain the largest plot, without prejudicing their claim
to other plots. If landlords refused to comply with the law they
would be treated as 'rebels'. If they did not present themselves
to the authorities within three days, IERAC was given the
authority to intervene on their estates.[82] Eventually, too,
peasant organizations secured the right to collective titles to
land; a measure that was subsequently favoured by the government and incorporated in the 1973 Agrarian Reform Law. Subsequently most former *precaristas* continued to work individual

plots of rice land, but the titles to this land were held by the cooperatives.

Velasco Ibarra, who was President of Ecuador for the fifth time when *Decreto 1001* was proclaimed, has provided his own version of what happened in December 1970. In an interview with the magazine *Nueva* he claimed that the reform was a sudden inspiration of his own, following a conversation with a member of his government whom he describes as a 'Communist'. He does not mention the landlords' reactions to *Decreto 373*, or the prospect of a colossal fall in production, as significant factors in the decision to abolish rice *precarismo*. He did claim that it marked a change in the relationship between the State and agriculture in Ecuador.[83] The introduction of the decree itself, however, is explained with true populist élan, in the following words:

A Communist came to me and said, 'look, Doctor, I want you to read this law. I am going to show you this law. If it seems all right to you then introduce it. If not reject it. Anyway, read it.' And I found, well, that I liked the law . . . it was our salvation. Agrarian reform is a delicate subject, *señor*, but what I did, at the instigation of a Communist, was to introduce a thoroughly admirable reform . . .[84]

1. According to the United Nations Food and Agriculture Organization (FAO), the Guayas River Basin alone is capable of providing enough food for twenty million people. *Nueva*, Quito, no. 12, October 1974, p. 38.

2. The average production annually between 1954 and 1957 was 1,055 kg per ha in Ecuador, 1988 kg per ha in Colombia, 2,655 kg per ha in Chile and 3,357 kg per ha in Argentina. ECLA, 1961, op. cit., Table 12, p. 71.

3. 'The typical Latin American diet is relatively high in calories but low in proteins, particularly those of high quality. Although rice has slightly less total protein than the other two important grains, maize and wheat, the quality of its protein is excellent. Hence, nutrition could be improved greatly if it were possible to substitute rice for a substantial part of the low protein plantain and/or cassava in the typical diet . . . Therefore, in terms of human nutrition and well being, increased rice production could play a vital role in the food economy of Latin America.' *Politicas Arroceras en América Latina*, Centro International de Agricultura Tropical, Cali, Colombia, 1972.

4. These changes are recorded in the records of *Cámara de Agricultura*, 2nd zone. Cattle ranching did not require heavy capital investment like irrigated rice cultivation. There was also less risk of land take-overs by the resident labour force. Zuvekas attributes the low value of rice estates to this risk in the 1960s, cf. Zuvekas, 1976, op. cit., p. 320.

5. Production fell from 2,500 kg per ha in 1967 to 1,286 kg per ha in 1968. See Table 16.

6. The Governor of Guayas, Sr Otto Carbo Avellan, held discussions with representatives of the *Banco Nacional de Fomento*, *Cámaras de Agricultura*, and the *Comisión Nacional de Arroz*. *El Comercio*, Quito, 27.9.68.

7. *Cámara de Agricultura*, 2nd zone, quoted in *El Comercio*, 27.9.68.

8. *El Universo*, Guayaquil, 27.9.68.

9. *El Comercio*, Quito, 10.11.68.

10. *El Comercio*, Quito, 12.11.68.

11. *El Telégrafo*, Guayaquil, 20.12.68.

12. *El Universo*, 1.1.69.

13. Ibid.

14. *El Universo*, 11.1.69.

15. *El Universo*, 16.1.69.

16. *El Universo*, 19.1.69.

17. It was calculated by AID that 'the rice crop was totally or partially lost roughly one year in every five because of the lack of irrigation', Zuvekas, 1976, p. 317 citing U.S.A.I.D. *Ecuador—Land Sale Guaranty*, Capital Assistance Paper, AID/DLC, p. 854, Washington, 1969.

18. *Babahoyo Irrigation Project Feasibility Report*, CEDEGE, Guayaquil, T. Ingledow and Associates/Guayaconsult, 1970.

19. *El Universo*, 3.2.71.

20. *El Universo*, 10.2.71.

21. *El Universo*, 3.2.71.

22. *Tenencia de la Tierra*, 1970, op. cit., p. 19.

23. *Babahoyo Irrigation Project*, 1970, op. cit., p. 41.

24. Quoted by Lautaro Ojeda, op. cit., p. 6.

25. Ibid., p. 6.

26. Ibid., p.7.

27. O.N.A.C. had been established by the government after pressure from landlords. Land values had, nominally, been very low as it was difficult to sell rice land (Zuvekas, 1976, op. cit.). This low valuation also meant that landlords avoided paying heavy taxes. The prospect of an agrarian reform, however, meant that landlords wanted their land to be revalued upwards, and compensation to be adjusted accordingly.

28. Ojeda, op. cit., p. 7.

29. *El Universo*, 3.2.71.

30. Ibid.

31. *El Universo*, 4.2.71.

32. Ojeda, op. cit., p. 10.

33. *El Universo*, 3.2.71. The feasibility studies for Daule-Peripa were eventually completed in 1973 but later contracts for further studies, worth 2·2 million U.S. dollars, were put out to tender (January 1975). At that time the Babahoyo scheme had cost 30 million U.S. dollars. *Latin American Economic Report*, vol. II, no. 3, 17 January 1975.

34. *Babahoyo Irrigation Project*, 1970, op. cit., p. 41.

35. Personal communication, Alfredo Mancero, CEDEGE, Deputy Technical Director, Guayaquil, 21.4.75.

36. 'CEDEGE: proyecto Babahoyo en marcha', *Mensajero*, Quito, October 1974, p. 21.

37. Between them IERAC and CEDEGE were to invest about 14 million U.S. dollars in rice cooperatives (1974/77). CEDEGE was to pay 4 million U.S.

dollars for cattle and machinery in connection with the Babahoyo Project. *El Telégrafo*, 15.2.74.

38. The first cooperative in Ecuador was the cooperative '*Bienestar Social Protector del Obrero*' founded in Guayaquil in 1919. Hurtado and Hereduk, op. cit., p. 31.

39. Ibid., p. 32.

40. *El Universo*, 5.2.69.

41. *El Universo*, 19.2.69.

42. Information from members of cooperative 'La Carmela', El Triunfo, 29.4.75.

43. Ojeda, op. cit., pp. 18–21.

44. Jaime Galarza, 1962, op. cit., p. 89.

45. Hurtado and Herudek, op. cit., p. 51.

46. This is described in detail in Blankstein and Zuvekas, 1973, op. cit.

47. Ibid., p. 88.

48. Ibid., p. 91.

49. Ibid., p. 92.

50. Ibid., p. 92.

51. Ibid., p. 92.

52. Antonio García, *Sociología de la Reforma Agraria en América Latina*, Ammorrortu Ediciones, Buenos Aires, 1973, p. 171.

53. *Memorandum*, AID office, Guayaquil, 1975.

54. Ibid.

55. Ibid. The financial mechanisms established under 'Land Sale Guaranty' were, in fact, never used. However, land had been bought with credit from the *Banco Nacional de Fomento*.

56. Charles Blankstein, personal communication, 14 June 1974.

57. Ortiz, op. cit., p. 126.

58. Ibid., p. 128.

59. Piedad y Alfredo Costales, *Historia social del Ecuador*, vol. 4: *Reforma Agraria*, Casa de la Cultura, Quito, 1971, p. 67.

60. Cesar Davila Torres, in *El Tiempo*, Quito, 25.12.73.

61. Hurtado and Herudek, op. cit., p. 101.

62. 'All we *campesinos* on the Ecuadorian Coast know about *Decreto 1001*. It is the decree by means of which we have expropriated an immense number of rice estates ... we know about it because it has cost us blood and struggle.' *Unidad Sindical* (ACAL) June 1975, p. 12.

63. Ojeda, op. cit., p. 28.

64. Galo Lara N. quoted in *Las Unidades Associativas Campesinas en el Ecuador* IERAC, Quito, October 1973 (mimeo), p. 34.

65. Ibid., p. 35.

66. Ibid., p. 36.

67. *El Universo*, 10.12.70.

68. *El Universo*, 11.21.70.

69. He went on to quote General McArthur, 'who had demanded that the Japanese abolish sharecropping in December 1945 ... and Professor "Doré" (sic) in his book published in 1958 showed that within ten years this one act had made the Japanese peasant human again. After ten or twelve years we, the Ecuadorian people, will be able to say the same thing with respect to the Ecuadorian peasant and the Law abolishing *precarismo* ... ' *El Universo*, 15.12.70.

70. *El Universo*, 30.12.70.

71. *El Universo*, 6.1.71.

72. *El Universo*, 10.1.71.

73. *El Universo*, 12.1.71. An evaluation of the land transferred under *Decreto 1001* is given in Chapter VII below.

74. Cf. Joseph R. Thome, 'Improving Land Tenure Security', Chapter I, in Peter Dorner (ed.), *Land Reform in Latin America*, University of Wisconsin, 1971.

75. Ibid., p. 229.

76. Marco A. Checa is one of the few Ecuadorian commentators to draw attention to the importance of this article. Marco Checa Cobo, *El Régimen de la Tierra en el Ecuador*, Ediciones Lexigrama, Quito, 1973, p. 260. Commenting on a fall in rice production of 16 per cent during 1970 throughout Latin America, the United Nations adds that ' . . . we can only deduce that agricultural output is increasingly deployed in meeting domestic demand, which translated itself into inflationary pressures which affect the masses most adversely.' *Estudio Económico de América Latina*, United Nations, 1971, p. 121.

77. Antonio García, op. cit., p. 28.

78. Article 7 of *Decreto 1001*, cf. Checa, op. cit., p. 261.

79. Under *Decreto 1001*, the *campesinos* also pay interest over the ten year period of 5 per cent per annum. The landlord is paid in Ecuadorian Government 'Agrarian Reform' bonds, which he receives in annual instalments over a five year period. It was even proposed at one stage that landlords should be able to use these bonds to buy back part of their estates (*El Universo*, 17.2.71).

80. Galo Lara, quoted in IERAC, 1973, op. cit., p. 37.

81. *El Universo*, 11.12.70.

82. *El Universo*, 22.12.70.

83. 'For the first time the *Banco Central* loaned money to the *Banco Nacional de Fomento*, and this bank gave credit to the *precaristas*, so that they could pay for the land.'

84. Ibid., p. 65. (*Nueva*, Quito, February 1975, p. 64.)

VI

PEASANT ORGANIZATION AND THE STATE

In the previous chapter it was argued that although landlord-peasant conflicts increased in 1968 and 1969 the abolition of rice *precarismo* was not a direct result of these conflicts in the rice zone. The principal motives for the introduction of *Decreto 1001* were economic, namely the desire to avoid further production crises, and the structural contradictions inherent in the way rice was being cultivated. It was shown that the government's interest in the rice zone was prompted by the importance of rice in the national diet, and the obstacles which tenurial institutions placed in the way of dramatic increases in production. Having established that landlord-peasant conflicts were not the main reason tenancy was abolished, this chapter examines the real significance of peasant organization on the Coast. It will be clear that social conflicts within the rice zone assumed greater importance after the announcement of *Decreto 1001* than before the decree was proclaimed.

In the early stages of the coastal agrarian reform the support of the *campesinos* was instrumental in guaranteeing that the Law was implemented, as the process of land adjudication was undertaken by IERAC in the face of widespread landlord opposition. After 1972, however, Ecuadorian oil revenues provided the State with more political authority and an enlarged bureaucracy with which to carry out the reform. The decree abolishing rice *precarismo* had been introduced because of economic necessity. The ability to carry out the agrarian reform, however, was a product of economic prosperity, and the opportunity to put into effect the development ideology which had taken shape in the early 1960s. The existence of adequate finance made it less likely that a radical agrarian reform would take place by diverting interest away from land expropriation. After 1972 *campesino* organizations became much more dependent on the bureaucracy, which they looked to for a better share of the available revenues allocated to agrarian development.

Orlando Fals Borda has distinguished two choices open to those who advocate change in Latin American rural societies.[1] On the one hand they can 'continue to support reformist programmes which only bring marginal changes, and which develop petty-bourgeoise attitudes among the peasantry'. In Fals Borda's view such programmes also contribute towards the future exploitation of new classes of rural workers. Alternatively, change can be brought about by adopting a more 'confrontationist' strategy towards landlords, and stimulating the local-level demands of *campesinos*.[2] The ideological inspiration for the Ecuadorian agrarian reform leads one to identify it as the former type of development strategy, which was undertaken 'to reinforce the existing social structure'.[3] It is clear that no attempt was made politically to mobilize peasant producers on the Coast, or develop their 'consciousness' of their interests. Nevertheless, we should not miss the significance of the coastal agrarian reform. At the regional level many traditional landlords have been displaced, and some groups of peasant producers have gained a measure of economic and political power. As a result it is possible to say that irrevocable changes have taken place in the agrarian structure of the rice zone.

We might choose to describe the 'incorporation' of the coastal peasantry by the Ecuadorian State as the substitution of one patron for another.[4] The early intervention of the Agency for International Development (AID) had helped to secure the land for the *campesino* and, at a later stage, the provision of credit and technical assistance by the State enabled it to gain a hold on the peasantry of the region. The peasant organizations discussed by Fals Borda had not attracted so much interest from third parties, least of all the Venezuelan, Colombian or Ecuadorian governments. The part played by official patronage in the Guayas Basin has to be recognized, and integrated into our analysis of the way peasant movements function.

The increasing control exercised by the Ecuadorian State over the peasant organizations on the Coast, should not lead us to draw too many facile conclusions, however. It would be wrong to envisage peasant organizations as having been deflected from their original goals by the intervention and 'co-optation' of interested third parties. Ojeda, in his comments on the work of AID, states that it had 'striven to develop the middle sectors by identifying the interests of small producers with those of the dominant social classes'.[5] This was certainly the effect of AID and FENACOOPARR's activities, and probably their intention; but we should recognize that it rested on a firm basis among the rice producers themselves. Rice *precaristas*, as we saw in chapter four, were petty entrepreneurs from their inception. It is significant that Ojeda, like Fals Borda, underestimates the importance of this ambiguous status in the development of the *precarista's* ideology, and the goals of the organizations they formed.

The early demands of the rice *precaristas* for land and agricultural credit, were shared by other tenants in the Coastal region. In seeking an amelioration of their conditions, however, rice tenants came to embrace different political positions. In some cases they were guaranteed a title to the land they worked, and access to the funds of the *Banco Nacional de Fomento*. In some cases outside organizations were slow to intervene on their behalf. Landlords reacted differently, too. Sometimes they were willing to sell their land to their tenants, and foresaw the opportunities that the agrarian reform provided for the realization of their own ambitions to 'modernize' their holdings. Other landlords ejected their tenants from their estates and tried to impede IERAC in the adjudication of land.

These differences in the responses of landlords were matched by differences between groups of peasants. Those who cultivated eight or nine hectares of land coveted the status of landowners, and resisted attempts to increase the wages paid to the labourers they employed.[6] Other *precaristas* cultivated less than one hectare of land, and were themselves dependent on the wages they received from other tenants. As the peasantry has become aligned to regional federations, these differences in the social composition of what are now cooperatives, have exacerbated relations between the former tenants. It has led also to peasant federations taking inconsistent political stances on a variety of issues because each federation contains former *precaristas* whose objective situation is different.

Finally, it needs to be emphasized that the willingness of former tenants to take radical political positions depends upon the 'stage' in the agrarian reform when they become organized. Many of the earlier cooperatives were formed for commercial reasons, by AID or FENACOOPARR. Today these cooperatives receive the bulk of financial and technical assistance. Some government bodies, like IERAC, believe that there would be no peasant organization if it were not for the intervention of the State.[7] The case studies that follow show this to be a fallacy. It is significant, however, that many tenants did not attract outside support because landlord opposition to their demands was strong, or the production possibilities of an estate made it less attractive to State *técnicos*. In the face of apparent disapproval or apathy, some of these *campesinos* have developed more 'confrontationist' ideologies and strategies. As Lehmann has observed, 'the consciousness of the peasantry at any given moment is composed of the stages through which it has passed, and as a result (peasant consciousness) comprises contradictions . . .'.[8] The adherence of some peasant organizations in the Guayas Basin to more global aims and beliefs, together with the more sectional interests of other *campesinos*, needs to be recognized before we can interpret their political behaviour. In broad terms the cooperatives that receive the lion's share of resources were the first to be organized, and politically are the least radical. On the other hand, the most 'class conscious' peasant organizations are normally the least advanced economically. The members of these more radical cooperatives are less confident that capital investment by the state will help to transform them into the beneficiaries of the Coastal agrarian reform, a new rural bourgeoisie.

CASE STUDIES IN PEASANT ORGANIZATION

Campesino unrest in the rice zone never found expression in a co-ordinated regional movement, but was restricted to largely spontaneous and localized conflicts which varied in intensity and spatial distribution. As we saw in chapter three, peasant uprisings had occurred when cocoa had been the principal coastal crop. Since the 1920s there had been a number of isolated rural uprisings. In July 1955 the *Federación de Trabajadores Agrícolas del Litoral* (FETAL), the Ecuadorian Communist Party's peasant organization, had combined with railway workers in calling for an agrarian reform and the release of imprisoned *campesinos*.[9] However, it was not until the drought years of 1968 and 1969 that peasant unrest reached anything like regional proportions.

At the beginning of 1969 the Press reported on the 'unease in agriculture' during the previous year.[10] There had been invasions of land, estate managers had been kidnapped near Balzar, and there were dire warnings of the imminence of rural guerrilla activity. Significantly, these manifestations of discontent were attributed not to individual grievances but to 'a general state of anarchy'. Throughout the coastal region 'the situation was equally tense'. In Guayas there had been a gunfight between police and *campesinos* working on Hacienda La Saiba, and six armed peasants had kidnapped another estate manager near Naranjal. Land invasions had increased, and 'huts made of branches, cardboard and tins had appeared suddenly on some estates'. It was recognized that the drought had contributed to this unrest, but it was alleged that behind the invaders were 'professional agitators and guerrillas' who were able to take advantage of the popular discontent. For the first time the tone of Press reports was ominous, even despairing, for these land invasions were being 'used in massive force, and without warning . . . and in the majority of cases have proved invincible'.

Periods of heightened peasant agitation coincided with general anxiety about bad harvests, and the hoarding of rice which was taking place. At the beginning of 1969 there were accusations in the press that IERAC was giving assistance to land invasions, an accusation which was to be repeated at intervals throughout the succeeding years. The Director of IERAC denied this charge, arguing that these land 'invasions' were not aggressive acts on the part of *campesinos* but merely organized resistance to attempts to eject them from estates.[11] A few days later the first 'sit-in' by *campesinos* took place at IERAC's offices in Guayaquil, when a hundred *precaristas* from Daule pressed their claims on officials.[12] During this occupation attention was drawn to the inconsistencies between the decrees governing the contracts of *precaristas* at the time, and the 1964 Agrarian Reform Law. Later the same protesters were ejected from an estate near Daule when the landowners called in the provincial authorities. It is interesting that the landowners claimed that the authorities should back them up 'until such time as the law was changed in favour of the *sembradores*'.[13] At the same time there were reports of peasant land invasions, and fights between wage labourers and *precaristas* in other parts of the Guayas Basin. In a visit to Daule, the scene of much of the trouble, the Minister of Social Provision promised that 'the government of José Maria Velasco Ibarra will bring about the necessary changes in the status of rice *precaristas* . . . peacefully'.[14]

The next wave of peasant militancy followed the passing of the decrees abolishing 'precarious tenancy' towards the end of 1970. This time *campesino* activity was in support of the government, which was trying to implement *Decreto 1001*, but once again it was also a spontaneous response to the widespread eviction of tenants by their landlords. A number of political organizations attempted to organize peasant disaffection. Representatives of the Christian left in the *Confederación Ecuatoriana de Obreros Católicos* (CEDOC), claimed that many *campesinos* had been turned off estates with police support, and expressed an interest in helping them form cooperatives.[15] The Ecuadorian Communist Party (PCE) alleged that landlords on the Coast were forming armed bands to resist the implementation of *Decreto 1001*. Already three peasant leaders had been murdered on estates as far apart as Urbino Jado, Vinces and Yaguachi. Houses had been burned and attempts made to kill peasants in at least seven other estates within the Guayas Basin.[16] Even in Babahoyo, where CEDEGE was active, there had been a build-up of land invasions and the expulsion of tenants. A CEDEGE report noted that, though isolated invasions could be contained, 'if larger numbers invade land . . . nobody can ensure a speedy resolution of the problem'.[17]

1. *Cooperative 'La Carmela' (Yaguachi).*[18]

This was one of the first rice cooperatives to be formed under the aegis of AID, and an interesting case study of landlord-tenant relations. 'La Carmela' seems to have existed as a 'pre-cooperative' in 1968, but even before this the tenants there were described as 'acting like a trade union' by neighbouring *campesinos*. Indeed, in 1965 the *precaristas* had employed lawyers to act for them in their wrangles with IERAC. It was claimed that the owner of the estate, Adolfo Rodriguez Urquites, did not possess a legal title to the land. This was later confirmed by IERAC officials, and authorization was given for the sale of 350 hectares of the estate's 1,200 hectares; this comprised almost all the land devoted to rice cultivation. Rodriguez was willing to sell no more than 250 hectares and only at a price that the tenants found unacceptable. The tenants were also instructed to pay their rent up to the end of 1966, which they had refused to do while the landlord would not sell them the land. Arguments followed about how much land should be sold, and at what price, before AID took an interest in the peasants' case.

Since 1972 the tenants on 'La Carmela' have paid off most of the debt they had incurred to the landlord, and with the assistance of FENACOOPARR, they have increased their capital assets to over £160,000. They claim that the landlord backed down eventually because he feared that if the *precaristas* did not take possession of the estate then his labourers (*jornaleros*) would. These labourers were—in the view of the ex-tenants—'anarchists and communists'. The landlord's first move had apparently been to try and sell the estate to another landlord, which incensed the tenants. During the most turbulent period they were threatened with imprisonment, and had to bribe IERAC officials. Eventually the dispute, which they saw as being prompted by the 'impropriety' of the landowner in trying to sell the land without their knowledge, had been resolved reasonably amicably. This was partly because they had been able to employ lawyers who challenged the legality of the landowner's title, and partly because of the active intervention of AID and FENACOOPARR. Today there are fifty families within the cooperative, cultivating between 5 and 30 *cuadras* of rice each, and employing *jornaleros* in much the same way as the landlord had before them.

2. *Urbino Jado*[19]

In contrast to 'La Carmela', conflict between landlords and tenants near Urbino Jado has been particularly bitter and sustained. Ojeda attributes this fact to the concentration of power in very few hands, and the united front that the landlords were able to maintain in the face of peasant unrest. In the Urbino Jado area landlords were able to prevent AID assisting the formation of cooperatives. After December 1970, when land began to be adjudicated, this unity broke down and landlords became more conciliatory towards the peasants. One landlord, named Freire, even helped the *campesinos* in their struggle with one of the dominant families, the Trianas. Peasants had been thrown off their land, their houses had been burned and their livestock slaughtered. Organized armed bands in the pay of the Triana family terrorized the *precaristas*, and were held to be responsible for the death of a peasant leader, Arnulfo Castro, on Hacienda Pachay on 18 June 1971. In a statement to the Civil and Military Governor of Guayas, Alejandro Jimenez, a labourer employed by the Trianas explained how the violence accelerated after the passing of *Decreto 1001*:

The idea of Teodulfo Triana was that six *jornaleros* on his estate ('La Fortuna') should set out to get the *precaristas* on Hacienda Pachay, which was the property of his son, Oswaldo Triana Morante. They had refused to pay their rent and had asked IERAC to intervene on their behalf. Triana thought that if he eliminated a few of the leaders (*dirigentes*) the peasants would be frightened to go to IERAC and ask for *Decreto 1001* to be implemented.[20]

3. *Daule*[21]

Like Urbino Jado, Daule was a centre of conflict before 1971, but the resistance of peasant leaders to landlord oppression was much more effective. Three landowning families, the Briones, Villegas and Carchi families, wielded considerable power in the area.[22] In 1965 the first conflict took place on Hacienda 'Clarisa' the property of the descendants of David Briones Salazár. A priest from the sierra, Carlos Cuadrado, had tried to form a cooperative on the 600 hectare estate, which he called 'San Isidro'. This attempt was countered by threats from local landowners to expel him from the area. Later the same man helped *precaristas* form 'cooperative Santa Monica' in the Peninsular del Animas near Daule. At this time there was an occupation of IERAC's offices in Guayaquil which was reported in the press, as we have seen above.

After the formation of the cooperatives 'San Isidro' and 'Santa Monica', the landlords employed 'criminals' to try and eject *precaristas* from their estates, according to the leaders of ACAL. The *campesinos* were also accused of stealing cattle, and went into hiding to evade capture by the police. In 1970 one member of cooperative 'Santa Monica', Francisco Acosta, was killed by a band of armed assassins while he was working his land. The culprits were never found, but it was alleged by the landlords that Acosta's death was the result of a dispute between the peasants.

The first two cooperatives had still not received official recognition when another cooperative, 'Victoria Definitiva' was formed 'to set the record straight once and for all', as one peasant leader expressed it. This was on 11 March 1971, three months after the proclamation of *Decreto 1001*. Meeting in Daule an assembly of all the members of cooperatives 'Santa Monica' and 'San Isidro' decided to unite and call the new cooperative so formed, 'Cooperative Francisco Acosta', in honour of their former comrade. Eventually other cooperatives were formed—'Santa Maria Linda de Jesus' and '15th of August'—the latter being the first cooperative in the area to be established under *Decreto 1001*. The present *dirigentes* remember these as the halcyon days of the peasants' movement in the area, every Sunday being spent in discussion about the next fight with the landlords.

In 1971 these cooperatives affiliated to the *Asociación de Cooperativas Agrícolas del Litoral* (ACAL), itself an arm of CEDOC, in an attempt to obtain credit from the *Banco Nacional de Fomento*. It was believed that affiliation to ACAL would bring technical assistance, and possibly short-term funds from the *Central Ecuatoriana de Servicios Agrícolas* (CESA). This did in fact happen; the first payment being made by CESA to the ubiquitous 'Victoria Definitiva'. By 1973 ACAL owned its own rice mill just to the north of Daule, and most of the cooperatives in the area which were affiliated to ACAL were selling some of their rice to it.

In the view of the local ACAL leadership, present-day conflicts elsewhere in the Guayas Basin are similar to those near Daule a decade earlier. Today ACAL leaders and organizers (*promotores*) spend most of their time travelling around the Coast spreading the word to fellow *campesinos*. The twenty-one cooperatives affiliated to ACAL in the Daule area are relatively rich in natural resources, and are located within the catchment area for CEDEGE's Daule-Peripa irrigation project. Meanwhile the violent phase of landlord-peasant conflict has moved elsewhere. In Vinces for example, to the north-east of Daule, the *Unión de Cooperativas de Vinces y Baba* has launched various sorties against the landowners, and its leaders regularly find themselves in prison.[23]

4. Cooperative 'Salamín'[24]

This cooperative had only been formed for seven months when I interviewed its members in May 1975. Originally the twenty families of rice *precaristas* on the estate had worked about 70 hectares of rice land. The owner of the estate decided to sell the land to another man, who expressed the intention of mechanizing rice production on the estate and introducing labourers from outside to work the land. The *precaristas* resisted the attempt to dislodge them and, in their own words, 'this was when the revolution started'. Eventually ACAL and CESA interceded on their behalf, and the land which had been worked by *precaristas* was transferred to the tenants. Today these tenants work this land in common, having divided it into three large plots. At the same time they continue to work for the landlord as labourers on land that is devoted to tobacco, where each family head is employed in a private capacity. This curious arrangement, under which part of the time is spent as members of a production cooperative and part of the time as independent wage-labourers, is not unusual in some parts of the Coast.

5. Cooperative 'Viva Alfaro' (Yaguachi)[25]

This cooperative was formed on an estate named 'Blanca Nieve', which had been owned by Eloy Grijalva Croella since 1953.

The tenants on this estate of over 500 hectares had each cultivated about three hectares of rice land, as well as other tropical crops. The number of tenants had originally been nine, but when this grew to about thirty the owner decided to appoint a *mayordomo* (overseer) to supervise the estate. This overseer kept a record of the amount of land worked by each tenant, and how much rent he had to pay, as well as any matter relating to his house; for example his rights to cut timber. Any dispute between the *mayordomo* and a tenant family was settled by simply dismissing the tenant from the estate, even though he might have worked there for ten years or more. According to IERAC, in its account of conflicts on the estate, the land which was not worked by tenants was abandoned altogether. The circumstances of the tenant families were 'similar to that of other tenants in the rice zone', and they were exploited by money-lenders as well as rice-mill owners and the landlord. They even hired the canoes they used to transport their rice, from townspeople who 'looked upon them with little sympathy for their situation'.

There was little unity among the tenants on the estate except between members of the same family or god-parents. Nor was the *campesino* organization in Yaguachi as developed as in some other areas of the Coast. When the landowner heard of the decrees abolishing *precarismo* he tried to dismiss the tenants, but only seven of the fifty-six families were prepared to leave. Both the owner and the *mayordomo* made attempts to prevent the tenants from working and making repairs to their houses. At this point the tenants took their protest to Yaguachi where they were met with abuse, and eventually thrown into prison. Nevertheless some of the peasant leaders heard of similar protests in Milagro, another town in the rice zone, and decided to take their complaints to the IERAC officials there. This was on 28 November 1970; by 15 December the regional office of IERAC in Guayaquil had heard the peasants' case and dispatched a brigade of men to verify what the *precaristas* had reported. Eventually IERAC undertook the adjudication of land to the cooperative that was formed, on the understanding that those tenants who became members would receive land. The cooperative, named 'Viva Alfaro', was formed on 11 February 1972.

6. Cooperative '22nd of October' (Baba)[26]

This estate of over two thousand hectares is typical of many that have been studied in the zone. The owner, Valeriano Cortez Vargas, was the owner of three *haciendas* in Santo Domingo, Quevedo and Guayas, as well as property in Los Rios. He is said to have acted 'like a gangster' and become wealthy overnight, inspiring fear in the *precaristas* he employed, who treated him 'like a god' according to Ojeda. Cortez always denied using *precaristas*, and claimed that those on his estate were invaders of his property. On a number of occasions he sought, and obtained, the help of the police in Babahoyo, and offered bribes to the peasant leaders if they agreed to end their struggle for the land.

The tactics employed by landowners when their tenants were on the offensive are illustrated by Cortez's attempt to sell part of the estate. This was in fact contrary to the law, but IERAC refused to intervene while the estate was being sold. A number of landlords in the area even came to the support of the *precaristas* on the estate, saying that if they were allowed to buy the land they would be prepared to sell it to the tenants. Eventually the cooperative was given the official authorization of IERAC on 11 October 1972, following an agreement on the part of the *campesinos* to buy five hundred hectares of the estate for the equivalent of £7,000.

It is possible to draw a number of conclusions from these and similar examples. In the majority of cases conflicts were long drawn-out and third parties only intervened after the *precaristas* had crossed swords with the landlord. This observation applies to the intervention of both the more politically radical ACAL and, in the early stages to AID and later, FENACOO-PARR. Often the dispute between landlord and tenant began when the land was being sold, or the landlord was proposing to make a substantial change in the way that the estate was run, such as employing wage-labourers in place of tenants. There are very few confirmed cases in which tenants actually 'invaded' land under these circumstances; generally *precaristas* refused to be ejected by the landlord or his agent. Once battle had been joined the landlords usually offered to sell at least part of the estate to the tenants, often at inflated prices. The 'carrot' of a quick sale was attractive to tenants who despaired of waiting while IERAC transferred the land to them. Often the time-consuming process of acquiring a title to land increased the tensions between tenants, and played into the hands of land-owners.

Landlords were also adept at using force to secure their ends, while the police usually kept out of what they regarded as domestic disputes between landlords and tenants. Sometimes landlords hired labourers to eject the *precaristas*, or they resorted to threats to the lives of peasant leaders. The roll-call of deaths among peasant organizers in the Guayas Basin since 1967 bears eloquent witness to the reality of these threats. It has also been suggested that, like many peasant movements in Latin America, peasant insurrection in the Guayas Basin was uncoordinated and localized. This was particularly true in the early stages of the struggle, although differences between *campesinos* have militated against concerted action even after peasant federations were formed. In the following section the reaction of landlords to the peasants' movement is discussed before examining the present-day configuration of the *campesino* organizations.

LANDLORD REACTION AND THE IDEOLOGY OF SIPPTAL

The political pressure mounted by landlords following a rumour of impending agrarian reform has been discussed in an earlier chapter. This predictable response to the slightest suspicion of a redistributive land reform has, since 1966, been manipulated by one landlord organization in particular, the *Sindicato de Productores y Trabajadores Agrícolas del Litoral* (SIPPTAL). In the previous section it was demonstrated that many landlords were willing to part with some of their land, provided they were offered what they considered reasonable compensation. Many landlords took advantage of the opportunities to 'modernize' their holdings, and at the same time evade the attention of IERAC officials. Any consideration by the government of a more global agrarian reform policy, however, met with landlord opposition. In August 1972, for example, the rumour that a new 'Agrarian Reform Ministry' was to be created led the members of the *Cámara de Agricultura* on the Coast to call a permanent session until an official government denial was issued. At that time the landlords declared:

We are not against an agrarian reform, nor are we against *precaristas*, provided that it is accompanied by technical advances, and not confined to the breaking-up of estates, as at the moment . . . but we cannot remain inactive in the face of this kind of threat, which seeks to liquidate private property and upset the prevailing economic system.[27]

A week later this provoked a statement from one of the *campesino* organizations, the *Federación Nacional de Organizaciones Campesinas* (FENOC), which called for a speeding up of land adjudication, and accused the *Cámaras* of 'tenaciously opposing, with menacing audacity, all the obligations that the law calls on them to fulfil'.[28]

SIPPTAL came into being in 1966 in an attempt to counteract the influence of AID on the *campesinos* of the Coast. According to one report, its birth 'created an incision in the bosom of the *Cámara de Agricultura*' which had traditionally been controlled by an 'aristocratic element among Coastal landlords'.[29] Since the fall of the military government in 1966 this group had gradually been replaced by a more intransigent coterie of landlords. The members of SIPPTAL were distinguished by their opposition to the activities of AID, which they saw as 'mobilizing' the Coastal peasantry. SIPPTAL was also suspicious of the approval with which the government looked upon both AID and FENACOOPARR. It was held that these organizations 'were acting as spokesmen for the *campesinos* in their relations with the government'.[30]

It is likely that SIPPTAL always represented an important section of landlord opinion, but it would be inaccurate to regard this sectional interest as synonymous with official opinion within the *Cámara de Agricultura* in Guayaquil. The official view of the *Cámara* was not as hostile to IERAC, and saw a role for rice cooperatives in conjuction with private holdings. The criticism of rice cooperatives most often made by *Cámara* representatives was that they were formed simply to obtain land, without any attempt being made to explain cooperative principles. It was possible to interpret the creation of what they called 'phantom cooperatives' as having nothing whatever to do with the activities of AID in the zone.[31] Indeed, one year after the *Cámara* had protested at the threat of an Agrarian Reform Ministry being created, the same body welcomed renewed interest in the suggestion. Dr. Valverde, Vice President of the *Cámara's* 2nd zone, pointed out that this suggestion might prevent an 'anarchic situation' developing on the Coast. He added that it would give the government more control of *campesino* organizations and . . .

. . . it would avoid the evils provoked by wrongly named 'pre-cooperatives', whose existence, in view of the anarchy they created, has provoked the deepest divisions between landowners, the executive organ (IERAC) and *campesino* organizations.[32]

The view propounded by SIPPTAL was much less conciliatory than that of the *Cámaras*, and much more critical of government policy generally, as one might expect from what was effectively a 'ginger group'. The ideology of the organization found expression in a number of pamphlets and a book by its leading theorist, Carlos Palacios Saenz.[33] In these publications it is alleged that AID officials boasted of their attempts 'to surround rice estates with cooperatives and invade the privately owned estates from these cooperatives'.[34] This had provoked a 'true civil war between landlords and tenants . . . in which *precaristas* themselves were thrown off the land by well-disciplined members of delinquent cooperatives and pre-cooperatives'.[35] The gradual increase in organized land invasions had the effect of discouraging landlords from using official credit to improve agricultural production. Palacios Saenz goes on to argue that the Planning Board's (*Junta de Planificación*) admission that the laws abolishing *precarismo* had failed to improve the standard of living of peasants, proved that 'the ardent campaign of bureaucrats and politicians for these laws . . . had fallen into an abyss'.[36]

Cooperatives were opposed by SIPPTAL because they had come under the control of IERAC. Both IERAC and the Ecuadorian Communist Party (P.C.E.) were accused of serving the interests of United States 'imperialism' by their complicity in supporting the agrarian reform legislation. The attacks on 'feudal' landlords were completely unfounded and inspired by the United States government, which wished to bring agricultural development under the control of the state.[37] It was important to resist so-called 'technical' solutions to agricultural problems, because these served 'imperialistic' interests.

The ideology of SIPPTAL was a curious one. The alternative it proposed to the machinations of IERAC, was termed the *'ciudad agraria'* (agro-city). This had first been advocated in 1968, and had been the central plank of SIPPTAL ever since. The 'agro-city' would hold land collectively and encourage its technification, so reducing the cost of the technical services that were being employed by IERAC on its existing cooperatives. The intention was to convert cooperatives from 'parastate entities which had to pay the state for technical assistance', to 'free enterprises directed by qualified members' which would function on the free market.[38] It was imperative, in the view of SIPPTAL, 'that after years of state planning which stopped private enterprise from creating more wealth and providing work for the legion of unemployed . . . the private sector should be allowed to organize its own development plan . . .'[39] This policy called for 'a single alliance between labour and capital' which would make agricultural development policy 'something other than the work of *técnicos* linked intimately with imperialist powers'.[40]

It is clear that SIPPTAL's momentum was derived not simply from its resistance to the Coastal peasant movement, but from opposition to the modernizing ambitions of successive Ecuadorian governments, and most of the *técnicos* employed by the state. Whether or not landlords supported, or even understood, the policies that it advocated, there can be little doubt that SIPPTAL canalized widespread discontent with the direction agrarian policy was taking. Recently concerted attempts have been made in the press to suggest that, as a result of considerable social mobility, the 'social composition of the coastal landowning families has changed within the last fifty years'.[41] Today landowners were a 'class of private entrepreneurs unrecognizable to their ancestors of half a century ago . . . who did not dream of being members of such a class'. The evidence to support these statements was not provided but they did serve to emphasize the legitimacy of Coastal landed interests. In a newspaper advertisement for SIPPTAL which appeared in February 1974 entitled 'What is a *latifundio*?' it is alleged that IERAC had expropriated efficient agricultural enterprises as well as 'feudal' estates. This distinguished the Ecuadorian agrarian reform from others in Latin America:

> The Ecuadorian agrarian reform is a new marxist agrarian reform, with solely political objectives, which has sought to begin where such reforms should not even end . . . with the confiscation of great agricultural enterprises, under the pretext that they are *latifundio*.[42]

The conclusion that one comes to from these and other pronouncements of SIPPTAL's, is that a defence of the existing distribution of land and power in Coastal rural society can no longer be based on unqualified support for institutions like the *latifundia*. It is necessary constantly to deny that *precarismo* exists at all.[43] Furthermore, in most cases the attack on government interference is directed against IERAC, rather than the *Banco Nacional de Fomento*, still less FENACOOPARR. That landlord opposition should take this form is itself evidence of the enlarged role of the State in agricultural development, particularly since 1972; a theme to which we return in the next chapter.

THE IDEOLOGY AND STRATEGY OF THE PEASANT FEDERATIONS

The *raisons d'être* of the second-level *campesino* federations are more varied than the cooperatives that lend them their support. In the case of FENACOOPARR the 'federation' itself is a private marketing organization, with its own salaried staff, to which the rice cooperatives are affiliated. By contrast another peasant federation, the *Federación de Trabajadores Agrícolas del Litoral* (FETAL) is the peasant movement of the Communist Party of Ecuador (PCE), and composed of *campesino* leaders linked to the P.C.E. A number of other *campesino* federations, such as the *Asociación de Cooperativas Arroceras del Ecuador* (ACAE)[44] and the *Unión Regional de Cooperativas Industriales de Mercadeo Arroceras* (URCIMA)[45] function largely as political pressure groups, and are led by unashamedly populist leaders.

Finally, there is the *Asociación de Cooperativas Agrícolas del Litoral* (ACAL), a highly political organization with a distinctive ideology, but heavily dependent on 'grass roots' organization for its support.[46]

(a) *Federación Nacional de Cooperativas Arroceras* (FENACOO-PARR)

FENACOOPARR is the natural successor to *Punto IV* and the Agency for International Development in Ecuador, and until recently the peasant federation most favoured by the government. It is a private marketing organization led by *técnicos* rather than a movement led by peasants. The origins of FENA-COOPARR can be traced back to a decision in 1965 by the Minister of Agriculture, to ask the advice of AID in organizing a series of cooperatives in the rice zone. In the report of this investigation it was stated that 'to obtain maximum production it is necessary to technify the land, and irrigate it, but in no case need this cost more than c. £100 per hectare'.[47] Following this report, Babahoyo, Daule and Yaguachi were chosen as pilot areas for the establishment of cooperatives, and an accountant and agricultural extensionist were appointed to each area. On the 6 October 1970 FENACOOPARR officially came into existence.

FENACOOPARR was the first commercial organization to buy rice from the ex-*precaristas*, de-husk the rice in its own rice-mills, extract the various sub-products, and sell the grain to the government. In doing so it rapidly exposed the inadequacies of the system of commercialization controlled by the landlords. From the beginning FENACOOPARR was prepared to buy rice from any source, including the highly mechanized private estates, as long as it was economically advantageous.

An *ex post facto* assessment of FENACOOPARR suggests that the indirect effects of its operations were more important than the direct effects. In order to maximize the available surplus from small rice producers these producers needed to receive agricultural credit, with which to support their families between harvests. This opened the way to increased contracts with the *Banco Nacional de Fomento*, and accountants working for FENACOOPARR acted as intermediaries between the ex-tenants and the bank. To obtain credit the ex-tenants needed titles to the land they worked, which in turn meant that FENACOOPARR put pressure on IERAC to adjudicate the land to them. The construction of large rice-mills, big enough to process and store all the available rice, necessitated good relations with the government, which channelled the loans to FENACOOPARR through the *Banco Nacional de Fomento*. Not surprisingly the leadership of FENACOOPARR was prepared to recognize its indebtedness to the State. Commenting on a rally of *campesinos* during May 1975 the press reported that:

The representative of F E N A C O O P A R R ... expressed his thanks for the agricultural policy followed by the Minister, through which it had been possible to gain an increase in rice production and to obtain excellent harvests, all of which had been achieved with credit from the *Banco Nacional de Fomento*. These words served to touch the sensibilities of the Minister, and tears could be seen rolling down his cheeks.[48]

It was never one of the principal aims of the FENACOO-PARR leaders to help mobilize the *campesino* population politically. Gustavo Riofrio, one of the founders of FENACOOPARR pointed to the indignities and economic exploitation to which the *precarista* was exposed at the hands of mill-owners, landlords and money-lenders. At the same time he believed that if the government acted decisively the landlords 'would be forced to comply with the law'. It was important that the law should be implemented swiftly and efficiently 'so that land agents and false leaders' did not take the initiative from organizations that were already active amongst *campesinos*.[49]

Close acquaintance with the methods of FENACOOPARR can leave the impression that it is an 'apolitical' organization. Most of the time spent by *técnicos* in the organization is dedicated to practical, day-to-day administrative problems. The cooperatives' members are given courses in accountancy and instruction in the use of better agricultural methods.[50] There are regular visits by lawyers and auditors to each of the seventy-six cooperatives which in 1975 were affiliated to the Federation. When asked to name the ways in which FENACOOPARR had helped them most, all those interviewed by García de Paladines thought that 'education in the principles of cooperation' was the most important. When asked to what use they would like to put future credit, 89 per cent of her informants cited the possibility of buying more land.[51]

The impression that their activities are apolitical is one that FENACOOPARR seeks to encourage. The leader of the department in charge of 'land-tenure' claims that 'relations with private estates are excellent, because they are modern enterprises, and the cooperatives have nothing to fear from them'.[52] The organization places emphasis on the sale of land, usually outside the terms of *Decreto 1001*, if this is at all possible. Of the 76 cooperatives affiliated to FENACOOPARR only 30 had been formed as a direct result of the application of *Decreto 1001*.[53] García noted that even in 1971 most land controlled by FENACOOPARR, over 7,000 *cuadras*, had been bought privately. A lawyer had already been employed, 'whose duties were to encourage cooperative members to comply with their financial obligations, once negotiations had been completed'.[54] Ojeda and his colleagues found that over 70 per cent of the land area acquired by FENACOOPARR cooperatives had been bought in private land transactions.[55]

In return for commercializing the production of its cooperatives, and providing them with access to bank credit, FENACOOPARR demands considerable loyalty.[56] Member cooperatives are not allowed to belong to any other organization, and have to promise to give preference to FENACOOPARR in the commercialization process, and the provision of technical services. The Federation still does not buy all the rice the cooperatives produce, and the burden of paying for the increased staff employed by FENACOOPARR can only be paid for with a higher turnover. In 1974 almost 90 per cent of the rice sold by FENACOOPARR was sold to the Ecuadorian government.[57] Following the government investigation of FENACOOPARR in March 1976 the future of the organization is uncertain, even if its political inheritance, in having contained *campesino* ambitions at least among member cooperatives, is assured.

(b) *Federación de Trabajadores Agrícolas del Litoral* (FETAL)

It is difficult to evalute the full contribution of FETAL to the peasants' movement of the Coast. Its strengths are those of a tight political organization with a well-defined political stance, as well as the kudos of belonging to the international Communist movement. Its weakness is that it commands few economic resources of its own; it does not own its own rice-mills or employ a large staff to supervise the activities of member cooperatives. In the view of one of its lawyers, FETAL 'has succeeded in entering the cooperative movement which was originally formed by North American imperialists with the objective of neutralizing the struggle for land'.[58] However, this diagnosis is not matched by clear alternative strategies which the rice cooperatives can follow.

FETAL supports the idea that the *campesinos* should sell their rice to the State-owned rice-mill (*'Piladora Modelo'*) rather than to privately owned mills, and those of FENACOOPARR and ACAL. It views FENACOOPARR as a 'business, rather than a peasant movement', and throws doubt on the sources of finance used by ACAL and CESA in their promotion of peasant organizations.[59] Furthermore URCIMA, as well as ACAL, is looked upon as a legitimate branch of CEDOC, the trade union movement with which the Ecuadorian Communist Party has in the past been prepared to form an alliance.[60] FETAL is unwilling to condemn all the senior employees of the *Banco Nacional de Fomento* and IERAC, and seeks to distinguish between 'people who are sympathetic to the *campesinos* and those who are not'.[61] Attempts are made to keep up the pressure on IERAC to continue to adjudicate the land, and to prevent the *Banco Nacional de Fomento* from providing agricultural credit to landowners as well as *campesinos*.

The strategy of FETAL is much more pragmatic than that of ACAL, without being as overtly commercial as that of FENACOOPARR. In principle FETAL is against cooperative members paying for the land under the agrarian reform, but it is prepared to defend the decision of some cooperatives to pay between 6 per cent and 10 per cent of the value of a piece of land in order to secure credit from the *Banco Nacional de Fomento*.[62]

Apparently the leaders of FETAL do not consider that such payments help legitimize the principle of paying for land. FETAL is equally reticent about pressing other demands on the government until 'the peasantry had achieved a higher level of consciousness'.[63] It maintains, however, that *campesino* representatives should be elected to the governing board of IERAC, and attempts to prevent FETAL leaders from expressing the organization's policies in public are resisted.[64] One such attempt in July 1975, at a rally of peasants which was addressed by the President of the Republic, provoked FETAL to an exegesis on government policies, linking the refusal to prolong *Decreto 1001* to the operations of the CIA and Texaco-Gulf in Ecuador.[65]

(c) *Asociación de Cooperativas Agrícolas del Litoral* (ACAL)

ACAL is the most combative of the peasant organizations on the Coast. In its public pronouncements ACAL interprets the agrarian reform as nothing less than 'a favour which (the government) has undertaken so that the oligarchy can improve its position'.[66] In its view the administration of IERAC is not merely ineffectual, it is in the hands of the landlords:

While so many important officials of I E R A C and the government make pompous declarations about the Agrarian Reform law, even this defective law is not systematically applied. More than that, the most corrupt functionaries of I E R A C are prepared to tell lies which prepare the ground for violent repression and the massive ejection of tenants . . . [67]

The leaders of FENACOOPARR are particularly bitterly resented. Their participation in manifestations of support for the government provokes the charge that they 'have ceded to bureaucratic pressure to mount "folklorical spectacles" that fail to convince anybody'.[68] Whether or not the government implements the 'agrarian reform', it is the promise of ACAL that 'the *campesinos* will undertake their own reform'.[69] This note of defiance is also demonstrated in the publicity ACAL gives to the imprisonment of *campesino* leaders, and the 'witch-hunts' that have followed the murder of landlords.[70]

The public pronouncements of ACAL are not inconsistent

with its private actions. Although the rice cooperatives which belong to the organization (and it claims there are 117 of them) work closely with *técnicos* from the *Central Ecuatoriana de Servicios Agrícolas* (CESA), the relationship between the two bodies is one of mutual respect rather than paternalism and dependence. The cooperatives which are affiliated to ACAL own one rice-mill, to which many of them sell their rice, but pay fees to CESA for the development work undertaken on their behalf. Like the *técnicos* working for FENACOOPARR and FETAL, the professionals from CESA who work with the *campesinos* receive lower salaries than they could obtain privately.

ACAL still holds to the view that the land that is transferred under the terms of *Decreto 1001* should not be paid for by the ex-*precaristas*. However, its member cooperatives are increasingly dependent on the *Banco Nacional de Fomento* for agricultural credit, as the funds available to CESA have been exhausted and the scale of its operations has increased. In June 1975 ACAL undertook, for the first time, to sell rice to the government from its mill north of Daule. Originally it had been planned to enter into a marketing arrangement with the trade unions associated with CEDOC, under which rice would be sold to the urban population. In the end this proposal was never put into effect. Today much of the work of ACAL leaders and organizers is promotional; courses are arranged for peasant leaders in conjunction with the *Instituto Ecuatoriano de Formación Sindical* (INEFOS), another organization linked to CEDOC.[71] These courses lay the emphasis on 'consciousness-raising' among the *campesino* population, drawing on the ideas of Paulo Freire amongst others.[72]

Campesino organizations on the Coast differ in important ways, notably in the political support they have given to the government since the military took power in 1972. Nevertheless as the agrarian reform has taken shape, each movement has become tied to the various compartments of the State bureaucracy, particularly IERAC and the *Banco Nacional de Fomento*. Although some organizations, principally ACAL, emphasize their independence of the government, active participation in the process through which land is transferred and agricultural credit obtained, has served to neutralize the more politically radical peasant organizations. Their relations with government are not so much 'bargaining relations', in which the peasantry exerts pressure on the government, as an unequal exchange under which peasants take their place in a queue.

Campesino organizations are made more politically compliant by their close economic relations with the State. It could be argued that they are also rendered less effective as interest groups. Each federation at the secondary level is made up of a number of cooperatives at different stages of economic and social development. Some cooperatives co-exist peacefully with large private estates, with which they share common geographical boundaries. Other cooperatives are still engaged in almost continuous conflict with landowners, or opposing groups of ex-tenants, to secure a title to the land.[73] It is, therefore, misguided to evaluate the strength of the various peasant federations in purely numerical terms, because the degree of each cooperative's adherence to the goals of the secondary organizations varies enormously.[74] Statements that imply a heightened class awareness among the Coastal peasantry have no basis in fact.[75] For such a consciousness to develop among the *campesino* population a prerequisite would be a realignment of social forces within, and between, the secondary movements that exist on the Coast today.

1. Orlando Fals Borda, 'Formación y deformación de la política cooperativa en América Latina', *Informaciones Cooperativas*, no. 4, International Labour Organization, Geneva, 1970.

2. Fals Borda developed this argument more fully in *El Reformismo Por Dentro en América Latina*, Siglo XXI, Mexico, 1972, and *Cooperatives and Rural Development in Latin America: an analytical report*, no. 71. 1, United Nations Research Institute for Social Development, Geneva, 1971.

3. Fals Borda, 1970, op. cit., p. 28.

4. D. B. Heath, 'New Patrons for Old: Changing Patron-Client Relations in the Bolivian Yungas', *Ethnology*, xxii (1973), pp. 75–98.

5. Ojeda, op. cit., p. 24.

6. Between 1972 and 1975 the daily wage (*jornal*) paid to labourers increased from twenty to fifty sucres a day (from *c*. £0.40 to £1). The price the producer received for rice has not matched this increase, consequently the small producer has been 'squeezed'.

7. *Las Unidades Asociativas Campesinas en el Ecuador*, IERAC, Quito, October 1973 (mimeo), p. 47.

8. David Lehmann, 'Hacia un analisis de la conciencia de los campesinos', in *El campesinado: clase y conciencia de clase*, Ediciones Nueva Vision, Buenos Aires, 1972, p. 84.

9. *El Comercio*, Quito, 30.7.55.

10. *El Universo*, Guayaquil, 1.1.69.

11. *El Universo*, 4.1.69.

12. *El Universo*, 7.1.69.

13. *El Universo*, 12.1.69.

14. *El Universo*, 22.1.69.

15. *El Universo*, 10.1.71.

16. *El Universo*, 13.2.71.

17. *Babahoyo Irrigation Project Feasibility Report*, CEDEGE, January 1970, p. 41.

18. The information in this section is taken from my own field interviews in April 1975, and Ojeda's report of a visit to 'La Carmela', Ojeda, op. cit., p. 57.

19. Information in this section is drawn from Ojeda, ibid., pp. 45–6.

20. Ojeda, ibid., p. 46.

21. Information from interviews with members of ACAL, Daule, April–May 1975.

22. Even after the intervention of IERAC and the expropriation of much of their land these families owned several sizeable estates in the area. According to ONAC records each estate was valued at between £60,000 and £70,000 in 1971/2, *Organización Nacional de Avaluación y Catastros*, valuation records, Quito.

23. More recently disputes ending in death have not been confined to landlords and tenants. On 20 March 1975 a fight took place between members of Cooperative 'Sentinela' near Palestinas. Several members had been expelled from the cooperative and during the struggle that ensued three people were killed.

24. Information from my interviews with the cooperative's members in April 1975.

25. Information from *Las Unidades Asociativas*, op. cit., pp. 1–9.

26. Information from Ojeda, op. cit., pp. 33–7.

27. *El Universo*, 4.8.72.

28. *El Comercio*, Quito, 12.8.72.

29. Ojeda, op. cit., p. 19.

30. Ibid.

31. This was the view expressed by José Torres Espinoza, secretary of the *Cámara de Agricultura*, 2nd zone, in an interview with me in Guayaquil (15.5.75).

32. *El Comercio*, Quito, 8.8.73.

33. Carlos Palacios Saenz, *El Problema Agrario*. Fray Jodoco Riche, Guayaquil, 1973.

34. Ibid., p. 8.

36. Ibid., p. 24.

37. Ibid., p. 37.

38. Ibid., p. 26.

39. Ibid., p. 37.

40. Ibid., p. 52.

41. Jorge Reyes in *El Comercio*, Quito, 12.9.73.

42. *El Universo*, Guayaquil, 8.2.74. and *El Tiempo*, Quito, 10.2.74.

43. Another article by Jorge Reyes states that, 'the interpretation of "precarious tenure" is nowhere understood because it is arbitrary. The logical thing would be to remove the designation *"precaria"* altogether', *El Comercio*, 18.10.73.

44. ACAE has considerable support in some areas such as Urbino Jado and Yaguachi. It has cooperated on many occasions with ACAL in anti-Government demonstrations, despite the fact that it is widely believed to be financed by IERAC.

Its leader, Efraín Robelly is said to have strong 'caudillo' tendencies. One notable innovation of ACAE's is the setting up of a direct rice marketing scheme to the urban slums of Guayaquil.

45. URCIMA is a movement that broke away from ACAL under the leadership of Adolfo Tutivén. It has secured considerable support in the Daule area, and broadcasts its own radio programme each evening. Tutivén has created *compadrazgo* (god-parent) relations with the leaders of many cooperatives in attempts to strengthen his position. The motive for breaking with ACAL was, reputedly, Tutiven's dislike of the bureaucratic work of the movement, and his demand for more 'confrontationist' tactics towards landlords.

46. There is another peasant federation, the *Federación Nacional de Campesinos Libres del Ecuador* (FENACLE), which is the official organ in Ecuador of the 'International Confederation of Free Trades Unions', to which the North American AFL–CIO is affiliated. It has little popular following.

47. Teresa García de Paladines, *Evaluación del Impacto de FENACOOPARR en diez Cooperativas Agrícolas*, thesis, University of Guayaquil, Faculty of Agronomy and Veterinary Studies, 1972, p. 25.

48. *El Universo*, 2.5.75. This mutual admiration did not last indefinitely. Several months later FENACOOPARR was 'investigated' by the Government because of alleged misappropriation of funds. Gustav Riofrio was accused of obtaining 80 million sucres on false pretences and, eventually, had to leave the country.

49. *El Universo*, 30.12.70.

50. There were 7,296 participants in a total of 193 courses between 1968 and 1971. Garcia, op. cit., p. 18.

51. Ibid., p. 33.

52. Interview with Galo Palacios Andrade (FENACOOPARR), Guayaquil, 24.4.75.

53. According to the estimation of FENACOOPARR in May 1975.

54. García, op. cit., p. 37.

55. Ojeda, op. cit., p. 23.

56. In the period before agricultural credit became more available (1968–1971) FENACOOPARR had secured from £8,000 (1968) to £40,000 (1971) for its 21 affiliated cooperatives, according to García, op. cit., p. 53.

57. Estimate from the *Programa Nacional de Arroz y Maiz*, Guayaquil, 17.7.75.

58. Interview with Dr Francisco Polit (FETAL), Guayaquil, 17.7.75.

59. The *Central Ecuatoriana de Servicios Agrícolas* (CESA) is funded by West German and Dutch church organizations.

60. For example, the Ecuadorian Communist Party's trade union organization (C.T.E.) and CEDOC opposed the dictatorship of Velasco Ibarra, and called for a general strike, in the late 1960s. Hurtado and Herudek, op. cit., p. 73.

61. Interview with Luis Castro Villana, Secretary of FETAL, Guayaquil, 18.7.75.

62. This entitles the cooperative members to a certificate of provisional land adjudication, a *titulo de afectación*.

63. Luis Castro Villana, op. cit.

64. 'The Ecuadorian Press has published a number of calumnies against the peasant movement in recent weeks, and has even attacked IERAC . . . as part of a campaign planned from abroad', *El Pueblo* (PCE newspaper), 31.7.75.

65. *El Universo*, 25.7.75.

66. *Unidad Sindical* (ACAL), May 1975, p. 8.

67. 'ACAL: al pueblo y al Gobierno del Ecuador', *Nueva*, Quito, June 1975, p. 106.

68. Ibid., p. 106.

69. *Unidad Sindical*, op. cit., p. 8.

70. This happened, for example, in Daule during July 1974 when Sixto Pasto Bajana, a prominent landowner, was murdered. *Unidad Sindical* (ACAL), August 1974, p. 8.

71. *Instituto Ecuatoriano de Formación Sindical* (INEFOS) is the adult education branch of CEDOC.

72. Paulo Freire, *?Extensión o Comunicación?: la concientización en el medio rural*, Siglo XXI, Buenos Aires, 1973.

73. It is the view of *técnicos* in CESA that today the cooperative members are more often in conflict with 'the institutional framework that envelops them', than the landlords organized as a class. Conflicts between cooperatives are also much more common than they were.

74. The numerical membership of federations given in this chapter are their own estimates in each case. They are very approximate. The estimates of some federations, for example URCIMA, are so inflated that they are useless.

75. For example, those of NACLA's report on Ecuador: 'The rural work-force in the highlands and on the Coast have not been fooled by official rhetoric. They are no longer waiting for the government to come through on its promises. Rather, the level of class struggle in the countryside is escalating, as the isolation of individual producers gives way to collective struggle and new organisational forms. Peasant cooperatives are being formed throughout the country to demand the division of the large *haciendas* . . . yet the bloody repression of the bourgeoisie has been met with greater unity among the peasantry, with stronger and more politicized forms of mass organisation and, most importantly, with a higher level of integration between the struggles of the working class in the cities and of rural labourers in the highlands and on the Coast.' 'Ecuador: oil up for grabs', *North American Congress on Latin America* (NACLA), vol. ix, no. 8, November 1975, p. 18.

VII

AGRARIAN REFORM IN THE RICE ZONE

It is now necessary to examine the implementation of agrarian reform in the rice zone and the agrarian structure that is coming into being in this 'national priority zone'.[1] Since 1970, and particularly since 1972, the *de facto* control of much of the land in the provinces of Guayas and Los Rios has passed from the landlords to the tenants. As we shall see this does not mean that large landowners are an insignificant political force dispossessed of economic resources and effective political representation. The agrarian reform that has brought benefits to many of the ex-*precaristas* has not simply tilted the balance of advantages away from the landlords. The provision of land titles and a new corporate identity as members of rice cooperatives increasingly dependent on the State has not prevented social differentiation within the rural population.[2] The political 'incorporation' of the coastal peasantry since 1970 had been bought at the cost of its independence, and has frustrated attempts to block those provisions of the agrarian reform which have been highly beneficial to landlords.[3] Despite the increased political dependence of coastal *campesinos*, however, it is misleading to claim that 'the distributive side of the agrarian reform in Ecuador has been decidedly abandoned, displaced by a strategy of cooperation between the government and landowners to raise production and revenues'.[4] This is a simplification of the effects of land distribution since 1970, which ignores the way in which both land and agricultural credit have been allocated to the ex-*precaristas*.

LAND DISTRIBUTION SINCE 1970

In an earlier chapter reference was made to the distribution of land in the rice zone before 1970. It was suggested that between 1954 and 1968 the number of small rice producers, most of whom were tenants, had increased dramatically. At the same time production on the largest estates, most of which employed wage-labour, had increased equally dramatically. Alongside the technification of rice production it would be possible to discern a process of cumulative social differentiation favouring large production units.[5]

Since 1970 the differences between the large private estates and the ex-tenanted sector have increased. Much of the growth in production has been concentrated on the large estates which are technically advanced, at the expense of smaller producers organized in cooperatives or pre-cooperatives. This kind of agrarian development in areas of rice cultivation cannot be explained simply in terms of technological advantages and economies of scale. In Japan, for example, mechanization has been of direct benefit to the four million family landholdings that make up almost 80 per cent of all farm households[6]. Even in Guyana, where rice production has been of increasing importance in recent years, tractors and combine harvesters were used in all of the government's settlement projects.[7] In Ecuador, by comparison, only 8·87 per cent of the land under rice cultivation in 1974 was devoted to the 'fully mechanized production' of the crop.[8] This has led officials in IERAC to talk of agricultural 'growth' (*crecimiento*) rather than 'development' (*desarrollo*) as characteristic of rice farming—a distinction that brings out something of their own disillusionment with what has been accomplished.

Using figures provided by the government's Rice Programme it is possible to compare the distribution of land between 1972 and 1974, the latest year for which there are available figures.[9] In 1972 the 'top' stratum of rice producers, those working more than 20 *cuadras* of land (c. 14 ha), made up 4·4 per cent of the total number of producers and worked 39·5 per cent of the land by area (see Tables 17 and 19). In 1974 2·5 per cent of producers were working more than 20 hectares of land, almost 36 per cent of the total amount of land under rice cultivation.[10] In 1972 the 'poorest' stratum of producers, those who worked less than 5 *cuadras* (3·5 ha), made up 73 per cent of the total number, and worked 27 per cent of the land devoted to rice (Tables 17 and 19). Two years later the nearest equivalent

Table 17. Distribution of land in the rice zone by size of holding (1972)*

Size of holding (cuadras)	Pro-Guayas		Pro-Los Rios	
	cuadras	%	cuadras	%
0– 4·9	10,430	14·16	9,014	12·24
5–19·9	14,346	19·48	9,705	13·18
20–49·9	6,836	9·28	3,988	5·42
50–99·9	5,130	6·97	2,879	3·91
more than 100	6,387	8·68	2,561	3·48
Total	43,131	58·57	28,148	38·23

*These figures refer to land actually devoted to rice cultivation, rather than the total extensions of 'rice' estates (cf. Tables to Chapter II above).
Source: Departamento de Comercialización, Programa Nacional del Arroz, Guayaquil, June 1972.

Table 18. Distribution of land in the rice zone by size of holding (1974)*

Size of holding (hectares)	Pro-Guayas		Pro-Los Rios	
	hectares	%	hectares	%
0– 4·9	18,611	29.92	6,700	10·77
5–19·9	8,977	14·43	5,143	8·27
20–49·9	3,372	5·42	2,227	3·58
50–99·9	4,274	6·87	2,052	3·30
more than 100	6,198	9·97	2,833	4·56
Total	41,435	66·61	18,958	30·48

*These figures refer to land actually devoted to rice cultivation, rather than the total extensions of 'rice' estates (cf. Tables to Chapter II above).
Source: Departamento de Comercialización, Programa Nacional del Arroz, Guayaquil, June 1974.

stratum (those working less than 5 ha) comprised 86 per cent of producers, who in turn worked 40 per cent of the land (Tables 18 and 20). These figures suggest that in the period of greatest agrarian reform activity, between 1972 and 1974, there has been little redistribution of land. Similarly, the average size of landholdings in the largest and smallest strata changed very little in this period. In 1974, as in 1972, the average size of landholdings in the 'poorest' stratum, those under 5 ha, was 1·5 hectares. The average-sized holding within the stratum of 'largest' holdings, those over 100 ha, was about 120 ha in both 1972 and 1974.[11]

Table 19. Distribution of rice producers in the rice zone by size of holding (1972)

Size of holding (cuadras)	Pro-Guayas		Pro-Los Rios	
	numbers	%	numbers	%
0–4·9	5,532	39·68	4,585	32·89
5–19·9	1,888	13·54	1,238	8·88
20–49·9	237	1·70	146	1·05
50–99·9	86	0·62	45	0·32
more than 100	31	0·32	14	0·10
Total	7,784	55·84	6,028	43·24

Source: Departamento de Comercialización, Programa Nacional del Arroz, Guayaquil, June 1972.

Table 20. Distribution of rice producers in the rice zone by size of holding (1974)

Size of holding (hectares)	Pro-Guayas		Pro-Los Rios	
	numbers	%	numbers	%
0– 4·9	12,955	63·73	4,670	22·97
5–19·9	1,321	6·50	806	3·97
20–49·9	147	0·72	108	0·53
50–99·9	76	0·37	44	0·22
more than 100	54	0·27	25	0·12
Total	14,553	71,59	5,653	27·81

Source: Departamento de Comercialización, Programa Nacional del Arroz, Guayaquil, June 1974.

It is clear from what has been written that between 1972 and 1974 land redistribution was not carried very far under the agrarian reform. During this period, however, the official status of the majority of small producers changed from that of 'tenant' to 'owner' although most former tenants had still not received titles to the land they worked.[12] The fact that the land adjudication process had been started, and that tenants no longer paid rent was *de facto* proof of this change in status. In

1972 there were 5,000 owners among the 15,000 rice producers on the Ecuadorian Coast, according to the official figures of the *Programa Nacional del Arroz*. By 1974 there were 20,000 producers, of whom 15,000 were owners of the land they worked (Tables 21 and 22). The principal effect of the land reform in these two years was the 'enfranchisement' of the *campesino* population, which ceased to be a largely tenant population and was increasingly made up of owner-occupiers. The process through

Table 21. Land tenure among rice producers (1972)

Province	Producers (total)		Owners		Tenants	
	numbers	%	numbers	%	numbers	%
Guayas	7,784	53·8	2,963	20·5	4,821	33·3
Los Rios	6,028	41·6	1,994	13·8	4,034	27·9
Other Provinces	656	4·6	367	2·5	289	2·0
National Total	14,468	100·0	5,324	36·8	9,144	63·2

Source: Departamento de Comercialización, Programa Nacional del Arroz, Guayaquil, June 1972.

Table 22. Land tenure among rice producers (1974)

Province	Producers (total)		Owners		Tenants	
	numbers	%	numbers	%	numbers	%
Guayas	14,553	65·1	10,505	46·9	4,048	18·1
Los Rios	5,653	25·3	3,633	16·3	2,020	9·0
Other Provinces	2,154	9·6	1,513	6·8	641	2·9
National Total	22,360	100·0	15,651	70·0	6,709	30·0

Source: Departamento de Comercialización, Programa Nacional del Arroz, Guayaquil, June 1974.

which this 'enfranchisement' was achieved did not bring about a major change in the distribution of land under the control of the different rural strata. Nevertheless, the change in status—from 'tenant' to 'owner'—was a visible sign of the official recognition of the former *precarista*, and his greatly increased access to State-provided credit and technical assistance.

Table 23. Distribution of land between owners and tenants in the rice zone
(1972)

Province	Total land sown		Extension owned		Extension tenanted	
	cuadras*	%	cuadras	%	cuadras	%
Guayas	43,131	55.27	23,101	29.61	20,029	25.67
Los Rios	28,148	36·07	11,714	15·01	16,434	21·06
Others	6,755	8·66	4,018	5·15	2,737	3·50
National Total	78,034	100·00	38,833	49·77	39,290	50·23

*1 cuadra = 0·70 hectares 'rounded' figures.
Source: Departamento de Comercialización, Programa Nacional del Arroz, Guayaquil,
June 1972.

Table 24. Distribution of land between owners and tenants in the rice zone
(1974)

Province	Total land sown		Extension owned		Extension tenanted	
	hectares*	%	hectares	%	hectares	%
Guayas	41,435	60·56	32·730	47·84	8,705	12·72
Los Rios	18,958	27·72	11,504	16·81	7,454	10·90
Others	1,803	11·73	5,455	7·97	2,566	3·76
National Total	68,416	100·00	49,689	72·62	18,726	27·38

*1 hectare = 1·41 cuadras 'rounded' figures.
Source: Departamento de Comercialización, Programa Nacional del Arroz, Guayaquil,
June 1974.

THE ADJUDICATION OF LAND UNDER 'DECRETO 1001'

In its 'Five Year Development Plan' the Ecuadorian government designated the Guayas Basin as the first 'priority zone' of
the agrarian reform programme. It states that the promulgation
of *Decreto 1001* prepared the way for the abolition of rice *precarismo* among the forty-six thousand tenant families in the
area.[13] These families were estimated to be working 160,000
hectares of land on rice estates under tenancy systems.[14] It was
proposed to redistribute very much more land than this, however, under the agrarian reform; the figure favoured by the
government being 480,000 hectares.[15] The way in which this
would be undertaken was described as follows:

Therefore the immediate action of the government in the area will consist of eliminating the speculative systems of credit, overcoming the imperfect market structure and proceeding to the expropriation of land in order to reorganize production on the new, reformed units.[16]

According to the same report 'a predisposition on the part of the area's *campesinos* towards cooperative forms of work' made it necessary to establish cooperatives as the new production units.[17]

Since the publication of the 'Five Year Plan' in 1972, the Coastal agrarian reform has been given a great deal of publicity. Newspaper headlines have proclaimed the fact that 'after ten years of work, 6,356 peasant families have been helped by IERAC'.[18] The significance of these figures is barely visible behind the political rhetoric and exaggerated claims. The tone of most of IERAC's publicity is conciliatory towards large landlords, while insisting on the vigour with which the agrarian reform is being implemented.[19] The impression created, and reinforced by the ferocity of landlord opposition to IERAC, is that the process of agrarian reform is well advanced in the Guayas Basin.

The private records kept by IERAC itself do not match up to the claims that are made in the press.[20] These records show that progress in finally adjudicating land to the former *precaristas* has been slow. According to IERAC's own figure only 45 estates in the rice zone were in 'the final stages of adjudication' in July 1975 (see Table 25). In about 70 per cent of these cases the *campesinos* on the former estates had received titles to the land. In another 356 cases the process of land adjudication was 'in the early stages of adjudication', the legal ownership of the estate was vested in IERAC, and measures were being taken to establish an officially recognized cooperative. A third category of estates, nearly three hundred of them, were under 'active consideration' by IERAC officials for adjudication under *Decreto 1001*. Thus of the total area of land judged appropriate for adjudication under *Decreto 1001* (170,000 ha) only about 12,000 ha was legally owned by the *campesinos* in the summer of 1975. In global terms only about 7 per cent of the land considered ripe for expropriation had been finally handed over to the ex-*precaristas* who had worked it.

Table 25. The progress of land adjudication under *Decreto 1001*
(1975)

(A)	Estates in the final stages of adjudication*		
Zones	Nos. of estates		Land expropriated
Guayaquil	18		7,237 ha
Daule	22		6,750 ha
Babahoyo	5		4,559 ha
Total	45		18,547 ha

(B)	Estates in the early stages of adjudication		
	Nos. of estates	Land expropriated	Possible beneficiaries
Guayaquil	144	44,986 ha	3,157
Daule	129	16,192 ha	1,933
Babahoyo	83	30,825 ha	2,558
Total	356	92,004 ha	7,648

(C)	Estates the expropriation of which is under consideration		
	Nos. of estates	Land expropriated	Possible beneficiaries
Guayaquil	79	26,814 ha	854
Daule	190	31,154 ha	1,453
Babahoyo	28	7,171 ha	65
Total	298	65,086 ha	2,372

Source: Plan Operativo Anual 1975, IERAC, Guayaquil.

Even the revelations of how little land has legally passed to the *campesinos* does not tell the entire story. Not all the land suitable for rice cultivation was considered appropriate for transference under *Decreto 1001*. The 170,000 hectares of land on rice estates represented about a third of the land originally surveyed by IERAC under the terms of *Decreto 1001* (530,000 ha). Two-thirds of the land on rice estates, roughly corresponding to the figure favoured by the government in its 'Development Plan', was left in the hands of the latifundists.

A number of explanations have been offered for the slowness of the land adjudication process. Lawyers working at the *Universidad Central* in Quito under Dr. Marcelo Ortiz, have suggested that changes in the highest echelons of IERAC account for the uneven pace of the agrarian reform since 1972:

In marked correlation with the loss of capable civil servants we see the increase of bureaucracy. It is as if the agrarian reform were something that adds desks and offices . . . [21]

But the unevenness of the process of land adjudication does not explain the slowness of IERAC's activity. Before land titles can be issued IERAC has to assess whether there are rice *precaristas* on an estate, and what priority should be given to their claims. It has been contended that 'the level of activity of IERAC officials depends more than anything else on the degree of pressure exerted by the *campesinos* and the gravity of conflict within an area'.[22] Delays in adjudicating land are thus attributed to the pressure exerted by landlords on IERAC officials and the threats that landlords have made to *campesinos* which have affected the willingness of the former tenants to press for their rights under the law. According to this interpretation the pressure mounted by social forces on IERAC have determined the outcome of the land reform process and the freedom of manoeuvre open to the State.

There can be little doubt that IERAC officials are pressurized by both sides during the long drawn-out process of agrarian reform, and have suffered from organizational and financial changes which have prejudiced their ability to act.[23] Piecemeal intervention on one estate after another has enabled landlords to hire lawyers to represent them in their dealings with IERAC, contrary to the intentions of those who framed *Decreto 1001*. Nevertheless, it would be disingenuous to assume that IERAC, as an arm of the government, was a disinterested party during the transference of land from one owner to another. In later sections of this chapter it is contended that a major expansion of government credit, and the selectivity with which it has been allocated, have enabled the Ecuadorian State to undertake a major task of social engineering in the Guayas Basin. Similarly, State control of the commercialization process has enabled the government to establish the conditions under which the agricultural surplus is transferred to urban centres. The formation of cooperatives under IERAC's jurisdiction might also be interpreted as one element in the Ecuadorian State's armoury of social control.

The dependence of the cooperatives on IERAC's goodwill in

seeking to reduce delays before they can receive land titles, is not merely an effect of their financial indebtedness to the State. This dependence is an intrinsic part of the institutional framework of the agrarian reform since the Agrarian Reform Law of 1973. Under the terms of this law *Organizaciones Campesinas de Reforma Agraria* (OCRAs) were created from what were previously described as 'pre-cooperatives'. As we have seen the ownership of the land on which OCRAs were formed was vested in IERAC. In most cases the *campesinos* affiliated to a second-level peasant federation, such as ACAL or FENACOO-PARR, so that they could receive help in securing credit and

Table 26. Campesino organizations established under the Agricultural Reform in the rice zone (OCRAs*)

		Organisations	Membership
(A)	*Officially approved*		
	Guayaquil	44	1,316
	Daule	87	2,903
	Babahoyo	24	914
(B)	*Awaiting approval*		
	Guayaquil	39	846
	Daule	128	3,104
	Babahoyo	73	2,212

*OCRA, *Organización Campesino Provisional de Reforma Agraria.*
Source: *Plan Operativo Anual 1975, IERAC,* Guayaquil.

technical assistance, while the land was being transferred to them. In order to meet IERAC's requirements the *campesinos* on an estate have to prove 'that they are capable of taking on the responsibility for the management of the enterprise, which requires modern agricultural methods'.[24] The suggestion in the 'Five Year Development Plan' that the *campesinos* of the Guayas Basin are predisposed to accept cooperatives is based on an interpretation of the situation on the part of *campesinos*.[25]

An analysis of the estates in which IERAC has intervened shows that they vary widely in size, and the number of tenants that they formerly employed. Of the 47 estates in the Babahoyo area, for example, only 7 were over a thousand hectares. In most cases about 200 to 300 ha of land is devoted to the cultivation of rice on estates of this size.[26] The number of tenant families employed on estates in the Babahoyo area varied between four and a hundred and sixty-two. The average size of the 47 estates was between 200 and 300 hectares, and the average number of tenant families was between 25 and 30.[27] Comparing estates at different stages of adjudication throughout the rice zone, there was little difference in the average size of estates which were 'in the early stages of adjudication' (300 ha) and those which were 'under active consideration' (320 ha), although estates in the later stages of adjudication were usually somewhat larger (500 ha).[28] The conclusion we must draw from these figures is that the slow progress of the agrarian reform has not favoured one particular group of landlords employing *precaristas*, whether identified by geographical area or size. Nor has the outcome of the agrarian reform been determined exclusively by the political pressure exerted by landlords and tenants. A satisfactory explanation of the course taken by the agrarian reform must consider the process of land adjudication in relation to the allocation of agricultural credit in the region. Only by considering both credit and land together can we appreciate the full political significance of the agrarian reform and the agrarian structure that is coming into being in the region.

THE EXPANSION OF AGRICULTURAL CREDIT

In an earlier chapter reference was made to the hold of money-lenders over tenants under the system of rice *precarismo*.[29] It was argued that the government's recognition of this economic dependence was a contributory factor in the decision to abolish rice tenancy altogether.[30] The inability of *precaristas* to obtain credit from the *Banco Nacional de Fomento* was given as one of the reasons for the intervention of the Agency for International Development (AID) in trying to establish cooperatives amongst small rice producers.[31] Clearly the measures taken by the government to provide a substitute for the funds that were traditionally manipulated by the *fomentadores* (money-lenders), must lie at the heart of the Coastal agrarian reform.

The principles of the Land Sale Guaranty programme introduced by AID were adopted in modified form by the military government in Ecuador after 1972, when oil revenues provided the State with the means to greatly expand the amount of agricultural credit. In 1972 and 1973 most of this credit was allocated to the cooperatives that were associated with the *Programa de Promoción de Empresas Agrícolas* which had been founded by AID under the Land Sale Guaranty scheme (see Table 27). Another outcome of AID's work was the establishment of FENACOOPARR, a private rice marketing organization which also negotiated on behalf of rice cooperatives for government credit.[32] Since 1972 a number of people involved with the allocation of agricultural credit have expressed their anxiety about the way government money is being used, and have argued forcibly for more control over the beneficiaries of official funds. In July 1975 the head of the *Banco Nacional de Fomento*, Carlos Camacho Sáa, emphasized that the bank 'could not be expected to continue to increase its operations at the pace of previous years'.[33] What was needed was not only closer supervision of cooperatives by financial institutions, but some understanding of the 'level of consciousness' that tenants had achieved.[34]

The growth in business undertaken by the *Banco Nacional de Fomento* has been spectacular by any standards. As recently as 1972 the bank provided only about a third of the agricultural credit in Ecuador. The following year the value of agricultural credit authorized by the B.N.F. increased by 89 per cent to a level that 'had never been reached before in the history of the institution'.[35] Between 1973 and 1974 it increased by nearly 300 per cent to a figure of 941 million *sucres* (c. £19 million).[36] Even more illuminating than these global figures are those for the credit distributed to agricultural cooperatives. In 1974 the *Banco Nacional de Fomento* in Guayaquil authorized credit amounting to over £5 million in the province of Guayas alone (see Table 27).

Within the rice zone the expansion of credit has been most dramatic. Between 1973 and 1974, the value of credit given to rice producers rose from c. £5 million to £10 million, and the amount of land cultivated with credit from the *Banco Nacional de Fomento* from 97,729 ha to 105,835 ha.[37] Among the recipients of this credit were 126 rice cooperatives in the Province of

Table 27. Agricultural credit to rice cooperative in the province of Guayas
(1972/75)

---

(1) *Authorized credit to rice cooperatives through the Banco Nacional de Fomento*
  1972   0·4 million sucres (*c.* £8,000)
  1973   45·6 million sucres
  1974   191·4 million sucres
  1975   (to May) 125·2 million sucres,
          (for year, estimated 300 million sucres, *c.* £6,000,000)

(2) *Authorized credit to rice cooperatives within the P.P.E.A.* for infrastructure*
  1972   3·3 million sucres (*c.* £66,000)
  1973   5·5 million sucres
  1974   71·3 million sucres
  1975   (to May) 51·9 million sucres,
          (for year, estimated 120 million sucres, *c.* £2,400,000)

---

*Programa de Promocion de Expresas Agrícolas.
Source: Banco Nacional de Fomento, Guayaquil Branch, July 1975.

Guayas. These cooperatives received funds from two main sources at the disposition of the *Banco Nacional de Fomento*. The most important sources were funds that the B.N.F. received from the Central Bank (*Banco Central*) on the basis of its proposed loans to the cooperatives. The other source of funds were those received directly from government development bodies, such as FONADE and FONAPRE. These are basically capital grants for agricultural investment.

The allocation of funds by the *Banco Nacional de Fomento* is also undertaken through two separate channels. Most of the agricultural credit that helps to meet the cooperatives' subsistence needs takes the form of a loan (the *préstamo capacitación*), which is calculated from the anticipated value of the harvest. As cooperatives acquire their own regular income the proportion of total subsistence needs provided by the BNF declines, the ultimate objective being self-sufficiency. The problem of recuperating loans, however, is such that this objective must remain a distant one for most cooperatives.[38]

It will be clear from Table 27 that the lion's share of agricultural credit going to rice cooperatives is taken by those affiliated to the *Programa de Promoción de Empresas Agrícolas* (P.P.E.A.).[39] Today there are 91 rice cooperatives affiliated to the PPEA in the Guayas Basin. The majority of these co-operatives (51) are in the 'first stage' of the PPEA's programme, which is designed to transform them into *'empresas agrícolas'* (agricultural enterprises). These fifty-one cooperatives only receive credit for the crop. When they have satisfied the *técnicos* in the PPEA that there are no obstacles to the realization of their full productive potential, they may also receive credit towards infrastructural development. Already another forty cooperatives receive credit towards infrastructure, such as levelling the land, irrigation and improved access roads. In 1975 these forty 'vanguard' cooperatives received the £2·5 million that was invested by the bank in infrastructure on PPEA cooperatives (see Table 27).

The cooperatives associated with the PPEA and the Ministry of Agriculture, are not representative of rice cooperatives generally in the Guayas Basin. The majority of them are endowed with better natural resources than the average cooperative, and they are better placed than the average cooperative to take advantage of advanced irrigation technology. In one survey it was established that a quarter of them had bought land from the previous owners outside the terms of *Decreto 1001*.[40] Most of these cooperatives had been associated with AID and FENACOOPARR, and there was little history of conflict between landlords and tenants before these third parties became interested in them. In 1975 the average length of time for which a *campesino* had been a member of one of the P.P.E.A. cooperatives was already nearly five years.[41] Three-quarters of the land within the cooperatives was worked communally by the members, a significantly higher proportion than elsewhere in the Guayas Basin.[42]

Of the cooperatives within the PPEA which have yet to receive credit towards infrastructure, some are very large in size. Of the seventeen cooperatives affiliated to the PPEA in the Milagro-Yaguachi area, for example, eight were over a thousand hectares.[43] Both the *técnicos* working for the PPEA and the *Banco Nacional de Fomento* officials, impress on the members of these cooperatives the technical and financial advantages of forming true production cooperatives. They explain that if land is worked communally it can be levelled and irrigated more easily, and mechanized harvesting can be undertaken. The advantages for the members are obvious; they have access to much more credit as well as priority in its allocation.[44] From the standpoint of the *técnicos* the programme has the advantage that it can be administered from offices in Guayaquil, and much closer financial and technical supervision of the cooperatives is possible.

The future evolution of the PPEA cooperatives can only widen the gap between the natural advantages possessed by some cooperatives, and the accumulation of disadvantages faced by others. Until their technification is complete, most PPEA cooperatives will continue to employ large numbers of seasonal workers, in contravention of Article Eight of IERAC's 'statutes for cooperatives'.[45] Members of PPEA cooperatives state that without employing outside labour they cannot contemplate working additional land—something that they are being constantly urged to do by their technical advisers.[46] Furthermore, the inability to repay debts incurred by PPEA cooperatives gives the Ministry of Agriculture, which supervises the PPEA, the power to take them over completely. This fact alone should lead one to treat with caution the claim made by the AID office that the PPEA acts solely as an 'intermediary'.[47]

STATE CONTROL OF THE COMMERCIALIZATION PROCESS

The activities of FENACOOPARR represent only one aspect of the commercialization of rice in Ecuador although the role of the organization has not diminished since 1972. What remains distinctive about FENACOOPARR is the vertical integration through which it produces, mills and markets rice within the same institution. Although in the words of one of its managers 'the mission of FENACOOPARR is to modernize archaic systems of production', there is little consensus of opinion about the objectives of FENACOOPARR.[48] The leaders of a rival organization, ACAL, accuse FENACOOPARR of paternalism, referring to Gustavo Riofrio rather disparagingly as 'Papa Riofrio'. The leader of the 'opposition' political party, the *Confederación de Fuerzas Populares* (C.F.P.), Assad Bucaram, has been even more scathing in his attacks on

FENACOOPARR and its alleged hoarding of rice.[49] Eventually, as we have seen, the government started its own investigations when allegations of financial mismanagement could not be ignored any longer.[50]

The formal apparatus of control over the processing and marketing of rice exercised by the Ecuadorian state has increased steadily since 1972. In that year the state first established the price which the rice mills (*piladoras*) paid the producer for the rice they bought. In 1973 *Decreto 914* was issued, which forced the *piladoras* to part with some of their rice to the government. The amount taken by the government varied with the size of the rice-mill, from 100 metric hundredweight to nearly 1,000 metric hundredweight a year. Since the rice harvest suffers from large seasonal variations there has been criticism of this system, which expresses what the mills must pay as a fixed amount rather than a proportion of the rice they handle.

Since 1975 the rice-mills have to pay between 180 *sucres* and 190 *sucres* (c. £4) for each metric hundredweight which they buy from the producers. Most of the rice eventually finds its way to Guayaquil, where nearly half of it is sold by the government's wholesale organization the *Empresa Nacional de Provisión y Transporte* (ENPROVIT).[51] The amount of rice 'in the husk' which the mills are allowed to sell for each metric hundredweight they buy, is also controlled.[52] As the price at which the rice-mills sell rice is controlled, in principle the operating margins of the rice-mills are dictated by the government.[53] Since 1975 the government's control of the commercialization process has been further strengthened by the establishment of the *Empresa Nacional de Almacemiento y Comercio* (ENAC), which buys and sells about 70 per cent of all the rice marketed at the wholesale level.

State control of rice marketing is, nevertheless, less advantageous to the small producer than might be imagined. The official prices dictated by the government were calculated by taking 'marginal production' as a base, that is the cost of production to the small producer. According to the Minister for Work and Social Welfare only 7 per cent of rice producers provide 25 per cent of total production, and they, therefore, receive a disproportionate amount of the benefit from guaranteed prices.[54] The lower costs of large mechanized producers, compared with those of 'marginal' producers, also means that they can take advantage of calculations based on the 'marginal' production unit.[55] In view of these facts it is easier to appreciate why so many large producers and rice-mill owners have been willing to cooperate with the government. One of them described the present system 'under which a dealer is paid more for his rice than the consumer is asked to pay', as a 'system of indirect subsidies which have been forced on the government under political pressure'.[56]

There is a further reason why the official system of controlled prices is less advantageous to the rice-producing cooperatives than it might seem at first. This is the inadequacy of existing storage facilities, which means that after a good harvest rice cooperatives are forced to sell their rice at prices below those established by the government. In July 1975 this 'black market' selling became common. There were reports in the press that 'supply' had outstripped 'demand' for rice, leaving the small producer with the impossible task of repaying the loans he had received. At the same time it was contended that the existence of this problem was a direct result of the ease with which cooperatives had been able to secure credit.[57]

Once the state had bought the rice that it could store, through the 'Piladora Modelo' and ENAC, 'the rest of the rice produced . . . would not be bought at the official prices'. In the view of the press 'this demonstrated that the fixing of prices to the consumer was a fiction . . . because the free play of supply and demand is a natural regulator of prices'.[58] The following day it was announced that the good harvest itself was largely explained by the 'extension of (the) agricultural frontier . . . as well as increased yields which were brought about by mechanization, the use of improved seeds and chemical fertilizers . . .'[59] Although attention was drawn to the effect of inadequate storage facilities on the ability to enforce price controls, the principal conclusion reached was that over-production would be 'even more of a problem in the future than it had been in the past'.[60]

Controversy over government control of the prices paid for rice was later given extra impetus by rumours that the government was contemplating the exportation of rice.[61] It was admitted that the last to benefit from the good harvest had been 'the fragile and modest economy of the *campesino* . . . because of the inadequacy of storage facilities'.[62] This fact notwithstanding, negotiations were initiated for the sale of 20,000 tons of rice to Peru and Chile.[63]

AN EVALUATION OF AGRARIAN REFORM IN THE GUAYAS BASIN

There are many criteria by which an agrarian reform can be judged successful or unsuccessful, and in this section an attempt is made to establish the merits of each of these sets of criteria. It is not proposed to review the voluminous literature on Latin American agrarian reform in a systematic fashion.[64] Rather, an attempt is made to establish what has happened in the course of the Ecuadorian agrarian reform in the light of experiences in Latin America as a whole.

We have seen that the roots of Ecuadorian agrarian policy lie both in an historical configuration of social forces that is specific to Ecuador, and partly in the effect of the Alliance for Progress ideology since the early 1960s. It is impossible to disentangle fully these influences on elite ideology, which should be seen in historical terms. Certainly, it would be misplaced to attribute distinct ideological perspectives to different 'endogenous' and 'exogenous' influences at work today. Within Ecuador, as elsewhere in Latin America, agrarian reform is conceived of by some as a means of securing social stability, while others look to agrarian reform as a way of changing society itself. The spectrum of opinion is a very wide one and there is only a limited consensus within the social groups that comprise it. This analysis will examine at what points this social consensus breaks down, and why, rather than present an exegesis on agrarian reform in general, or a taxonomical guide to Latin American reforms within which we can 'fit' the Ecuadorian experience.[65]

The classic liberal statement about agrarian reform is that it is 'a means of speeding the transformation from a feudal to a capitalistic (or a socialistic) society'.[66] Conceived in this way even the most 'incrementalist' agrarian reform, that is one which puts increased production well before income redistribution, represents an historic advance from which both the individual and the economy reap some benefit.[67] For a time in the 1960s it almost looked as if advocates of agrarian reform in Latin American countries, having learned from the CIDA Reports that the *latifundia/minifundia* complex was a barrier to increased agricultural production, had resolved the contradiction between 'the two goals of efficiency and justice' by urging a redistributive agrarian reform.[68] As Barraclough has pointed out the failure to reconcile efficiency and equity 'stems from real differences in values concerning the aims of development' as well as 'a substantial divergence in the interpretation of available evidence about the effects of manifestly unjust land systems on economic performance'.[69]

It is the experience of Ecuador, like other Latin American countries, that both economic development and social justice are not easily realized within a framework of capitalist development. Few people would dissent from the general tenor of Dorner's statement that:

... experience over the past decade seems to indicate that the questions of increased agricultural production and a more equitable distribution of the fruits of that production must be viewed as parts of the same process.[70]

The problem lies in putting this prescription into effect. When policies are implemented and new institutions fashioned, the social objectives of land reforms are often forgotten.[71] The people who pay the price for inability to measure 'the most important relationships between reform and development' by economic indices alone, are often the masses of landless labourers which are often created by the agrarian reform process itself.[72]

There is much less consensus about the broader political objectives of an agrarian reform. According to Jacques Chonchol a distinction can be made between 'structural' agrarian reforms, and what he terms 'apparent' agrarian reforms.[73] Among the essential preconditions of 'structural' reforms are widespread popular support for 'substantial institutional change'. Such 'structural' reforms involve enormous capital investment on

the part of the state, and enable the 'massive, rapid and profound redistribution of rights over land and water'.[74] The
emphasis which Chonchol places on adequate finance for
agrarian reform is shared by Edmundo Flores, amongst others.[75]

The resources available to the state, of course, vary with the
level of economic development that an individual country has
achieved. Antonio García points out that most European and
North American perspectives on Latin America's 'agrarian
problem' overlook 'the nature of the process of historical
change' in Latin America, and take as their point of comparison
the historical experience of agriculture in developed countries.[76]
This ignores the relationship between agricultural production
systems in Latin America and the global development of world
capitalism.[77] Eric Hanley, in an important contribution to the
discussion of this relationship, draws attention to the way in
which rice farmers in Guyana 'are part of the international
commodity-producing system' since most of what they produce
is marketed in other Caribbean countries.[78]

Finally, any evaluation of agrarian reform must necessarily
be placed within the broader rural-urban context of a particular country, where the 'terms of trade' between agriculture
and industry are critical in determining the value of the
marketed agricultural surplus.[79] Agrarian reforms are not
necessarily undertaken primarily with agricultural objectives
in mind; indeed they are rarely undertaken for agricultural
objectives alone. The most enthusiastic supporters of agrarian
reforms are often urban interests. This inevitably means that in
evaluating an agrarian reform one must consider the class
structure of a country. As Lehmann has written:

Predictions about the consequences of a redistribution of land are
vacuous unless it is specified which elites inspire it or carry it out,
what their long-term aims are, and what class interests they represent.[80]

It is clear, then, that any consensus which might have existed
about the desirability of changing the existing agrarian structure
cannot be sustained for very long. If the frustrating history of
post-Alliance for Progress reforms were not enough to divide
the advocates of agrarian reform, then much of the intellectual

debate about agrarian reform would have done so very effectively.

It is clear that the evaluation of an agrarian reform has at least as much to do with ideological factors as it has with what happens 'on the ground'. The evaluation of the Coastal agrarian reform that follows is thus interpretative rather than 'objective' and, *inter alia*, provisional.

First, it is suggested that the Coastal agrarian reform was not principally a response to *campesino* demands, nor has the Ecuadorian state attempted to mobilize the peasantry since 1970. Peasant unrest was a contributory factor in the abolition of rice *precarismo*, but organized dissent acted as a catalyst and no more. It would also be a simplification to say that the agrarian reform was pressed on the government by an urban bourgeoisie, as in many other parts of Latin America. As one of the least industrialized countries in the area, Ecuadorian politics have not been dominated by conflicts of interest between emerging entrepreneurial classes and established landed interests. It would be more accurate to see the Ecuadorian agrarian reform as carried out as part of a strategy to create an urban bourgeoisie, a strategy that was made possible by expanding foreign exchange revenues.

Second, although the power of some landlords in the rice zone has been checked, it has not been destroyed. Instead, the traditional landlord class has had its energies diverted into new activities consistent with the expansion of modern capitalist farming. As Guillermo Navarro has argued:

> ... the structural changes in the country's agrarian sector mean nothing more than the change of 'semi-feudal relations of production to capitalist forms ... with the consequent consolidation of these relations of production and the Ecuadorian bourgeoisie.[81]

Third, the available evidence suggests that there has been no significant redistribution of land within the rice zone. What has occurred has been a change in the status of former tenants. It has been argued that this change in the status of the tenants has afforded them the legal recognition without which they would not have access to agricultural credit and technical assistance. In its turn this has given the state a greater hold over the 'enfranchised' peasantry, not only politically and financially, but through the selective introduction of sophisticated agricultural technology on some of the former estates. The important issue today is who controls the technology, and to what use it is being put.[82]

Fourth, the slowness with which the agrarian reform on the Coast has been carried out is not entirely explicable in terms of landlord pressure on the Land Reform Institute (IERAC). It should be recalled that ex-tenants only receive land if they are prepared to form 'cooperatives' which have sought official approval. Until they are members of such cooperatives the ex-tenants are not qualified to receive government credit. Under these circumstances it is hardly surprising that official recognition of cooperatives frequently takes as long as it does. The possession of both a carrot and a whip has enabled the state to dictate the form that the new agrarian structure has taken in the Guayas Basin. In the previous chapter it was argued that the secondary peasant organizations themselves are 'queueing' for benefits rather than 'bargaining' with the state. In view of the anticipated contraction in the amount of agricultural credit available to them, the queue is likely to be a longer one in the future.

The economic advances that have been gained by some former rice tenants in the Guayas Basin are not insignificant, but they have not been gained as a result of a strengthening of the ex-tenant's position within Ecuadorian society. Factors outside the control of the former tenants could put many of the gains of the Coastal agrarian reform in jeopardy. It is also unlikely that the benefits of agrarian reform will spread to other groups of Coastal *campesinos*. The absence of effective political representation, or wider class alliances with urban social groups, thus makes the eventual outcome of the agrarian reform problematical.

---

1. 'With the purpose of concentrating the country's scarce human resources during the transformation process, it is necessary to declare ... priority zones for the agrarian reform, and gradually expand the reform from these zones to include the whole national territory.' *Ecuador: Plan Integral de Transformación y Desarrollo 1973/77 Resumen General*, Quito, 1972, p. 94.

2. Social differentiation in the rice zone before 1970 was discussed in Chapter III pp. 53–8 above.

3. For a discussion of the political 'incorporation' of the Chilean peasantry, cf. David Lehmann, 'Political Incorporation versus political Stability; the case of the Chilean Agrarian Reform, 1965–1970', *Journal of Development Studies*, vol. 7, no. 4. July 1971.

4. *Ecuador: oil up for grabs*, NACLA, op. cit., p. 18.

5. For an excellent discussion of a comparable situation elsewhere on the South American continent cf. Eric R. Hanley, 'Rice, politics and development in Guyana' in I. Oxaal, T. Barnett and D. Booth (eds.), *Beyond the Sociology of Development*, Routledge and Kegan Paul, London, 1975.

6. Between 1960 and 1970 the number of power tillers used in Japanese rice cultivation increased from 746,000 to 3,448,000. Motosuke Kaihara, *The Changing Structure of Agriculture in Japan: Effects on Rice Farming*, Land Tenure Centre Special Paper, 1976, University of Wisconsin, Madison.

7. James W. Vine, 'The Rice Economy of Government Settlement Schemes in Guyana', *Inter-American Economic Affairs*, vol. 29, no. 1, Summer 1975, p. 14; cf. also Hanley, op. cit., p. 140.

8. In 1972 only 5·3 per cent of the land under rice cultivation was employing 'full mechanization'. This term was defined as: mechanical ploughing and harvesting on 'levelled' land. *Programa Nacional de Arroz* figures, June 1972 and June 1974, Guayaquil, Ecuador.

9. The 1974 Agricultural Census is not yet available.

10. Note that the 1972 figures are given in *cuadras*, and those for 1974 in hectares. (1 *cuadra* = 0·70 ha).

11. Allowing for conversion from *cuadras* to hectares for 1972 figures.

12. The estates are managed by IERAC in the interim period. This is discussed on p. 30 below.

13. *Ecuador: Plan Integral* . . . op. cit., p. 95.

14. Ibid., p. 95.

15. Ibid., p. 96.

16. Ibid., p. 96.

17. The evidence for the assertion that *campesinos* themselves favoured cooperatives is not presented. Most people with any knowledge of the situation agree that the peasants favoured cooperatives as a means of gaining ownership of the land.

18. *El Universo*, Guayaquil, 8.8.72.

19. 'During the years 1972 to 1974 IERAC, through its Regional Office has intensified its activity in applying the law . . . guaranteeing the peasantry its possession of land by legal means . . . and simultaneously guaranteeing the private property of those landowners who have shown they are working the land efficiently.' *El Campesino*, IERAC, Quito, no. 16, January 1975, p. 3.

20. *Plan Operativo Anual*, 1975, IERAC, Guayaquil (unpublished).

21. El. Marcelo Ortiz, quoted in *El Tiempo*, Quito, 25.12.73.

22. Vicente Abarca Villegas, Jaime Nuques Becerra and Jaime Paladines Moran, *Evaluación de la aplicación de la ley de Abolición del Trabajo Precario en las provincias del Guayas y los Rios, con relación a la tenancia de la tierra*, Thesis, Faculty of Agronomy, University of Guayaquil, 1974, p. 77.

23. See Chapter II, p. 26 above.

24. *Instructivo para promotores de Reforma Agraria*, IERAC, 1974, p. 4.

25. 'One of the reasons for the limited success achieved by cooperatives is the false idea, prevalent among peasants, that cooperatives . . . are a simple means of acquiring private parcels of land, rather like housing cooperatives.' Ibid., p. 3.

One IERAC official remarked to me that the *campesinos* 'were so hungry for land that even those who had always worked five hectares would like to work a hundred (hectares)'.

26. On more technically advanced estates a much higher proportion of the land is devoted to rice production. Several privately owned estates of over 2,000 ha near Samborondon devote over half their land area to the cultivation of rice. These include those belonging to the Compania Agricola Buijo and Camarte Barbero, *Oficina Nacional de Avaluación y Catastros*, Quito, 1975.

27. *Plan Operativo Anual*, op. cit.

28. Ibid.

29. Chapter IV, pp. 68–70 above. Cf. also Keith Griffin's argument that the difference between the price at which the producer sells rice, and the price at which the consumer buys it, is not necessarily attributable to excessive profits on the part of middle-men. K. Griffin, *The Political Economy of Agrarian Change: an essay on the Green Revolution*, Macmillan, London, 1974, pp. 131–8.

30. Chapter V, p. 74 above. CIDA had commented briefly on this situation, too. *Inventory of Information to the planning of agricultural development in Ecuador*, CIDA, 1965, Washington D.C., p. 57.

31. Chapter V, p. 81 above.

32. Chapter VI, p. 82 above.

33. *El Universo*, 17.7.75.

34. Personal communication, Carlos Camacho Sáa, Quito, 10.4.75.

35. Hurtado and Herudek, op. cit., p. 102.

36. *El Universo*, 23.7.75.

37. Ibid. These figures include both cooperatives and independent producers.

38. The *Banco Nacional de Fomento* calculates that it recuperates between 70 per cent and 75 per cent of the agricultural credit it allocates to cooperatives,

39. Credit for large private landholdings is provided by the private banks, rather than the BNF.

40. E. Bajana Rivera and Francisco Macias Zapata, *Estudio del Sistema de Acción de un Programa del Ministerio de Agricultura y Ganadería de Crédito Externo: Programa de Promoción de Empresas Agrícolas*, Faculty of Agronomy, University of Guayaquil, 1975, p. 57.

41. Ibid., p. 59. It is still too early to judge the way in which these 'production' cooperatives will be organized. For example, how the 'profits' of the enterprise are divided and work allocated within the cooperatives. Equipment and infrastructure is communally owned.

42. Ibid., p. 57.

43. *P.P.E.A.* figures, Guayaquil, July, 1975.

44. Bajana and Macias found that, not surprisingly, most members were enthusiastic about participating in the PPEA scheme, and 96 per cent thought they could work more land if credit was available. Bajana and Macias, op. cit., p. 35.

45. 'The Cooperative can only employ wage-labourers occasionally. In cases where they are employed preference must be given to the spouses or close relatives of members.' *Estatutos de las Cooperativas*, Capitulo II, Articulo 8, IERAC, Quito (undated). Cf. also a similar experience in Chile discussed by Lehmann, in Lehmann (ed.), 1974 op. cit.

46. Bajana and Macias, op. cit., p. 53.

47. Interview with Frederick Hubig, then AID Representative, Guayaquil, 23.4.75.

48. Galo Palacios Andrade, head of the Department of Land Tenure, FENACOOPARR, interviewed, Guayaquil, 27.4.75.

49. 'They talk about price control and the prices are controlled in accordance with the producer's interests. Rice, the bread of the poor, has increased in price by a third . . . and it is the hoarders of rice who have dictated the price rise. FENA-COOPARR is one of the biggest hoarders of rice. In the newspapers they themselves have said, "we are storing rice". The most important hoarding is done by FENACOOPARR and the "Piladora Modelo". Instead of looking after six million Ecuadorians who consume rice, we are satisfying certain producers . . . the consumer has no association to defend his interests.' Assad Bucaram, interviewed in *Nueva*, Quito, June 1975, p. 51.

50. See Chapter VI, p. 113 below.

51. In 1974 approximately 24 per cent of the rice being sold in Guayaquil was bought by the state rice-mill (the Piladora 'Modelo'), 20 per cent by FENA-COOPARR, 28·5 per cent by private rice-mills and 28·5 per cent by dealers. *Programa Nacional de Arroz*, estimates, Guayaquil, 1975.

52. For every 100 lb (metric hundredweight) of rice it processes, the rice-mill must pay the producer for 154 metric lb of rice 'in the husk'. This is *c*. £6 for each metric cwt of rice purchases.

53. The dealers who buy rice from the mills pay between 360 and 390 sucres (£7 and £8) per metric cwt. Thus the mills are allowed an operating margin of about 60 sucres (£1) a metric cwt.

54. The Minister was quoted in *El Comercio*, Quito, 23.5.75. It was claimed that a 'first group' of very large producers (7 per cent of the total number) contributed 25 per cent to total production. A 'second group' of small and medium sized producers (70 per cent), receiving credit from the *Banco Nacional de Fomento*, contributed 55 per cent to total production. Small producers in a 'third group' (23 per cent) produced 20 per cent of total rice production. No sources for these figures were given by the Minister.

55. Gonzalo Enderica commented that: '. . . it is clear that the results of this method of fixing prices are unjust, as the least numerous producers will receive the greatest benefit, while small producers in the last group, who are three times as numerous as the largest producers, will receive least benefit'. *El Universo*, 30.5.75.

56. Miguel Salazar Barragán, President of the *Asociación Nacional de Industriales Arroceras* (ANIA), interviewed, Guayaquil, 28.5.75.

57. *El Universo*, 17.7.75.

58. Ibid.

59. *El Universo*, 18.7.75.

60. Ibid.

61. Gustavo Riofrio, the former head of FENACOOPARR, then Under Secretary at the Ministry of Agriculture, announced that the Government was considering this on 1 August 1975 (*El Tiempo*, Quito, 2.8.75.). On 6 August 1975 the Minister of Agriculture inspected various rice mills on the Coast, and announced that there was a surplus of 1,500,000 metric cwt of rice in the country (*El Comercio*, Quito, 7.8.75.)

62. *El Universo*, Guayaquil, 11.8.75.

63. *Lloyds Bank and BOLSA Review*, vol. 9, no. 12, December 1975.

64. The bibliographies of most of the works cited in this section provide an adequate review of this literature. For Ecuador, see *Economic Aspects of Agricultural Development in Ecuador: A Bibliography*, Land Tenure Center, University of Wisconsin, 1972.

65. Among the best of these 'classificatory' guides are: Oscar Delgado, *Las Reformas Agrarias en América Latina*, Mexico, 1965, and Antonia García, *Sociología de la Reforma Agraria*, Amorrortu Ediciones, Buenos Aires, 1973.

66. Barraclough, 1973, op. cit., p. 38.

67. The distinction between 'incrementalist' and 'redistributive' agrarian reforms is made by James Petras and R. La Porte, 'Modernization from above versus reform from below: U.S. policy towards Latin American agricultural development', in J. Petras, *Politics and Social Structure in Latin America*, Monthly Review Press, 1970. Ernest Feder refers to the proponents of such reforms as 'Technocrats' and 'Reformers' respectively (Feder, 1971, op. cit., pp. 259–92).

68. Barraclough, 1973, op. cit., p. xxv.

69. Ibid., p. xxv.

70. Ibid., p. xxvii.

71. Dorner later concedes this point: 'although a primary goal of agrarian reform must be to provide more secure opportunities on the land, this employment objective is too often ignored, and reforms are evaluated only in terms of possible or potential consequences'. Ibid., p. xix.

72. The phrase in quotation marks is Barraclough's (op. cit., p. 38). The latent effects of the Mexican Agrarian Reform demonstrate this point perfectly, cf. Marco Antonio Durán, *El Agrarismo Mexicano*, Siglo XXI, Mexico City, 1967. In this context, too, cf. Feder, writing about the effects of changes in the law favourable to tenants in Colombia and Ecuador: 'We should not overlook the fact that while land reform institutes were distributing land to the peasants, on whatever small scale this may have occurred, the landed elite was evicting peasants from their estates, and from the land to which they had access under some sort of lease arrangement, in order to prevent the peasants from claiming land to which the legislation gave them certain rights.' Feder, 1971, op. cit., p. 253.

73. Jacques Chonchol, *El desarrollo de América Latina y la reforma agraria*, Santiago, ICIRA, 1965.

74. Ibid., p. 79.

75. Edmundo Flores, *La economía de la reforma agraria y el desarrollo agrícola*, Vinar del Mar, VIII Congreso Latinoamericana Sobre la Agricultura y la Alimentación (undated).

76. García, 1973, op. cit., p. 7.

77. Differing interpretations of the articulation of capitalist and non-capitalist modes of production formed the core of the debate between Frank and Laclau. (A. G. Frank, *Latin America: Underdevelopment or Revolution*, New York, 1969, and Ernesto Laclau, 'Feudalism and capitalism in Latin America', *New Left Review*, 67, 1971, pp. 19–38).

78. Hanley, 1975, op. cit., p. 134.

79 Cf. T. J. Byres, 'Land Reform, Industrialization and the Marketed Surplus in India: an Essay on the Power of Rural Bias', in D. Lehmann (ed.), *Agrarian Reform and Agrarian Reformism*, Faber, 1974.

80. D. Lehmann 'Introduction' in Lehmann (ed.) ibid., p. 14.

81. Navarro's analysis is valuable in establishing the degree of concentration of capital in Ecuador. (Although it has been criticized by people sympathetic to his political position, for its dependence on the returns of the *Superintendencia de Companias*.) However, he does not consider the agrarian sector in any detail, and ignores the Coastal agrarian reform altogether. Guillermo Navarro Jimenez, *La Concentración de Capitales en el Ecuador*, Universidad Centra, 1975, p. 102.

82. Cf. Lehmann's remark that: 'collective agriculture is not . . . a sufficient defining characteristic of socialism, nor is peasant farming an insurmountable stumbling block to be avoided at all costs in the period of transition'. Lehmann (ed.), op. cit., p. 22.

VIII

AGRARIAN REFORM ON A RICE COOPERATIVE

Most accounts of agrarian reform provide a national, or at most a regional, perspective on changes in rural society. The evaluation of agrarian policy consists of emphasizing the relative advantages of an agrarian reform to urban and rural classes, the likelihood that it will facilitate industrialization or bring a country greater economic self-sufficiency and a more favourable position in its balance of payments. Usually agrarian reform is also expected to produce certain intangible benefits of a more qualitative kind which are difficult, if not impossible, to measure. *Campesinos* may become free from the coercion of landlords and have access, for the first time, to the sources of greater personal security and independence of action. Better medical facilities, and the possibility of real educational opportunity and improved housing conditions are existential as well as concrete gains for which an agrarian reform may be the prerequisite. At the same time the provision of new opportunities for the rural poor requires a degree of planning which may conflict with individual and group interests among peasants as well as large landowners. The social pressure mounted by an oppressed peasantry is only one of several contending social forces which might create the conditions for a radical restructuring of society. Finally, it cannot be assumed that all *campesinos* share the same objective interests.

The contradictions inherent in the transition from rice *precarismo* to the establishment of agricultural cooperatives have been described by one of the *técnicos* employed by the *Central Ecuatoriana de Servicios Agrícolas* (CESA). Noting the extent to which *precarismo* had produced individualistic attitudes among small producers in the rice zone Ramón Espinel claims that . . .

. . . peasant organization in production cooperatives represents a superior form of social structure for the *campesino*. The change implies a diminution in the value attached to individualism in the ethical scale of the peasantry. This is brought about precisely because in the productive process new socialistic elements are introduced, provoking a rationalized division of labour that permits greater efficiency in attaining the objectives that are pursued by the new organizations. Nevertheless, we must not lose sight of the fact that the fundamental cohesive element is not social production, but the necessity that is shared by each of the individuals making up a cooperative to obtain the ownership of the land ... In this very process of struggling to secure the land flowers the individualistic nature of the campesino.[1]

This chapter analyses the contradictions between individualism and collectivism on one rice cooperative in the Guayas Basin, Cooperative 'Francisco Rule', and examines the implications of development problems at this level for the agrarian reform on the Coast.[2] Without claiming that 'Pancho Rule' is representative of all rice cooperatives, it is demonstrated that many of the internal conflicts and divisions on 'Pancho Rule' have their roots in the previous system of agricultural production as well as the nature of the present agrarian reform. If solutions are to be found to these problems it is essential that the contradictions in the goals pursued by the peasants' movement should be demonstrated, and the response of *campesinos* at the local level set against the various objectives of *técnicos* and peasant leaders alike.

THE HISTORY OF 'PANCHO RULE'

Cooperative 'Francisco Rule' is situated ninety kilometres north of Guayaquil, in the province of Guayas. The nearest town, Balzár, is about five kilometres to the north of the cooperative, where the rice zone gives way to the commercial production of bananas and cocoa. Today the cooperative is composed of a hundred and sixty members and their families, making approximately a thousand people all told. These members cultivate about 400 hectares of rice land, the total extension of the cooperative being more than two thousand hectares. Following the course of the river Daule, a tributary of the Guayas, one boundary of the cooperative stretches for about thirteen kilometres, the other for about ten kilometres. To reach the cooperative one has to travel by road and canoe; to traverse it one must travel on horseback. Even by the standards of rice cooperatives in the Guayas Basin, many of which are very large, 'Pancho Rule' is exceptional in being so immense.

The present cooperative is composed of what was formerly three estates which were at one time administered and owned separately. Today their names designate the three administrative units into which the cooperative is subdivided: 'Naranjal', 'Javiera' and 'Perinado'. Originally the estate named 'Naranjal' extended beyond the present limits of the cooperative to include land which is still owned privately on a neighbouring *hacienda* called 'San Vicente'. Cooperative 'Francisco Rule' was formed on the 4 October 1971 by mutual agreement of the former owners, members of the Salesian Order of priests, and the *precaristas* and their families resident on the estate. The agreement to sell the estate to the tenant families had been voluntarily entered into by the Salesians through the mediation of CESA, itself a Church organization. It will be recalled that private land transactions of this kind were particularly common in the rice zone, and account for a significant proportion of the estates which have changed hands under the 'agrarian reform'.[3]

The name 'Pancho Rule' is derived from the estate's owner between 1946 and 1949, a Mexican who is reputed to have had large landholdings in Ecuador. According to popular belief this man had been caught in a storm at sea which resulted in a shipwreck from which he was one of the few survivors. It is said that Pancho Rule attributed his survival to divine intervention and showed his gratitude to the Church by donating the estate to the Salesian order. Before Pancho Rule the estate had been owned by a General Venegas, who had ruled the *hacienda* for many years but left no son to inherit the land. Accordingly, Pancho Rule bought the estate from Venegas although he never took an active part in administering it. He appears to have sold it to the Salesians. Everybody on the cooperative today is agreed that Francisco Rule never envisaged the estate passing to the tenants who worked it.

The Salesians seem to have administered the estate as benevolent despots. There were rarely more than five of them resident

in the old *hacienda* building, but their influence on the management of the *hacienda* was subtle and enduring. This was particularly true of their influence on private behaviour. The
Salesians were insistent that every common-law marriage
should be made legal in the eyes of the Church, something
very unusual in Coastal Ecuador. It was also thought important
that the children on the estate should be brought up in an
atmosphere of religious devotion. The priests interested themselves in the education of the children, establishing a school
which they paid for themselves, and obtaining from the charity
'*Caritas*' a regular supply of foodstuffs for the schoolchildren.
Not surprisingly the cooperative's members were reluctant to
lose these benefits when they took over the estate from the
Salesians.

The consensus of opinion on the cooperative today is that the
Salesians were ambivalent about leaving the entire estate to the
tenant families. A significant amount of cocoa and coffee was
grown along the river bank at this time and it is suggested that
the priests wanted to retain ownership of the land on which
these crops grew. During the time of General Venegas there had
been up to five thousand head of cattle grazing on the *hacienda*,
and even under the Salesians the estate was self-sufficient in
milk products. Consequently, it is likely that the Salesians also
wanted to retain this land, only transferring the land under rice
cultivation to the *precaristas*. The families on the estate paid
about one-tenth of their rice harvest, three metric hundredweight per *cuadra*, to the Salesians. Discretion was exercised in
collecting the rents however; it is generally conceded that the
Salesians did not exact the full rent if a family was in great
difficulties and could not afford to pay.

There is little doubt that under the paternalistic administration of the Salesian Order some families benefited much
more than others. There were about half a dozen favoured
families who were given the rank of supervisors or *mayordomos* on
the estate and received special privileges from the Salesians.
Some of these families had electric light installed in their houses
when the priests bought a generator for the cooperative, and
others even had concrete houses built for them. These families
also assisted the Salesians in religious ceremonials, and even

today they are marked out by their religiosity and superior education.

The circumstances under which the Salesians eventually parted with the estate are not clear, but it seems to have been an amicable arrangement. Today the cooperative's members are paying the Salesian Order the equivalent of £20 a *cuadra* per annum to clear the debt, only a fraction of the amount they would pay under the terms of *Decreto 1001*. The total debt is said to be in the region of £20,000 and it was anticipated that the members could pay this off within the space of ten years. It is interesting that today the same proportion of total rice production is allocated to paying off this debt, as was formerly paid in rent to the Salesians.

SOCIAL STRATIFICATION WITHIN THE COOPERATIVE

In any discussion of the differences in status and wealth between members of an agricultural cooperative a number of different variables must be considered. Although differences in the amount of land under rice cultivation is the best single indicator of socio-economic distinctions, these differences alone do not provide a comprehensive picture of social differentiation on the cooperative. It has already been suggested that certain families on the estate occupied a privileged position by virtue of their closeness to the Salesians. On the whole these families retained their material advantages after the cooperative was formed in 1971, although their rights within the cooperative are nominally the same as those of other members.

André Beteille has argued that in discussing rural stratification 'the identification of persistent groups and categories in a society is only the first step'.[4] It remains to consider 'the relations of these groups with each other in terms of a series of socially defined rights and obligations'.[5] It is usually understood that the relations between landlords and tenants do not conform simply to legal definitions of their respective roles. However, contractual definitions of social status have even less application to social relations between peasants, and these status differentials can take on an even greater degree of subtlety and complexity.[6] In considering social stratification on 'Pancho

Rule' we must consider the relational aspects of status as well as the objective differences in wealth between cooperative members, although the content of social relationships is closely associated with discrete differences in material resources. The differing perceptions of peasant families as to the future of the co-operative, and the relations between the cooperative and outside organizations, are the principal focus of our analysis.[7]

Table 28 gives figures for the distribution of rice land within 'Pancho Rule'. It is clear that the delineation of separate agricultural strata from these figures is extremely difficult. It

Table 28. The distribution of rice land on cooperative 'Pancho Rule' (1975)

Less than 1 *cuadra**	16 members	
1–1·99 *cuadras*	60 members	
2–2·99 *cuadras*	43 members	
3–3.99 *cuadras*	15 members	
4–4·99 *cuadras*	13 members	
More than 5 *cuadras*	5 members	(3 of whom own 7 *cuadras*, 1 of whom owns 8 *cuadras* and 1 of whom owns 10 *cuadras*)
Total: 312½ *cuadras*	152 members	

*1 *cuadra* = 0·70 ha.

Note: These figures represent the *minimum* amount of land devoted to rice cultivation. In a normal year approximately 500 ha might be used for rice.

should be recalled, too, that the amount of land devoted to rice cultivation varies widely according to rainfall. Cooperative members say 'our plans are ruined by too much rain as well as too little'.[8] Nevertheless in an average year the amount of land on which rice is grown significantly increases the differences between poorer and better-off members of the cooperative. Those families with a minimum of two or three hectares of rice land can cultivate twice this amount in an average year. At the same time families with a minimum landholding of four or five hectares can usually cultivate twice this amount, and in an exceptional year may even triple or quadruple the amount of land devoted to growing rice. The distribution of rice land within the cooperative is thus much more unequal than the minimum figures alone would suggest.

Those families with the most land under rice cultivation also own most of the cooperative's livestock. It was once suggested by Lenin that the ownership of livestock, particularly draught animals, is a better guide to stratification in peasant societies than land ownership alone.[9] Whatever the general validity of this comment it needs to be noted that of the six hundred head of cattle owned by cooperative members almost all are in the possession of less than a dozen families. These families pasture their animals on one of the three pieces of grazing land (*potreros*) owned collectively by the cooperative. Their share of a communal resource is therefore much greater than their numerical importance within the cooperative alone would indicate.

For the better-off members of the cooperative it can be difficult finding sufficient labour to work the land. Labour is invariably drawn from outside the family, usually from other former tenant families. However, the employment of non-family labour during peak periods of the agricultural calendar is not confined to better-off families. At least during the harvest most cooperative members rely on the assistance of other families' labour, and the sub-letting of land to other people within the cooperative is not uncommon. For poorer families, however, the need to find employment for their children is a constant problem. A family with seven or eight children cannot employ all of them on a two-hectare plot of land, and work has to be found off the family holding. This is a regular occurrence made worse by seasonal variations in the demand for labour for which no immediate solution is available. Not surprisingly the poorest families are most anxious that more of the land suitable for rice cultivation should be brought into production and worked on a communal basis. At the present time only about thirty hectares of land is owned and worked communally (the *lote comunal*) but it has been suggested that a further eight hundred hectares could be brought into cultivation. In order to level and irrigate this land technical assistance has to be sought from one of a number of outside organizations. There is general agreement within the cooperative that bringing this land into production would be a desirable course of action for the cooperative to take. Better-off families regard the extension of the *lote communal* as an essential step in the technification of production, rather than an experiment in socialist agriculture. For their part poorer families see it both as a way of guaranteeing employment to their sons and a way of redressing private inequalities within the cooperative.

The redistribution of privately held land within the cooperative has never been seriously advocated by members of the cooperative, although it is the policy of ACAL, the peasant federation to which 'Pancho Rule' is affiliated. Some members also claim, mistakenly, that equality of land ownership is one of the stated goals of cooperative legislation. To bring about greater equality in private landholding would involve taking land off a number of families without whose support the cooperative could not survive. It would also be difficult to enforce a 'ceiling' for maximum private landownership when many members of the cooperative sub-let parts of their plots to other members.[10] Reducing private inequality in landholding is regarded by poor and better-off alike as both less feasible and less desirable than increasing the amount of land which is worked as a production cooperative.

If the amount of land that is owned and worked communally increased we might anticipate a number of consequences, only some of which members themselves are aware of. First, many of the sons of poorer families would spend most of their working lives on the *lote comunal*, and receive regular wages rather than contribute their labour to the family's plot. The difficulties of combining the payment of wages with private production for the market have received considerable attention from scholars interested in the Chilean *asentamientos*.[11] The intention of most members on 'Pancho Rule' is that workers on the *lote comunal* should continue to be paid a daily wage which would be subtracted from the profits of the *lote comunal*. The rest of the income from the communally-worked land would be reinvested in capital equipment and public works on the cooperative. Obviously the advantage of this investment in the cooperative would be shared by families who did not contribute to the *lote comunal* as well as those who did. It is a condition of recognition by IERAC that a cooperative only employs outside labour 'occasionally . . . and then only when preference has been given to the wives and families of members'.[12] In practice other cooperatives do employ considerable outside labour, as we have seen already. However, it is a cherished right of members to give their families priority if additional labour is required. The exercise of this right, by producing a regular salaried work-force on the *lote comunal*, made up of the sons of poorer members, might eventually serve to increase rather than diminish differentials in wealth among peasant families. It might also be expected to increase the financial independence of children within the farming household.

THE ADMINISTRATION OF THE COOPERATIVE

Day-to-day authority for administering 'Pancho Rule' is vested in a ruling body (the *Junta Administrativa*) composed of thirteen elected members. This body is responsible to the total membership of the cooperative, which meets as an assembly once every month. The most important office-holders are the President, Secretary and Treasurer, each of whom works for the cooperative without pay. When officers visit Guayaquil, however, which they do at least once a week, they are paid the costs of their journey by the cooperative. These visits and attendance at rallies and conferences are financed by levying 20 *sucres* (forty pence) a week on each member.

Many members of the cooperative resent having to pay the expenses of office-holders when they are carrying out cooperative business elsewhere, and there are frequent allegations that the cooperative's funds are being embezzled by one or other leader. Mismanagement of the cooperative's finances is a common event, and when this has been detected in the past a meeting of all the members has been called to pronounce judgement. This meeting can and does bring about the resignation of office-holders, but there are limits to how far disciplinary action can be taken. There are few members with enough experience of accountancy, and who are sufficiently literate, to undertake the necessary administrative work. Although ACAL and CESA take an interest in what happens within the cooperative, decisions are left to members, and unlike the cooperatives administered by FENACOOPARR, outside advice is only sought occasionally.

Weekly meetings of the *Junta Administrativa* are usually devoted to settling disputes between members, and establishing the ground rules for the use of communal resources. Applications to join the cooperative, although rare, are made at these meetings. Sometimes problems connected with the use of the pasture land are debated, the respective rights of members to use wells (*pozos*) or the two communally owned water pumps. Members who have not been paying their contribution to the cooperative's debt, which as we saw is approximately one-tenth of each family's rice production, also have sanctions applied to them on these occasions. The opportunity is taken to assert the authority of the *Junta* but dissenting voices are frequently heard after a ruling has been made. At one meeting a member was criticized for spreading the view that the cooperative was 'robbing its members to pay its debts'. The offending individual was subjected to so much criticism that he ended the session in tears. Finally a decision was taken to fine him for a 'breach of members' confidence in the cooperative'. Even members who have been disciplined are referred to as '*compañero*' ('comrade'), however, and the application of sanctions for their behaviour is usually left to public disapproval rather than fines. Members are invariably exhorted to behave in a more socially responsible way in future.

Outside 'Pancho Rule' there is considerable criticism of the way that the cooperative is run; it is said to be 'anarchic' and to lack internal cohesion. To some extent these criticisms are echoed by members themselves, who admit that there is less unity than there should be. Conversations and interviews with a large number of members reveal that unity is valued primarily because it is seen as a means of obtaining technical and financial help from outside organizations like CESA and the *Banco Nacional de Fomento*. There is said to be more unity than there was in the past, as 'the past' is taken to mean the period before the formation of a cooperative. At the same time it is admitted that the large size of the cooperative, and the existence of a number of relatively well-off families, made its establishment extremely difficult.

The present-day enthusiasm for 'cooperation' does not entirely obscure an older, religious tradition. There is still abundant evidence of the cooperative's former history in the way that members behave. Many members make the sign of the cross when entering the building, formerly a chapel, used for meetings of the *Junta Administrativa*. The *hacienda* building is still referred to as 'the *hacienda*' by a majority of members, and the cooperative is called 'the cooperative of the *hacienda*'. When a priest visits the cooperative communion is celebrated, although only a minority of members attend.

It is recognized that the cooperative came into existence primarily as a way of securing the ownership of the land, rather than as a conscious social experiment on the part of members. This does not mean that there is no interest in the principles of cooperation, even if these usually confuse what Espinel terms the 'means and the ends to liberation'.[13] Loyalty to the cooperative is regarded very highly, as is loyalty to the peasant federation, ACAL. Inevitably, conflicts between the individual's self-interest and that of the cooperative mean that this loyalty does not always find expression in action. Most members are agreed that more unity is a precondition for receiving assistance from outside the cooperative, and that the technical development of the cooperative is essential if capital is to be generated. The cooperative's freedom from financial indebtedness is looked upon as a long-term objective by most of the members. People on 'Pancho Rule' look warily at other cooperatives which are apparently in a healthier financial position, like 'San Felipe' across the river Daule, because they regard such cooperatives as much more financially dependent on outside organizations. At the same time they are envious of the successes of other cooperatives, and attribute this to their members' restraint.

The unity and independence of 'Pancho Rule' are important to most members, but there is little agreement about how they might be achieved. Since confidence in leaders is usually short-lived as we have seen, there are frequent changes in office-holders. Most members are cautious of taking corporate initiatives, such as hiring machinery to level the land. They are also prone to regard CESA as an inexhaustible source of assistance and funds, despite the financial precariousness of that organization. This has created a certain amount of ill-feeling between *técnicos* and the leadership of the cooperative. People on 'Pancho Rule' say that they face two immediate tasks; the first is 'to provide a livelihood for ourselves' and the second is 'to struggle to control ourselves'. These expressions sum up the crisis of confidence and the ambivalent loyalties that each member and his family face.

IDEOLOGY AND PRACTICE IN THE RUNNING OF A COOPERATIVE

Agricultural cooperatives do not provide 'ideal' solutions to specific problems but merely an institutional framework within which people can interact. The nature of a country's agricultural cooperatives will depend upon the development strategy of a particular country at a particular time. Traditions concerning cooperation cannot, as Fals Borda has rightly insisted, be imported into one continent from another regardless of the social structure of the country concerned.[14] Nor are cooperatives necessarily socialistic institutions. Worsley reminds us of this in writing that:

... the cooperative, in so far as it is a coming together of individual private producers ... is thus not especially either collectivistic or equalizing. It does not imply the elimination of private property, nor even of the profit-oriented mode of economy.[15]

A number of Latin American writers have also reminded us that cooperatives take their cues from the society in which they are located, and the opportunities provided by that society for autonomous development. Hermitte and Herran, for example, have shown that the paternalistic attitudes generated by the landlord relating with his tenant, do not disappear overnight when agricultural cooperatives are formed.[16] A failure to take account of the peasant's dependence on the landlord only contributes to an increased dependence on new power holders, even the leaders of rural syndicates.[17] In these circumstances the most that can be hoped for is that new vertical linkages will not impede the development of horizontal links between groups of peasants; providing what Singleman describes as 'the triangle with a base'.[18]

A recent United Nations survey of rural cooperatives in the Less Developed Countries suggested that 'especially in Latin America cooperatives seem to have been used on occasion as instruments to contain and control potentially dangerous or revolutionary situations'.[19] Their role was more often counter-revolutionary than revolutionary. At their most successful, as we have seen, cooperatives have been credited with producing only 'marginal changes'.[20] According to Thomas Carroll:

> . . . it seems clear that where the tenure system is grossly inequitable cooperatives, even if they manage to get established and survive, are not expected to become a force for structural reform. In such a situation the best that can be expected is successful adaptation to the existing social system and some protection of its members from the more onerous forms of exploitation.[21]

On the Ecuadorian Coast the formation of cooperatives began as a response to grass-roots pressure for changes in land tenure rather than as a deliberate act of social engineering. The experience of North American sponsored cooperatives prior to 1970 served as an example for the Ecuadorian government on how popular pressure could be contained and channelled.

The most important aspect of peasant organization in the Guayas Basin today is not the institutional form which it is taking but the differences within the peasantry, differences which are derived from unequal access to the economic resources controlled by the state, as well as inequalities in the rice zone prior to 1970. The process through which both the accumulation of wealth and the pauperization of the rural population march hand-in-hand has been eloquently documented for other parts of Latin America.[22] This process of social differentiation is in no way incompatible with particular institutional reforms, such as the introduction of agricultural cooperatives. Furthermore, the existence of a cooperative movement may only contribute to the mystification of agrarian reform principles. Cooperatives like those in the Guayas Basin are then conceived of as 'a deformation, in cover form of reality . . . serving to justify the existence of capitalism'.[23]

What emerges clearly from a consideration of the problems facing the ex-tenants of 'Pancho Rule' is that no development strategy will suit all the families within the cooperative. In the unlikely event that such a strategy was advocated then its implementation would suffer, in the course of time, from internal dissent and opposition. Just as the structural situation of the peasantry in the Guayas Basin varies between groups of former tenants, so the structural position of different families within a single cooperative leaves them at odds with each other. At the present time no objective basis exists for independent collective action on the part of groups of former tenants, beyond the desire to obtain land and agricultural credit. Lacking organizational solidarity and common interests, the first generation of cooperative members is unable to provide sufficient pressure on second-level peasant organizations to carry through a radical, integrated agrarian reform.

1. Ramón Espinel Martinez, *CESA, el movimiento campesino y la comercialización: aporte teórico para la discusión en la reunión funcional de comercialización*, CESA Litoral, Guayaquil, August 1975 (mimeo), p. 6. It will be clear that 'Pancho Rule' is by no means a 'production cooperative'.

2. Drawing on field observations and interviews during May and June 1975.

3. Cf. Chapter VI, p. 113 above.

4. A. Beteille, *Studies in Agrarian Social Structure*, O.U.P., London, 1974, p. 8.

5. Ibid., p. 9.

6. Cf., for example, the discussion of reciprocity and status in European peasant communities in F. G. Bailey (ed.), *Gifts and Poison: the politics of reputation*, Blackwell, Oxford, 1971.

7. In the absence of large landowners *campesinos* do not exhibit 'deferential' behaviour as discussed by Howard Newby, 'The Deferential Dialectic', *Comparative Studies in Society and History*, vol. 17, no. 2, April 1975.

8. In Spanish: '*fracasamos con el exceso de lluvia tanto que la falta. . .*'

9. V. I. Lenin, 'The Development of Capitalism in Russia', *Collected Works*, vol. 3, Lawrence and Wishart, 1972, pp. 73 and 74.

For a general discussion of this question cf. A. Beteille, *Six Essays in Comparative Sociology*, O.U.P., 1974, and chapter 5 of B. Galeski, *Basic Concepts of Rural Sociology*, Manchester U.P., 1972.

10. At the moment labour contracts during harvesting, for example, are expressed as piece-work. Thus thirty cartloads of rice represents one '*tarea*' (job), the labourer being paid one *sucre* (*c*. two pence) for each cartload. One *tarea* is more or less equivalent to a day's work, although some of the land within a rice plot may also be let to the labourer 'to give him an interest in the work' as one person expressed it.

11. David Lehmann, 'Agrarian Reform in Chile, 1965–1972', in D. Lehmann (ed.), *Agrarian Reform and Agrarian Reformism*, Faber, 1974. This question has also been debated at great length in relation to Russia and East European countries,

cf. Ian Hill, 'Some problems concerning the categorisation of the Soviet agricultural population', *Sociologia Ruralis*, xv, no. 1/2, 1975.

12. Article 8 of the *Statutes of Production Cooperatives*, IERAC, Quito, 1973.

13. Espinel argues that both *técnicos* and *campesino* leaders in the Guayas Basin have become attached to technical solutions and the market economy and have lost their interest in longer-term objectives. He gives as an instance the case of the commercialization of rice where 'the inability to perceive (the commercialization process) in its relationship to the whole produces the idea of immediate objectives, whose characteristics are defined in terms of their immediate utility . . . as a consequence the "means" have replaced the "ends"'. Espinel, 1975, op. cit., p. 11.

14. Orlando Fals Borda, 1970, op. cit.; cf. also Ortiz Villacis, 1970, op. cit.

15. Peter Worsley in the 'Introduction' to P. Worsley (ed.), *Two Blades of Grass: rural cooperatives in agricultural modernisation*, Manchester U.P., 1971, p. 5.

16. Esther Hermitte and Carlos Herran, 'Patronazgo o cooperativismo? obstaculos a la modificación del sistema social en una comunidad del noroeste argentino', *Revista Latinoamericana de Sociologia*, 1970, no. 2.

17. D. B. Heath, 'New patrons for old: changing patron-client relationships in the Bolivian Yungas', *Ethnology*, vol. XIII, no. 1, 1973.

18. Peter Singleman, 'The Closing Triangle: Critical Notes on a Model for Peasant Mobilization in Latin America', *Comparative Studies in Society and History*, vol. 17, no. 4, October 1975.

19. *Rural cooperatives as agents of change: a research report and a debate*, UNRISD, vol. VIII, Geneva, 1975, p. 12.

20. O. Fals Borda, 1971, op. cit., and 1972, op. cit.

21. Thomas Carroll, 'Peasant Cooperatives in Latin America', in P. Worsley (ed.), 1971, op. cit., p. 237.

22. For example, the Alta Sorocabana area of São Paulo state, Brazil. Maria Conceição d'incao e mello, *O Bóia Fria: acumulação e miséria*, Editora Vozes, Petropolis, Brazil, 1976.

23. Espinel, 1975, op. cit., p. 12.

IX

CONCLUSION

At the beginning of this book changes in the agrarian structure of the Ecuadorian Coast were described within an historical and political context. Reference was made to the conflicts between social forces in the highlands and the Coast in the first decades of this century. The last fifteen years has seen the evolution of a development ideology, prompted by the Alliance for Progress, which represents a threat to neither the traditional landowning groups in the Sierra nor the Coastal interests involved in international trade. For most of this period overseas economists and technical assistance personnel made little impact on the course that agrarian development has taken in Ecuador.

The changes that occurred in the rice zone following the abolition of rice *precarismo*, and the use to which oil revenues have been put since 1972, have served to modify this picture of Ecuadorian development. It is suggested that the abolition of rice-tenancy has proved to be more than a short-term innovation to meet exceptionally bad harvests and rural unrest. The agrarian reform which has been carried out in the rice zone is seen as a significant move in the realization of development objectives on the part of the Ecuadorian state. In return for the distribution of land titles the state bureaucracy expected to increase their control over the marketed surplus of rice, on which most of the urban population depended. By selective inputs of agricultural technology and the close management of rice cultivation it was also hoped to increase rice production dramatically.

In the longer term wider development objectives were envisaged. It was hoped to reduce the value of the agricultural surplus, keep down urban wages and stimulate industrial production. Foreign exchange could also be saved by substituting domestic production for imported foodstuffs. From this perspective the political crisis provoked by widespread peasant unrest and production shortages proved opportune for introducing a reform which gave practical effect to longstanding development objectives. The proclamation of *Decreto 1001* marked the expression of a newer, more confident policy of state intervention in the agrarian sector which was given added impetus after 1972 by the petroleum revenues.

Although the political and economic factors that contributed to the abolition of rice *precarismo* have wider significance, the analysis of agrarian change in Latin America cannot proceed on the basis of observable shifts in ideology and policy alone. It is also important to pay careful attention to the deep-rooted processes at work within the agrarian structure of an area, and the kinds of group and class 'consciousness' to which tenurial relations contribute. The analysis of agrarian change in a region like the Ecuadorian rice zone can only be fully understood by considering the specific historical experience of social groups as well as the overall momentum of macro-development policy.

There are a number of reasons why we should avoid too sweeping a view of the part played by coastal exporting interests and highland landlords in influencing the coastal agrarian reform. First, it is essential to consider the class 'physiognomy' of the rural population on the Ecuadorian Coast. It has been shown that *campesinos* on the Coast participate in a number of very different agrarian production systems, and that as a consequence there is an absence of universal, clear-cut class divisions. The class interests of most individual producers —labourers, tenants and small owners—are linked to the crops which they grow. In many cases it is changes in world demand, and the policies followed by the multi-national companies that buy their crops, which most directly affect their livelihoods. For this reason divisions between groups of producers are often as important as tenurial status on the Ecuadorian Coast.

It has also been shown that social differentiation within the rice zone exists within the reformed sector, as well as between the reformed sector and the large privately owned sector. The differences between large and small landholdings prior to 1970 have been intensified since the urban bureaucracy has made selective use of the oil revenues. Within the 'reformed sector' the most technically advanced 'cooperatives' have become most dependent on the state for technical and financial resources, and it would be otiose to describe them as having a community of interest with the poorer, marginalized *campesinos* in the zone. The relations between different cooperatives and the state, rather than global 'class' interests shared by former tenants, provide the key to understanding the process of capitalist development within agriculture in the region.

There is a second reason why generalizations about the national class structure do not provide an adequate explanation of the forces behind the agrarian reform. In Latin America redistributive agrarian reform policies have usually been attempted by governments which have not possessed important foreign exchange revenues. On the contrary, the possession of adequate financial resources has enabled governments to avoid confronting the need for a radical restructuring of the agrarian sector. This has been the case since 1958 with the Venezuelan 'agrarian reform' programme, for example. The alignments of social classes responsible for radical agrarian reforms were either the product of traumatic social revolution, as in Mexico and Bolivia, or the outcome of more gradual shifts in power towards urban groups, as in Peru.[1] Although the reports of the Economic Commission for Latin America (ECLA) and the Inter-American Committee for Agricultural Development (CIDA) advocated redistributive agrarian reform as a means of creating an industrial sector, this policy was never consistently applied in the 1960s.[2] Far more common than serious attempts at agrarian reform were the numerous efforts Latin American countries made to assist colonization of jungle areas and encourage foreign capital investment in agriculture.

In the case of Ecuador the opposition of landowning groups, in the Sierra and on the Coast, makes it clear that they were never the chief instigators of the modest agrarian reform programme. It is clear, too, that the industrial bourgeoisie in Ecuador was far too weak to act in this capacity.[3] The origins of the agrarian reform must be sought in the opportunity oil revenues provided for the creation of industrialization, rather than the goals of a well-developed 'national' or 'industrial' bourgeoisie. As we have seen the changes that followed the introduction of *Decreto 1001* have enabled Ecuador to reduce its dependence on imported rice, and hold the prospect of future price reductions for urban consumers. The agrarian reform has provided the state with a bigger hand in determining the 'terms of trade' between manufactures and domestically produced foodstuffs. It has also given the government effective political control over the producers of an important national resource. It could, of course, be objected that the foreign exchange which has been channelled into the rice zone might have been spent on imported rice, without the need for even a modest 'incrementalist' agrarian reform. Had this been done, however, the foreign advisers and *técnicos* working for, and with, the Ecuadorian government would have lost the opportunity to implement the development policies that had been advocated in Ecuador since 1964. Another factor which undoubtedly entered into the government's calculations was the prospect of heightened social conflict in the rice zone if a reform was not undertaken.

The agrarian reform on the Coast had political and economic advantages whatever government was in power. The reform helped to create a 'reformed sector' which was politically compliant and imbued with the same development goals as the greatly expanded bureaucracy. The abolition of rice *precarismo* was thus entirely consistent with the objectives of agricultural modernization to which successive Ecuadorian governments have been committed. Rice *precarismo* was a system of land tenure and agricultural production unsuited to technological innovation. The control that landlords exerted over marketing the product made it difficult for the state to control the distribution and the size of the agricultural 'surplus'. With the abolition of rice *precarismo* a fillip was given to modern capitalist relations of production which, as we have seen, were already in existence in the zone. The changes in agricultural production and marketing within the 'reformed sector', moreover, would have no adverse effect on private estates which were managed 'efficiently' according to the demands of 'the social functions of property'.

A further objection could be made to this version of the role played by the state in the Coastal agrarian reform. It can be argued that, since no significant redistribution of land took place, the 'agrarian reform' is a reform only in name. Titles were distributed to some groups of beneficiaries and marketing arrangements were improved, but there was no real redistribution of power while most land on the Coast remained in private hands. All that happened in the rice zone, it might be objected, was that family producers within a 'deformed capitalist mode of production' had made the transition to a properly constituted rural bourgeoisie.

This interpretation of events overlooks several important aspects of agrarian reform on the Coast which cannot be left out of the account. First, the state bureaucracy in the rice zone had intervened in an unprecedented way, temporarily displacing the landlords in much of the rice zone. Second, the effect of state intervention was to shift political control to a new strata of *técnicos* who were by no means dependent on the approval of local landlords. Third, the way in which the 'reformed sector' took shape effectively excluded the *campesinos* from democratic participation in the reform. The most economically successful became progressively more dependent on state assistance. This factor alone makes them distinguishable from a class of 'kulak' peasants. As we have seen, social differentiation within the agrarian structure of the rice zone has served to intensify existing divisions within the organizational context provided by the Ecuadorian state.

By recognizing the importance of the state within the process of capitalist agrarian development we are making an important modification to 'classical' theory about the 'polarization of the countryside'.[4] We can see that social differentiation within the peasantry does not only take the form of forced conversion to the status of 'proletarian'. This kind of transformation may well occur, but today it is often linked with shifts in the control of the state over new capital resources. As a result of selective capital investment by the state, and moves to control marketing arrangements, new corporate groups of former tenants come into being. These corporate groups make short-term economic gains, in some cases, but they simultaneously lose entrepreneurial control over their enterprises. This institutional differentiation reduces the effectiveness of the peasantry as a political force and, at the same time, increases the ability of the state bureaucracy to pursue its wider development goals.

1. Military authoritarianism and the increased power of the state in Peru, where sectoral interests are much more highly developed, are discussed in David Collier, *Squatters and Oligarchs: authoritarian rule and policy change in Peru*, Johns Hopkins U.P., 1976. It is worth noting that in Ecuador, unlike Peru, the military have not set themselves the task of breaking a political power base such as that of APRA. Marx's view of the 'Bonapartist' state is given in 'The Eighteenth Brumaire of Louis Bonaparte', in K. Marx and F. Engels, *Selected Works*, vol. 1, Lawrence and Wishart, 1950. Theory of the state in Latin America is heavily indebted to Fernando Henrique Cardoso and Enzo Faletto, *Dependencia y Desarrollo en América Latina: ensayo de interpretación sociológica*, Siglo XXI, Mexico, 1969.

2. *El proceso de industrialización en América Latina*, Comision Económica para América Latina (CEPAL), Santiago, 1965. *Land Tenure Conditions and Socio-Economic Development* (in the seven CIDA countries), Union Panamericana, Washington D.C., 1966–70. The failure of the CIDA and CEPAL reports to affect Governments is discussed by Jorge Dandler, A. Eugene Havens, Carlos Samaniego and Bernardo Sorj, 'La estructura agraria en America Latina: un modelo de analisis', *Revista Mexicana de Sociología*, vol. xxxviii, no. 1, Enero-Marzo 1976.

3. Cf. Zeitlin and Ratcliff's conclusion, from Chilean material, that 'The contradictions between agrarian and industrial capital, and the clashes over state policies affecting them, where these have led to political rivalries within the dominant class in Chile in recent decades, did not arise between separate onto-logically "real" class segments of large landowners and capitalists. For contradictory interests and social cleavages within the dominant class did not coincide; rather, the dominant agrarian and industrial elements were internally related, if not "fused", in so complex a pattern that neither of them possessed a specific autonomy or distinctive social indentity'. Maurice Zeitlin and Richard Earl Ratcliff, 'Research Methods for the Analysis of the Internal Structure of Dominant Classes: the case of landlords and capitalists in Chile', *Latin American Research Review*, vol. 10, no. 3. Fall 1975.

4. V. I. Lenin, 'The Development of Capitalism in Russia: the process of the formation of a Home Market for Large-Scale Industry', *Collected Works*, vol. 3, Lawrence and Wishart, 1972, see especially Chapter II, pp. 172–91 and Chapter IV, pp. 310–18.

BIBLIOGRAPHY

Abarca Villegas, Vicente, Becerra, Jaime Nuques and Moran, Jaime Paladines, *Evaluación de la aplicación de la ley de Abolición del Trabajo Precario en las provincias del Guayas y los Rios*, Thesis, Faculty of Agronomy, University of Guayaquil, 1974.

AID (Agency for International Development), memorandum (undated), Guayaquil.

U.S.A.I.D. Ecuador—land sale guaranty, Capital Assistance Paper, AID/DLC, Washington D.C., 1969, p. 854.

Albornoz, Oswaldo, *Historia de la acción clerical en el Ecuador*, Ediciones Espejo, Quito, 1963.

Albornoz P., Oswaldo, *Del Crimén de El Ejido a la Revolución del 9 de Julio de 1925*, Editorial 'Claridad', (PCE) Guayaquil, 1969.

Albuja Punina, Jose Ignacio, *Estructura Agraria y Estructura Social*, Quito, 1964.

Althusser, L. and Balibar, E., *Reading Capital*, Pantheon Books, New York, 1970.

Amin, S. and Vergopoulos, K., *La Question Paysanne et le Capitalisme*, Paris, Anthropos, 1974.

Andrade Pavo, Jorge, 1975. Thesis in preparation, Guayaquil. (*Programa Nacional de Arroz*.)

Anuario Estadistica, Quito, 1968.

Area Handbook for Ecuador, Foreign Area Studies, Washington D.C., 1966.

Baez, René, 'Hacia un Subdesarrollo "moderno"', in *Ecuador: pasado y presente*, Instituto de Investigaciones Economicas, Quito, Universidad Central, 1975.

Bailey F. G. (ed.), *Gifts and Poison: the politics of reputation*, Blackwell, Oxford, 1971.

Banjana Rivera, E. and Marcias Zapata, F., *Estudio del Sistema de Acción de un Programa del Ministerio de Agricultura y Ganaderia de Credito Externo: Programa de Promoción de Empresas Agrícolas*, Faculty of Agronomy, University of Guayaquil, 1975.

Banco Central del Ecuador, *Reforma Agraria y Desarrollo Economico en el Ecuador*, Quito, 1960.

Banco Nacional de Fomento (unpublished figures), 1975, Guayaquil.

Bajana Rivera, E. and Macias Zapata, P., 1975, *Estudio del sistema de Acción de un Programa del Ministerio de Agricultura y Ganaderia de Credito Externo: Programa de Promoción de Empresas Agrícolas*, Faculty of Agronomy, University of Guayaquil.

Baraona, Rafael, 'Cambios en Tenencia de la Tierra y la demanda externa: algunas observaciones sobre la Costa Ecuatoriana', *Les Problems Agraires de Amerique Latine*, CNSR, Paris, 1965.

Baraona, R. and Delgado, O., 1972, 'El sistema de tenencia precaria y la explotacion del trabajo de los aparceros', in *El Proyecto de Reforma Agraria en la Region Arrocera del Ecuador*, FAO, Santiago.

Barraclough, Solon, *Agrarian Structure in Latin America*, D. C. Heath, Massachusetts, 1973.

Barraclough, S. and Domike, A., 'Agrarian Structure in Seven Latin American Countries', *Land Tenure Centre Reprint*, no. 25, LTC, University of Wisconsin, Madison, November 1966.

Beckford, G., 'Persistent Poverty', *Underdevelopment in Plantation Economies of the Third World*, O.U.P., New York, 1972.

Beteille, A., *Studies in Agrarian Social Structure*, O.U.P., London, 1974.

—, *Six Essays in Comparative Sociology*, O.U.P. 1974.

Blankstein, C. and Zuvekas, C., 1973 (and 1974), 'Agrarian Reform in Ecuador: an evaluation of past efforts and the development of a new approach', *Economic Development and Cultural Change*, vol. 22, no. 1, 1973.

—, 'Agrarian Reform in Ecuador', *Land Tenure Center Paper*, University of Wisconsin, 1974.

Bonifaz, Emilio, 'La Población Marginada de la Sierra Ecuatoriana', *Ecuador: poblacion y crisis*, Comite de Informatión y Contacto para Empresarios Privados (CICE), Quito, 1975.

Booth, David, 'André Gunder Frank: an introduction and appreciation', in I. Oxaal *et al.* (eds.), *Beyond the Sociology of Development*, RKP, 1975.

Bottomley, A., 'Monopolistic rent determination in underdeveloped rural areas', *Kyklos*, vol. xix, 1966, pp. 106–17.

Bottomley, A., 'Agricultural Employment Policy in Developing Countries—the case of Ecuador', *Inter-American Economic Affairs*, 20 (Spring 1966), 53–79.

Brandão Lopes, Juarez, 'Capitalist Development and Agrarian Structure in Brazil', paper given to the conference of the *Urban and Regional Studies Committee* of the International Sociological Association, Messina, Sicily, March 1976.

Bromley, Raymond J., *Bibliografía del Ecuador: Ciencias Sociales, Economicas y Geograficas*, Junta de Planificación, Quito, 1970.

Bromley, Rosemary D. F. and Bromley, R. J., 'The Debate on Sunday Markets in Nineteenth Century Ecuador', *Journal of Latin American Studies*, vol. 7, part 1, May 1975.

Brown, M., 1971, 'Private Efforts and Reform', in Peter Dorner(ed.), *Land Reform in Latin America*, University of Wisconsin, Madison.

Brownrigg, Leslie Ann, 'Interest Groups in Regime Changes in Ecuador', *Inter-American Economic Affairs*, vol. 28, no. 1, 1974.

Burgos Guevara, Hugo, *Relaciones Interétnicas en Riobamba*, Mexico, 1970.

Byres, T. J., 'Land Reform, Industrialisation and the Marketed Surplus in India: an essay on the power of rural bias', in D. Lehmann (ed.), *Agrarian Reform and Agrarian Reformism*, Faber, 1974.

Caicedo, Emiliano, *El Canton Daule en la Exposición Internacional de Quito*, Guayaquil, 1908.

Cámara de Agricultura, Register of Landholding. 1964–1975. Primera Zona (Guayaquil).

Cárdenas, Jose C. 'Reforma Agraria y Desarrollo Económico en el Ecuador', *El Trimestre Economico*, Julio–Septiembre 1954.

Cardoso, Fernando Henrique and Faletto, Enzo, *Dependencia y Desarrollo en América Latina: ensayo de interpretación sociologica*, Siglo xxi, Mexico, 1969.

Carroll, Thomas, 'Peasant Cooperatives in Latin America', in P. Worsley (ed.), *Two Blades of Grass*, Manchester U.P., 1971.

Casals, Juan, 'La Estructura Agraria del Ecuador', *Revista Interamericana de Ciencias Socias Sociales*, 1963.

—, 'Ecuador: la estructura agraria', in Oscar Delgado (ed.), *Reformas Agrarias en la América Latina*, Fondo de Culture Economico, Mexico, 1965.

CEDEGE, 1970a (Comisión de Estudios para el Desarrollo de la Cuenca del Rio Guayas), *Tenencia de la Tierra y Reforma Agraria —un estudio socio-economico y legal*, T. Ingledow and Associates Ltd/Guayaconsult, Guayaquil.

CEDEGE, 1970b, *Babahoyo Irrigation Feasibility Report*, T. Ingledow and Associates Ltd/Guayaconsult, Guayaquil.

CEDEGE, *Proyecto de Propósito Multiple Guayas*, Resumen de los Estudios Realizados, Guayaquil, March 1975.

Censo Agropecuario, 1954, Quito.

Censo Agropecuario (Encuesta) 1968, Quito.

Centro International de Agricultura Tropical, *Políticas Arroceras en América Latina*, Cali, Colombia, 1972.

CEPAL, *El proceso de industrialización en América Latina*, Comision Economica para America Latina (CEPAL), Santiago, 1965.

CESA (Central Ecuatoriana de Servicios Agrícolas), *Informe de la Encuesta sobre la cómercialización por el campesino de la Costa*, Guayaquil, 1971.

CESA, *Una Experiencia en Desarrollo Rural*, Quito, 1974.

Checa Cobo, Marco, *El Régimen de la Propiedad de la Tierra en el Ecuador*, Ediciones Lexigrama, Quito, 1973.

Cheung, Steven N. S., *The Theory of Share Tenancy*, University of Chicago Press, 1970.

Chonchol, Jacques, *El desarrollo de América Latina y la reforma agraria*, ICIRA, Santiago, 1965.

CICE (Comite de Información y contacto Externo para Empresario Privados), *Ecuador: población y crisis*, Quito, 1975.

CIDA (Comite Interamericano de Desarrollo Agrícola), *Inventory of Information Basic to the Planning of Agricultural Development in Latin America*, Washington D.C., 1963.

CIDA, 1965, *Ecuador: Tenencia de la Tierra y Desarrollo socio-Economica del Sector Agricola*, Washington D.C.

CIDA, *Péru: Tenencia de la Tierra y Desarrollo Socio-Económico del Sector Agrícola*, Washington D.C., 1966.

Collier, David, *Squatters and Oligarchs: authoritarian rule and policy change in Peru*, Johns Hopkins U.P., 1976.

Corral, S., 1967. *El Cuento de Don Mateo*, Casa de la Cultura, Quito.

Costales, Piedad, *El Huasipungo*, Quito, 1962

Costales, Piedad and Alfredo, *Historia Social del Ecuador: tomo iv, Reforma Agraria*, Casa de la Cultura, Quito, 1971.

Crespi, Muriel, 'Changing power relations: the rise of peasant unions on traditional Ecuadorian haciendas', *Cuadernos Americanos*, vol. 44, no. 4, October 1971.

Cueva, Agustín, *El proceso de dominación política en Ecuador*, Ediciones Critica, Quito, 1973.

—, 'La crisis de los años "60"', in *Ecuador: pasado y presente*, Universidad Central, Quito, 1975.

Curtis, William Elroy, *The Capitals of Spanish America*, Praeger, New York, 1969.

De la Cuadra, José, 1937, 'El Montuvio Ecuatoriano', in *Obras Completas de José de la Cuadra*, Ediciones Casa de la Cultura, Quito, 1958.

Delavaud, Anne Collin, 'La Banane et la Colonisation de la Côte Centrale Equatorienne', Paper presented to Symposium on Regions and Regionalism, *International Congress of Americanists*, Mexico, 1974.

Delgado, Oscar, *Las Reformas Agrárias en América Latina*, Mexico, 1965.

Documentos: IX Congreso, Ecuadorian Communist Party, November 1973.

Durán, Marcos Antonio, *El Agrarismo Mexicano*, Siglo XXI, Mexico City, 1967.

ECLA (United Nations), *Economic Bulletin for Latin America*, 'Productivity of the agricultural sector in Ecuador', vol. vi, no. 2, 1961, pp. 65–92.

Ecuador: pasado y presente, Instituto de Investigaciones Economicas, Universidad Central, Quito, 1975.

El Comercio, Quito, 1966–1975.

El Telegrafo, Guayaquil, 1968–1975.

El Universo, Guayaquil 1968–1975.

Emmanuel, A. (ed.), *Unequal Exchange*, New Left Books, 1973.

Encuesta Agropecuario Nacional, 1968, Quito.

Erasmus, C., 1967, 'Upper Limits of Peasantry and Agrarian Reform: Bolivia, Venezuela and Mexico compared', *Ethnology*, vol. vi, no. 4, October.

Erasmus, Charles J., 'Agrarian Reform versus Land Reform: three Latin American countries', in Dwight B. Heath (ed.), *Contemporary Cultures and Societies of Latin America*, 1974.

Erneholm, Ivar, *Cocoa Production of South America: historical development and present geographical distribution*, Gothenburg, 1948.

Espinel Martinez, Ramón, *CESA, El movimiento campesino y la comercialización: aporte téorico para la discusión en la reunión funcional de comercialización*, CESA Litoral, Guayaquil, August 1975 (mimeo).

Espinosa Z, Javier, *La Introducción de la Sociología en el Ecuador*, Casa de la Cultura, Guayaquil, 1972.

Etram, Juan, 'Militarismo: nueva ideologia?', *Nueva*, nos. 19 and 20, (June and July) 1975, Quito.

Fals Borda, Orlando, 'Formación y deformación de la política cooperativa en América Latina', *Informaciones Cooperativas*, no. 4, International Labour Organization (ILO), Geneva, 1970.

—, *El Reformismo por Dentro*, Siglo XXI, Mexico, 1972.

FAO (Food and Agriculture Organization), *Commodity Review and Outlook*, Rome, 1972/3.

Feder, Ernest, *The Rape of the Peasantry*, Anchor Books, New York, 1971.

—, 'The New World Bank Programme for the Self-Liquidisation of the Third World Peasantry', *The Journal of Peasant Studies*, vol. 3, no. 3, April 1976.

Filosofía y plan de Acción del Gobierno Revolucionario y Nacionalista del Ecuador, Quito, 10 March 1972.

Fitzgerald, E. V. K., 'The Political Economy of Peru 1968–75', *Development and Change*, 7 (1976), pp. 7–33.

Flores, Edmundo, *La economía de la reforma agraria y el desarrollo agrícola*, VIII Congreso Latinoamericana sobre Agricultura y la Alimentacion, Viñar del Mar (undated).

Foster-Carter, Aidan, 'Neo-Marxist Approaches to Development and Underdevelopment', in Emanuel de Kadt and Gavin Williams (eds.), *Sociology and Development*, Tavistock, 1974.

Frank, A. G., *Capitalism and Underdevelopment in Latin America*, Monthly Review Press, 1969.

—, *Latin America: Underdevelopment or Revolution*, New York, 1969.

Frieire, Paulo, *Extensión o Comunicación? : la concientización en el medio rural*, Siglo XXI, Buenos Aires, 1973.

Furtado, Celso, *Economic Development of Latin America*, Cambridge University Press, 1970.

Galarza, Jaime, *El Yugo Feudal, Visión del campo Ecuatoriano*, Quito, 1962.

—, *El Festín del Petróleo*, Ediciones Solitierra, Quito, 1972.

—, *Los Campesinos de Loja y Zamora*, Universidad Central Quito, 1973.

Galeski, B., *Basic Concepts of Rural Sociology*, Manchester U.P., 1972.

Galjart, Benno, 'Peasant cooperation, consciousness and solidarity', *Development and Change*, vol. VI, no. 4, October 1975.

García, Antonio, *Reforma Agraria y Economia Empresarial en América Latina*, Santiago, 1967.

—, *Sociología de la Reforma Agraria en América Latina*, Amorrortu Ediciones, Buenos Aires, 1973.

García de Paladines, T., 'Evaluación de impacto de FENACOO-PARR en diez cooperativas agrícolas', Thesis, Faculty of Agronomy, University of Guayaquil, 1972.

Geertz, Clifford, *Agricultural Involution*, University of California Press, 1971.

Greaves, Thomas C., 'The Andean Rural Proletarians', *Anthropological Quarterly*, vol. 45, no. 2, 1972.

Griffin, Keith, *The Political Economy of Agrarian Change*, Macmillan, 1974.

—, *Land Concentration and Rural Poverty*, Macmillan, 1976.

Guayaquil Economico, Instituto de Investigaciones Economicas y Politicas, Universidad de Guayaquil, 1971.

Hamerly, Michael T., *A Social and Economic History of the City and District of Guayaquil during the late Colonial and Independence Periods*, Unpublished Ph.D. thesis, Gainsville, Florida, 1970.

174   BIBLIOGRAPHY

—, *Historia social y económica de la antigua provincia de Guayaquil, 1763–1842*, Guayaquil, 1973.

Hanley, Eric, 'Rice, politics and development in Guyana', in I. Oxaal, T. Barnett and D. Booth (eds.), *Beyond the Sociology of Development*, Routledge and Kegan Paul, 1975.

Harding, Colin, 'Land Reform and Social Conflict in Peru', in Abraham F. Lowenthal (ed.), *The Peruvian Experiment*, Princeton U.P., 1975.

Hayami, Y. and Ruttan, U. W., *Agricultural Development*, Johns Hopkins U.P., Baltimore, 1971.

Heath, Dwight B., Erasmus, Charles and Buechler, Hans, *Land Reform and Social Revolution in Bolivia*, Praeger, New York, 1969.

Heath, Dwight B., 'New Patrons for old: changing patron-client relations in the Bolivian Yungas', *Ethnology*, xii, 1973.

Hermitte, Esther and Herran, Carlos, 'Patronazgo o cooperativismo? —obstáculos a la modificación del sistema social en una comunidad del noroeste argentino', *Revista Latinoamericana de Sociología*, 1970, no. 2.

Herrera Vasconez, Cesar, *El Cultivo del Banano en el Ecuador*, 1963 (unpublished), Junta Nacional de Planificación, Quito.

Hill, Ian, 'Some problems concerning the categorisation of the Soviet agricultural population', *Sociologia Ruralis*, vol. xv, nos. 1/2, 1975.

Hobsbawm, E. J., 'Peru: the "Peculiar" Revolution', *New York Review of Books*, 16 December 1971.

Humphreys, R. A. (ed.), *British Consular Reports on the Trade and Politics of Latin America, 1824–1826*, London, 1940.

Hurtado, Oswaldo, *Dos Mundos Superpuestos* (ensayo diagnóstico de la realidad ecuatoriana), INEDES (Instituto Ecuatoriano para el Desarrollo Social), Quito, 1971.

Hurtado, Oswaldo and Herudek, J., *La organización popular en el Ecuador*, Instituto Ecuatoriano para el Desarrollo Social), Quito, INDES, 1974.

Icaza, Jorge, *Huasipungo*, Editorial Losada, Buenos Aires, 1953.

D'Incao e Mello, Maria Conceicão, *O Bóia Fria: Acumulacão Miséria*, Editora Vozes, Petropolis, Brazil, 1976.

IERAC (Instituto Ecuatoriano de Reforma Agraria y Colonisación), *Las Unidades Asociativas Campesinas en el Ecuador*, Quito, October 1973 (mimeo).

—, *Estadisticas de lad Adjudicaciones Legalizadas en Reforma Agraria y Colonización*, Quito, 1973.

—, *Instructivo para promotores de Reforma Agraria*, Quito, 1974.
—, *El Campesino*, January 1975, no. 16.
—, *Plan Operativo Anual*, Guayaquil, 1975.
—, *Estatutos de las Cooperativas*, Quito, 1973.
Instituto de Investigaciones Económicas, Universidad Central, Quito, *Visión de Ecuador*, 1975 (mimeo).
James, William R., 'Subsistence, survival and capitalist agriculture: aspects of the mode of production among a Colombian proletariat', *Latin American Perspectives*, vol. 11, no. 3, Fall 1975.
Johnson, A. W., *Sharecroppers of the Sertão*, Stanford U.P., 1971.
Junta Nacional de Planificación, *Plan General de Desarrollo*, Quito, 1963.
—, *Lineamientos fundamentales del plan integral de transformación y desarrollo*, Quito, 1972.
—, *Ecuador: Plan Integral de Transformación y Desarrollo 1973–77* (Resumen General), Quito, 1972.
—, *Estadísticas Económicas*, Quito, 1967.
—, *El Estrato Popular Urbano*, 1973.
Katzman, Martin T., 'The Brazilian Frontier in Comparative Perspective', *Comparative Studies in Society and History*, vol. 17, no. 3, July 1975, p. 273.
Kay, Cristóbal, *Comparative Development of the European Manorial System and the Latin American Hacienda System*, University of Sussex, D.Phil. thesis, 1971.
Laclau, Ernesto, 'Feudalism and Capitalism in Latin America', *New Left Review*, vol. 67, 1971.
Land Tenure Center, *Economic Aspects of Agricultural Development in Ecuador: a bibliography*, University of Wisconsin, Madison, Training and Methods Series, no, 21, December 1972.
Latin American Economic Report, vol. 11, no. 3, 17 January 1975.
Lehmann, David, 'Political Incorporation versus Political Stability: the case of the Chilean Agrarian Reform, 1965–1970', *Journal of Development Studies*, vol. 7, no. 4, July 1971.
—, 'Hacia un análisis de la conciencia de los campesinos' in *El Campesinado: clase y conciencia ed clase*, Ediciones Nueva Vision, Buenos Aires, 1972.
—, 'Introduction', in D. Lehmann (ed.), *Agrarian Reform and Agrarian Reformism*, Faber, 1974.
—, 'Agrarian Reform in Chile, 1965–1972', in D. Lehmann (ed.), *Agrarian Reform and Agrarian Reformism*, Faber, 1974.
—, 'Agrarian Structure: typology and paths of transformation in Latin America', *Peasants Seminar*, Centre for International and Area Studies, University of London, 11 June 1976.

Lenin, V. I., 'The development of Capitalism in Russia: the process of the formation of a home market for large-scale industry', in *Collected Works*, vol. 3, Lawrence and Wishart, 1972.

Ley de Reforma Agraria y Colonización, Decreto 1480, Registro Oficial (23.7.64).

Ley de Reforma Agraria, Registro Oficial no. 410, Quito (15.10.73).

Linke, Lilo, *Ecuador, Country of Contrasts*, O.U.P., 1967.

Lloyds Bank and BOLSA Review, vol. 9, no. 12, December 1975.

Maier, Georg, *The Ecuadorian Presidential Election of June 2nd 1968: an analysis*, Institute for the Comparative Study of Political Systems, Washington D.C., 1969.

Martinez-Alier, Juan, 'Landowners and Peasants in the Central Sierra of Peru', paper delivered to the *Symposium on Landlords and Peasants in Latin America and the Caribbean*, University of Cambridge, 1972.

—, 'Peasants and Labourers in Southern Spain, Cuba and Highland Peru', *Journal of Peasants Studies*, vol. 1, no. 2 (January).

Marx, K. and Engels, F., 'The Eighteenth Brumaire of Louis Bonaparte', in *Selected Works*, vol. 1. Lawrence and Wishart, 1950.

Marx, Karl, Preface to *A contribution to the critique of political Economy*, in *Selected Works* (Marx and Engels), Lawrence and Wishart, 1970.

Marzal, Manuel M., 'El Indio y la Tierra en el Ecuador', *América Indigena*, Enero 1963.

Meillassoux, C., 'From reproduction to production: a Marxist approach to economic anthropology', *Economy and Society*, vol. 1, no. 1, 1972.

Mensajero, 'CEDEGE: projecto Babahoyo en marcha', Quito, October 1974

Mensajero, 'La Reforma Agraria en el Perú', Quito, October 1974.

Moreano, Alejandro, 'Capitalismo y lucha de clases en la primera mitad del siglo xx', in *Ecuador: pasado y presente*, Instituto de Investigaciones Economicas, Universidad Central, Quito, 1975.

Morel, Eduardo, 'La Reforma Agraria en el Ecuador', *Mensajero*, Quito, July 1973.

Morena, Claudio, 'Peru 1968–1969: transformación de las estructuras del subdesarrollo y de la dependencia', *Mensajero*, Quito, January 1974.

Moncada, José, *Pasado y presente de la Planificación en el Ecuador*, Quito, 1973.

Moreno, Alberto Cornejo, *Ecuador: capitalismo y dependencia*, Edic. Amanecer, Quito, 1973 (2 vols.)

Motosuke, Kaihara, *The Changing Structure of Agriculture in Japan: effects on rice farming*, Land Tenure Centre Special Paper, University of Winconsin, Madison, 1976.

Mouzelis, N., 'Capitalism and the Development of Agriculture' (Review Article), *Journal of Peasants Studies*, vol. 3, no. 4, July 1976.

NACLA (North American Congress on Latin America), 'Ecuador: oil up for grabs', vol. ix, no. 8, November 1975.

Navarro, Guillermo, *La Concentración de Capitales en el Ecuador*, Universidad Central, Quito, 1975.

Nett, E. M., 'The Servant Class in a Developing Country: Ecuador', *Journal of Inter-American Studies*, vol. 8, no. 3, 1966.

Newby, Howard, 'The Deferential Dialectic', *Comparative Studies in Society and History*, vol. 17, no. 2, April 1975.

New York Times, New York.

NUEVA, 'ACAL: al pueblo y al Gobierno del Ecuador', no. 20, Junio 1975, Quito.

NUEVA, 'Agro: justicia o rebelión?', no. 19, Mayo 1975, Quito.

NUEVA, Quito, 1974/5.

O'Brien, Philip, 'A critique of Latin American theories of dependency', in I. Oxaal *et al.* (eds.), *Beyond the Sociology of Development*, Routledge and Kegan Paul, 1975.

Ojeda, L. *et al.*, *Dominación política en la Cuenca del Guayas* (unpublished), Quito, 1971.

Organización Nacional de Avaluación y Catastros (ONAC), land valuation records, Quito, 1971/5.

Ortiz Villacis, Marcelo, *El Cooperativismo: un mito de la democracia representiva*, Universidad Central, Quito, 1970.

Palacios, Saenz, *El Problema Agrario*, Fray Jodoco Riche, Guayaquil, 1973.

Pearse, Andrew, 'Metropolis and peasant: the expansion of the urban-industrial complex and the changing rural structure', in T. Shanin (ed.), *Peasants and Peasant Societies*, 1971.

—, *The Latin American Peasant*, Frank Cass, London, 1975.

Petras, J. and LaPorte, R., 'Modernisation from above versus reform from below', in J. Petras, *Politics and Social Structure in Latin America*, Monthly Review Press.

—, *Cultivating Revolution: the United States and Agrarian Reform in Latin America*, Random House, New York, 1971.

Plan Integral de Transformación y Desarrollo, 1973–77, Resumen General, Quito, 1972.

Plan de Acción, 'Plan Integral de Transformación y Desarrollo' 1973–77, Military Government of Ecuador, 1972.

Powell, John D., *Political Mobilization of the Venezuelan Peasant*, Cambridge, Mass., 1971.

Primer Censo Agropecuario Nacional, 1954, Quito.

Primer Congreso de Estudiantes de Ciencias Agrícolas del Ecuador (Proceedings), University of Guayaquil, March 1972.

Programa Nacional de Arroz, Raiz y Control de Piladores y Molinos, Departmento de Comercialización, Guayaquil (unpublished figures), 1975.

Programa de Promoción de Empresas Agrícolas, 'Explanatory Notes' (undated).

Programa de Promoción de Empresas Agrícolas (PPEA), statistics, Guayaquil, 1975.

Pyne, Peter, 'The Politics of Instability in Ecuador', *Journal of Latin American Studies*, vol. 7, part 1, May 1975.

Quintana, M. E. and Palacios, L. A., *Monografía y Album de Los Rios*, Quito, 1937.

Redclift, M. R., *El papel de las cooperativas agrícolas en la transformación del campesinado de la Cuenca del Guayas, Ecuador*, Central Ecuatoriana de Servicios Agrícolas (CESA), Guayaquil, 1975.

—, 'Agrarian Reform and Peasant Organisation in the Guayas Basin, Ecuador', paper given to the *Peasants Seminar*, Centre of International and Area Studies, University of London, January 1976.

—, 'Agrarian Reform and Peasant Organisation in the Guayas Basin, Ecuador', *Inter-American Economic Affairs*, vol. xxx, no. 1, Summer 1976.

Reyes, Oscar Efrén, *Breve Historia General del Ecuador*, vol. 2 (1809–1940), Quito, 1942.

Roseberry, W., 'Rent, Differentiation and the Development of Capitalism among Peasants', *American Anthropologist*, vol. 78, no. 1, 1976.

Rover, James B., 'Ecuador's Cocoa', *Tropical Agriculture*, vol. 3, no. 3, 1926.

Rubio Orbe, Gonzalo, *La Población Rural Ecuatoriana*, Quito. 1966.

Saad, Pedro, 'La Reforma Agraria', *Revista Bandera, Roja* no. 1, January–February 1961, Quito.

—, *La Realidad Agropecuaria del Ecuador*, Ediciones Claridad, Guayaquil, 1972.

—, 'Nueva Ley de Reforma Agraria del Ecuador', *Documentos IX Congreso, Partido Comunista del Ecuador*, November 1973.

Saunders, J. V. D., 'Man-Land Relations in Ecuador', *Rural Sociology*, 26.1.1961.

Singleman, Peter, 'The Closing Triangle: Critical notes on a model for peasant mobilization in Latin America', *Comparative Studies in Society and History*, vol. 17, no. 4, October 1975.

Stavenhagen, R., 'Changing functions of the community in underdeveloped countries', in H. Bernstein (ed.), *Underdevelopment and Development*, Penguin, 1973.

Tama Paz, Cyrano, *Petróleo: drama ecuatoriano*, Guayaquil, 1970.

Thome, Joseph R., 'Improving Land Tenure Security', in Peter Dorner (ed.), *Land Reform in Latin America*, University of Wisconsin, Madison, 1971.

The Times, London.

Torres Caicedo, Reinaldo, *Los Estratos Socioeconómicos del Ecuador*, Junta Nacional de Planificación, Quito, 1960.

Uggen, J. F., 'Peasant mobilization in Ecuador: a case study of Guayas Province', unpublished Ph.D. dissertation, University of Miami, 1974.

Unidad Sindical. Asociación de Cooperativas Agrícolas del Litoral (ACAL), June and August, 1974.

United Nations, *Economic Survey of Latin America* (1966), New York, 1968.

United Nations, *Estudio Económico de América Latina*, 1971.

UNRISD (United Nations Research Institute for Social Development), *Cooperatives and Rural Development in Latin America; an analytical report*, Geneva, 1971.

—, *Rural Cooperatives as agents of change: a research report and a debate*, vol. VIII, Geneva.

van den Bergh, 'The Interconnection between Processes of State and Class formation: problems of conceptualisation', *Institute of Social Studies*, Occasional papers, 1975.

Vera Arrata, G., *Historia de un triste banano*, Imprenta Abad, Guayaquil, 1972.

Villavicencio, X., *Geografía del Ecuador*, Quito, 1860.

Vine, James W., 'The Rice Economy of Government Settlement Schemes in Guyana', *Inter-American Economic Affairs*, vol. 29, no. 2, Summer 1975.

Weber, Max, *The Methodology of the Social Sciences*, Glencoe, 1949.

Whitten, Norman E., 'Strategies of adaptive mobility on the Colombian-Ecuadorian Litoral', *American Anthropologist*, vol. 71, 1969.

—, *Black Frontiersmen, a South American Case*, Schenkman, Cambridge, Mass., 1974.

Whymper, Edward, *Travels Amongst the Great Andes of the Equator* (ed. E. Shipton), Charles Knight, London, 1972.

Wolf, Teodoro, *Geografía y Geología del Ecuador*, Leipzig, 1892.

Womack, John, *Zapata and the Mexican Revolution*, Penguin, 1972.

Worsley, Peter, 'Introduction', in P. Worsley (ed.), *Two Blades of Grass: rural cooperatives in agricultural modernisation*, Manchester U.P., 1971.

Zeitlin, Maurice and Ratcliff, Richard Earl, 'Research Methods for the analysis of the internal structure of the dominant classes, the case of landlords and capitalists in Chile', *Latin American Research Review*, vol. 10, no. 3, Fall 1975.

Zuvekas, Clarence, 'Agrarian Reform in Ecuador's Guayas River Basin', *Land Economics*, vol. 52, no. 3, August 1976.

INDEX